A. F. Carl Wiese Descendants

O'Levia Neil Wilson Wiese

HERITAGE BOOKS
2009

HERITAGE BOOKS
AN IMPRINT OF HERITAGE BOOKS, INC.

Books, CDs, and more—Worldwide

For our listing of thousands of titles see our website
at
www.HeritageBooks.com

Published 2009 by
HERITAGE BOOKS, INC.
Publishing Division
100 Railroad Ave. #104
Westminster, Maryland 21157

Other Heritage Books by O'Levia Neil Wilson Wiese:
Cemetery Records of Greene County, Alabama, and Related Areas
A. F. Carl Wiese Descendants
The Woodville Republican: Mississippi's Oldest Existing Newspaper:
Volume 1: December 18, 1823 - December 17, 1839
Volume 2: January 4, 1840 - October 30, 1847
Volume 3: January 8, 1848 - January 9, 1855
Volume 4: June 22, 1878 - December 25, 1880
Volume 5: January 1, 1881 - December 22, 1883
Volume 6: January 5, 1884 - December 26, 1891
CD: *The Woodville Republican, Volumes 1-5*

Cover Art by Gary Dodgen

International Standard Book Numbers
Paperbound: 978-0-7884-0831-1
Clothbound: 978-0-7884-8299-1

CONTENTS

Introduction ii

Acknowledgments iii

Dedication iv

Genealogical Table
  Wiese and Meyer v

Ship List ix

U.S. Census x

Church Records xiii

Brenham Map xv

History of Wiese Family xvi

August Friedrick Carl Wiese xvii

Synopsis of Will xix

Chapter I (Fritz) 1

Chapter II (William) 3

Chapter III (Henry) 28

Henry Holle Descendents 46

Chapter IV (Louise) 61

Chapter V (Caroline) 71

Chapter VI (Carl) 74

Chapter VII (Wilhelmina) 85

Chapter IX (Henrietta) 89

Additional Information 91

The beginning of this book on the ancestory of the Wiese Family
was the outgrowth of a family reunion of the children of Fred and
Hulda Wiese. It was originally to cover just the immediate family;
however, once this information was obtained, it was a natural
impulse to continue the search.

The result is the accumulation of information--both hazy memories
as well as documented evidence.Much information was given by the
living children and grandchildren of Carl and Minna Wiese who came
to the United States from Germany in 1869,leaving a farm that had
been registered since 1689, and is still today, in the possession
of a Chris Wiese.

The reader must take into consideration that if time and age have
distorted facts and truths, these memories are better than knowing
nothing.

> "Somebody labored years ago
> Whose name I do not know
> Ploughed ground or sailed the open sea
> And loved a maiden that I might be...
> --Edgar Guest

ACKNOWLEDGMENTS

This book could not have been written without the assistance of my "co-pilot", Lydia Wiese Hodel, who traveled many miles with me while searching for information; Ben and Hulda Bishoff Wiese whose memories provided me with clues to the history of the family; Uncle Fritz and Aunt Hulda Wiese Goessler whose assistance and hospitality cannot be measured; Adolph and Anita Thim Boedeker's warm hospitality; Ella Hausler of Brockum, Germany, who was my "friend-in-need" to do the research in that country; and my friend Dieter Hiersig who translated the material for me. To all of these helpers, I say thank you!

> ...For name by name I find no sign
> Of hero in this distant life,
> But only men as calm as snow
> Who took some faithful girl as wife,
>
> Who labored while the drought, the flood
> Crisscrossed the fickle summer air,
> Who built great barns and propped their lives
> Upon a slow heart-breaking care.
>
> Why do I love them as I do,
> Who dared no glory, won no fame?
> In a harsh land that lies subdued,
> They are the good boughs of my name.
>
> If music sailed their dreams at all,
> They were not heroes, and slept on;
> As one by one they left the small
> Accomplished, till the great was done.
>
> MARY OLIVER

To my husband,Ernest Ray Wiese,I dedicate this book
for without his patience and forbearance this could
not have been written.

January,1979

OUR PRINTERS: The off-set printing classes of WISD

Steven Collins,Darla Padgett,Jimmy Duarte,Ophelia Hawthorne,
David Chamberlain,Frank Nettles and Freddie Montgomery. Mrs.
Edna Williams, instructor.

Bethine Dawson,Irene Hernandez,Rachel Tijerina,Mark Stroud,
Mitchell Williams,Mark Shaw,Joe Gutierrez, and Kenneth Dixon.

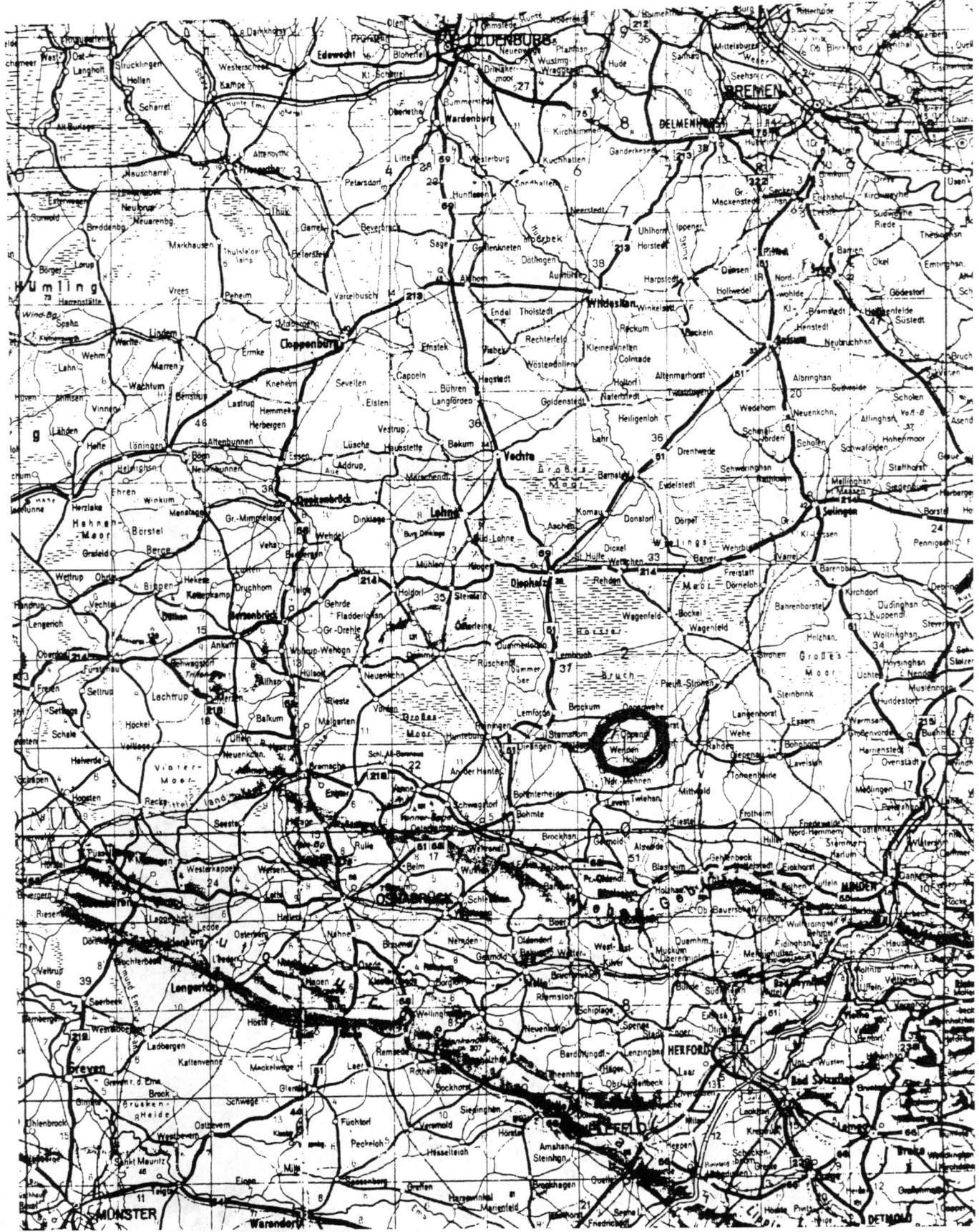

WIESE
August Friedrich Carl
b.May 8,1820 bpt.May 14
m.Charlotte Wilhelmine
Meier,also called Schwietermeier
on April 7,1842

Father Hermann Henrich Wiese
b.Aug.22,k774 bpt.Aug.28 d.Aug.1,1848
burial Aug.4.Reg.62.Farmer at Grossenholze
Wehdem 181,Died of weakness of old age.Left
wife and 3 of 8 adult children

Married Nov.4,1803 Reg.27.to..
MotherMetz,Margaretha Charlotte
from the Birchbushes.b.1782 d.Apr.13,
1849 from a chest illness which she had for
14 days.Doctor Brosin,Wehdem.

Grandfather born Fricke.Took the name
of Wiese.died Dec.18,1799 of dropsy
Widower.Reg.50 married Sept.5,1753 to
Grandmother Maria Sophia Wiese b.Oct.
7,1732 bapt.Oct.12,d.June 3,1782 of a
chest illness.Reg.32

Grandfather: Johann Friedrich Metz

Grandmother: Marie Elizabeth
            Schmalgemeier

The GENEALOGICAL RECORD OF AUGUST FRIEDRICH CARL WIESE who emmigrated to the
United States of America in 1869 along with his wife and children.
Research from the older Church books and Farm Register.(p.1) cont...

v

Great,Great,Great,grandfather WIESE
Johann Wiese was the owner of a farm
number 3 in Wehdem.He was 51 years
of age at registration.
Registered farm in 1682

Great,Great,grandfather WIESE
Johann Henrich b. Oct.13,1671
reg.#71,d.March 18,1726 reg.#24

Great,grandfather WIESE
Johann Hermann in the Birchbushes
bapt.1708 reg.#8,d.Oct.30,1769
of the colic. reg.#41

Great,grandmother Eickhoff,
Catharine Margarethe from Arnkamp,
county of Diehlingen,d.June 1,
1772 of weakness of old age
reg.# 43

The GENEALOGICAL RECORD OF AUGUST FRIEDRICH CARL WIESE who emmigrated to the

United States of America in 1869 along with his wife and children.Research

from the older Church books and Farm Register.(p.2) cont...

Grandfather: Meier,also called
Schwietermeier,Hermann Henrich
b.Nov.9,1754,bapt.#11,married
1st:Feb.8,1786,reg.#2
2nd:July 29,1789,reg.#14 to
Aukamp Ilsabein,Haldem
d. July 14,1819,burial July 16
Narrow chested,reg# 37.

Grandmother: Aukamp Haldem
Catharina Adelheit d.Aug.25,
1788,reg.# 41
At 25 years died of a chest
illness.Married Feb.8,1786
1 son&1 dau.who died.

Grandfather: Lehde,Gerd Henrich
b.June 17,1748,bapt.June 2
reg.# 39,married Nov.1786 reg.# 25
died Dec.16,1812 reg.#124,
27 yrs. of marriage, 2 sons,
7 daughters.Still living: 1 son
and 1 dau.

Grandmother: Rohling,Marie Elisabeth
b.June 8,1748,d.Feb.9,1835 reg.# 11
died to weakness of old age.From
9 children,3 are still living.
4 children are left behind.

Col.Westrup 4

Father:Meier,also called Schwietermeier
Johann Henrich: Manager
b.April 12,1790,bapt.April 18,reg.#40
died of weakness of old age,Nov.17,1864
burial Nov.21,1864.Left behind 7 from
12 children born.

Mother: Lehde,Marie Elisabeth
b.Feb.28,1791,bapt.March 6,reg.#16
married Oct.11,1811,reg.#20.
d.Nov.14,1854 burial Nov.18,reg.#90
Died of colic,left behind 6 adult
children and 1 minor child

MEIER,also called SCHWIETERMEIER
Charlotte Wilhelmine Dorothee
b.Nov.30,1822,bapt.Dec.8,reg.#23
Westrup No.4,Married August
Friedrich Carl Wiese on Dec.7,1842
reg.#34.

The GENEALOGICAL RECORD OF CHARLOTTE WILHELMINE DOROTHEE MEIER
who emmigrated to the United States of America in 1869 along with
her husband and children.Research from the older Church books
and Farm Register.(p.3)cont..

Great,Great,Great,grandfather:Henry Meyer
Owner of a farm listed as Farm No.4 in
Westrup. In 1682 when he registered the
farm,he was 35 years of age.

Great,Great,grandfather: Johann Wilhelm Meyer
b.Oct.9,1694,reg.#36.
Married 1st: Margarete Ilsabein Schapers
June 27,1717,reg.11
Married 2nd: Anna Hedewig Holts
May 2,1720,reg.#20

Great,Great,grandmother: Margarete Ilsabein
Schapers on June 27,1717,reg.#11
She died 1719 at the age of 24

Great,grandfather: Meier,also called
Schwietermeier.Johann Henrich born
about 1719-20,died June 28,1784 at
64 years of age,reg.#41.
Married Oct.5,1747 reg.#13, to
Elisabeth Grube who died in 1760
Married 2nd to Margarethe Engel
Henke from Ilwede Reg.#1,Jan.14,1761
Died Sept.19,1784,reg.#37

Great,grandmother: Grube,Elisabeth
died Jan.26,1760 at the age of 35½
years of age,reg.#6.
Great,grandfather: Lehde,Johann Friedrich

Great,grandfather: Rohling,Johann Friedrich

Great,grandmother: Rohling,Margarete

The GENEALOGICAL RECORD OF CHARLOTTE WILHELMINE DOROTHEE MEIER who emmigrated to the United States of
America in 1869 along with her husband and children.Research from the older Church books and Farm
Register.(p.4).

COPIES OF LIST OF PASSENGERS ARRIVING AT MISCELLANEOUS PORTS
ON THE ATLANTIC AND GULF PORTS AND AT PORTS ON THE GREAT LAKES.

1820-1873:Roll 3....Galveston,Texas

Ship WESER

December 31,1869, page 14

(Farmer)

29	Carl	Wise	Farmer	50	
30	Wilhelmine	Wise		49	
31	Christof	Wise		10	
32	Carl	"		7	
33	August	"		15	
34	Wilhelmine	"			
35	Henrietta	"		4	
36	Louise	"			
37	Carolina				
38	Wilhelm Bohls Meyer				
	Carl Gücke				

1870   Wiese,   Fritz 28 b. Prussia

              Caroline 29 b. Prussia

              Alonzo 7   b. Texas

              Minna 9, b. Prussia

1880   Wiese,   Fritz 37
              Caroline 40
              Anna Loesch(Losh)

       Wiese,   Carl 64
              Mina 58
              Carl 19
              August 18
              Mina 18
              Setta 16

       Wiese,   Henry 34
              Sophie 34
              Fred 13
              Melinda 11
              Mina 9
              Charlie 4
              Betty 4
              Lidia 2
              Christe 2
              male unnamed 1mo.old

       Wiese,   William 35
              Minnie 35
              Betty 10
              Charlie 8
              Louise 6
              Anna 4
              Mena 1

       Wiese,   W.L. 21 b. Texas
              Lottie 18 b. Germany

       Wiese,   Christine 30 b. Germany
              Mary 26
              Albert 3 months

       Boney   C.(Chris) 25
              Caroline 23
              Carl 2
              Minnie 1

<u>1900</u>   Wiese,   Henry b.Nov.1845 54 years old:married 33 yrs.
              Sophie b.Dec.1845 54 years old
              13 children, 11 living in 1900
              Chas.H. b.Jan.1876 24
              Henry C. b.June 1881 19
              Willie b. Oct.1882 17
              Lydia b.Oct.1882 17

              Anna b.Feb.1885 15   (Emma)
              Sophie b.Feb.1887 13

       Wiese, Christph b.Feb.1877 22
               Augusta b.Jan.1880 20
               Johnnie b. June 1899 11mo.
               Married one year

       Wiese, Lonie b.Feb.1859 41 b.Texas
               Lottie b.Dec.1862 37
               Married 20 years, ehildren,8 living
               John b. Feb.1882 19
               William b.Oct.1884 15
               Roy b. July 1886 13
               Joseph b. July 1889 11
               Loney b.Apr.1894 6
               Thomas b.Feb.1897 3

               James b.Nov.1899 6 mo.

       Wiese, August b.June 1862 37
               Louise b.Sept.1866 33
               Married 15 years

               Louise b. Aug.1886 13
               Emma b.Nov.1889 12
               Ernest b. Jan.1889 11
               August b.Aug.1890 9
               Ida b.Feb.1892 8
               Minna b.May 1893 7
               Heneretta b.Feb.1896 4

       Wiese   Charles b. Mar.1872 28
               Mathilda b.Aug.1877 22
               Married 3 years
               Heneretta b. 1897 2
       Wiese   Son b. May 1900 1mo.
               William(brother) b.Feb.1883 17

1900   Wiese,   Fredrick b.April 1867 33 b.Texas
                  Hulda b.Aug.1871 28   b.Texas
                  Fred,son,b.Oct.1892 7
                  Otto,son,b.Sept.1894 5
                  Willie,son,b.Nov.1896 3
                  Henry,son,b.Jan.1898 2
                  Lydia,dau b.Oct.1899 7 mo.

        Neumann,   Fredricke,Mother of Hulda,b.Mar.1837
                  63 years old.Immigrated 1860(along with
                  husband Sigmund, step-sons William,Adolph,
                  and Hermine.Port Lenzen to Brenham on ship
                  FORTUNA)

        Spinn,   William b.Aug.1874 25 b.Texas
                  Malinda b.Aug.1876 23 b.Texas
                  Married 5 years, 4 children,1 living
                  Herman b.Apr.1898 2

        Wiese,   Charles b.Feb.1861 39 Immigrated 1869
                  Louise b.July 1864 35 Immigrated 1869
                  Married 15 years. 5 children,5 living
                  William b.Oct.1886 13
                  Fritz b.Feb.1888 12
                  Minnie b.June 1891 9
                  Anna b.Sept.1892 7
                  Ben b.Aug.1894 5

  Brockermeyer, Henry b.Dec.1869 30 Immigrated 1872
                  Minna b.July 1871 28 b.Texas
                  Sophie b.Aug.1892 7
                  Henry Jr.b.Feb.1894 6
                  Robert b.Oct.1895 4
                  Charles b.Aug.1897 2
                  William b. 1899 3 months old.

CHARTER MEMBERS, May 28, 1877
(Age at time of organization is given in Parenthesis)

William Holle (29)

Carl A. F. Wiese (57)

Mrs. Carl Wiese (59) (Minna Meye

J. H. (51) & Margareth (Stegmann) Lippe (55)

Henry (29) & Minna (Schulze) Reue (24)

J. Wilhelm (33) & (32)
Dorothea (Meier) Wiese

Chris (52) & Lucie Schulte (52)

Henry (30) & Sophie (Holle) Wiese (31)

EARLY YEARS AT PRAIRIE HILL

Pastor F. Ernst

A Deed for 10 acres of land was signed Sept. 29, 1875, from H. H. Daily to Henry Wiese and Wm. Holle, trustees of St. John's Evangelical Lutheran Church for $100 in gold.

Lutheran Pastor Friedrich Ernst of Wiedeville (1875-79) held worship services in homes of Prairie Hill families during 1876.

The first church building was dedicated January 7, 1877 (Pictured below)

First resident pastor, Christian C. Rudi, age 50, moved from Swiss Alp and served May 13, 1877 to July, 1880.

Pastor C.C. Rudi

A Constitution was adopted May 28, 1877, and the congregation was re-organized with 12 heads of families as charter members.

Wilhelm Holle, 1847-1932	Fritz Schramme, 1826-1900
J.H. Lippe, 1825-1905	Christian Schulte, 1824-1908
Christoph Loesch, 1846-1922	A. F. Carl Wiese, 1820-1902
Heinrich Quebe, 1848-1925	Henry F. Wiese, 1846-1922
Henry Reue, 1847-1928	J. Wilhelm Wiese, 1843-83
Wm. Schlottmann, Jr. 1851-1902	Fried. Wilhelm Wist, 1832-86

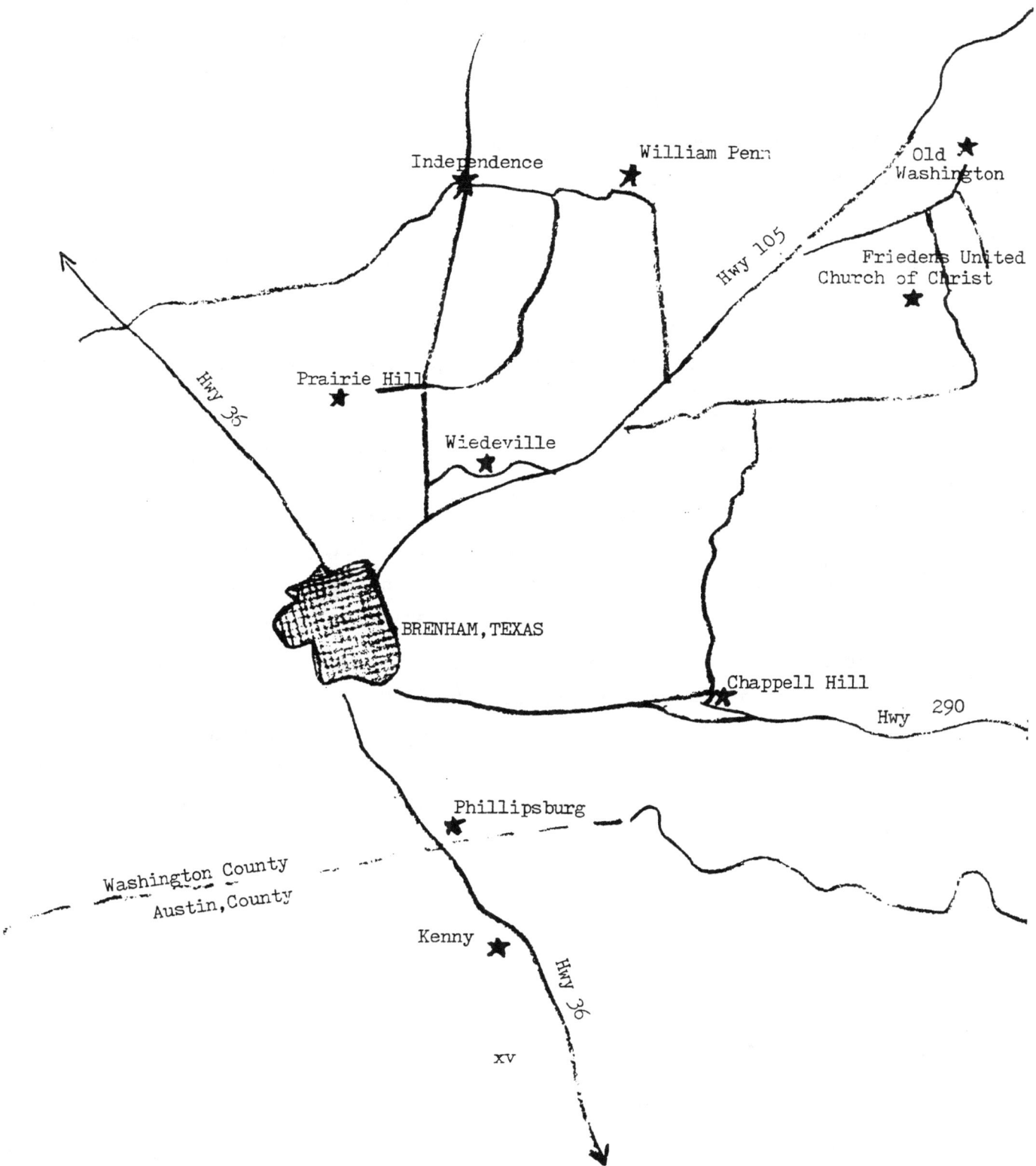

Independence ★

William Penn ★

Old ★
Washington

Hwy 105

Frieders United
Church of Christ ★

Hwy 36

Prairie Hill ★

Wiedeville ★

BRENHAM, TEXAS

Chappell Hill ★

Hwy 290

Phillipsburg ★

Washington County
Austin, County

Kenny ★

Hwy 36

xv

During the pre-Civil War years many Germans came to Washington County, Texas, in search of good farming land and political freedom. Realizing that the Wiese family were farmers and that Germany was going through a transition period, one could assume it was for these reasons that Carl and Minna Wiese immigrated to this section of the United States.

Their four oldest sons had preceded them: Fritz in 1859, William and Henry in 1860, and Herman in 1866. The advent of the War Between the States closed the ports and no ships sailed. It was not until December 31, 1869, that the mother and father could bring their younger children, Louise, Caroline, Chris, Carl, August, Wilhelmena and Heneretta to Texas.

They sailed from Bremen, a port of embarkation in Germany, and after a sixteen-week journey, eventually landed in Galveston, Texas. From their ship the WESER, they transferred to a smaller ship to travel into the bay in order to reach their destination, Indianola. From there they continued on to Prairie Hill, a community six miles northwest of Brenham, Texas, the county seat of Washington County.

There, alongside their sons who had married, they reared their younger children; and, in 1872, for $1,501.50 in gold Carl bought two tracts of farming land adjacent to his sons, William and Henry. Herman had died in 1868 in a tragic accident, and Fritz had bought land in the Post Oak community which would later become known as Wiedeville.

August Friedrich Carl Wiese,who immigrated to the United States of
America, was the son of Herman Henrich Wiese and Margrete Charlotte,
nee Metz. Residence: Wehdem im Grossen Holz,No.181.

Carl was born May 8,1820 and baptized on May 14,1820, died in
Prairie Hill,Texas on Oct.12,1902. Married December 7,1842 to
Charlotte Wilhelmine Dorothee Schwietermeier, daughter of Johann
Heinrich Schwietermeier and Marie Elisabeth,nee Lehde. Born Nov.30,
1822,baptized: December 12,1822, died in Prairie Hill, Texas on
December 26,1896. (Marriage records 1842,No.34) Both buried in
St.John's Cemetery at Prairie Hill.

Carl and Minna had fifteen children,eight sons and seven daughters.
Nine would marry and have children. From these nine, many descendents
are scattered all over the United States.

CHILDREN

#1 : Hermann Friedrich Wilhelm,b.Feb.18,1843,bpt.Feb.26.d. June 3,
1908. Known as Fritz.Married Caroline Branning and adopted
her son Alonzo,and gave him his name of Wiese.He and Caroline
reared Anna Loesch who became the mother of Bertha,Martha,
Annie,Lillie and Herman Burmeister.

Anna was the child of Louise, Fritz's sister , and after being
widowed again, Louise remarried:to Herman Grube. Louise died
in childbirth leaving 3 more children. Fritz reared her baby of
the first marriage.Charlie Loesch later married Lora Wiese, the
daughter of Alonzo.

Fritz's sister Caroline (Bohne) took the second child,Bertha
Loesch who married William Goessler.

#2 : William Johann Friedrich,b.Aug.14,1844,bpt.Aug.20,1844,d.
Aug.28,1883. Married Wilhelmina Maier and reared 5 children,
Bertha,Carl,Louise,Annie and William. Minnia has died as a child.
William died at the age of 39 and his widow married Wm.Quebe.
After bearing him a child,Malinda,Minna also died and Mr.Quebe
married again.

#3.: Heinrich Friedrich Wilhelm.b. Nov.22,1845,bapt.Nov.30,1845.
d. Aug. 20,1922.Married Sophie Holle and reared 12 children:
Fred,Melinda,Wilhelmina,Charlie,Betty,Lidia, Christe,Will,
Lydia,Henry, Emma and Sophie.

#4 : Marie Wilhelmine Henriette b.Jan.3,1847,bpt. Jan.10,1847 and
died in Germany on Feb.13,1847.

5: Carl Hermann Wilhelm b. Nov.16,1848,bpt.Nov.26,1848 and
died Feb.8,1868 in a tragic accident soon after arriving
from Germany.

6: Henriette Louise Caroline b. Feb.10,1851, bpt.Feb.16,1851 and
died Dec.2,1884. Married 1st to Herman Loesch and bore three
children;Bertha,Anna,and Charlie.Married 2nd after Herman Loesch
died, to Herman Grube. Louise died in childbirth and left
three more children.The two that her brother August took to
rear,died of diptheria along with one child of August. The
other child,Fritz Grube was reared by Louise's sister,Minna
Wehmeyer. Herman Grube returned to Germany and died in 1910.

7: Henriette Wilhelmine Charlotte b. May 26,1854,bpt.June 5,
1854 and died Aug.11,1855 in Germany.

8: Henriette Luise Caroline, b. Oct.18,1856, bpt.Nov.2,1856
and died in Jan.22,1941. Married Crist Willian Bohne and
reared 11 children;Minnie,Emma, Karl,Fritz,Minnie;Henry,Lena,
Emma,Bertha, Annie and Willie. They made their home in Old
Washington.

9: (Twins) Christoph Heinrich Wilhelm,b.March 30,1859,Time:1 AM
bpt.April 10, and died July 16,1878 in Prairie Hill,Texas.
Nothing is known concerning his death.

#10: (Twin to Chris) b. March 30,1859,Time: 2 AM,bpt.April 10,
1859 and died Jan.3,1860 Germany.(Carl Friedrich Wilhelm)

#11: Heinrich Friedrich Carl, b. Feb.7,1861,bpt.May 5,1861, and
died March 15,1940 McGregor,Texas.Married Louise Wehmeyer
an reared 5 children;William,Fred,Minna,Anna, and Ben.
Ben and Fred still live in McGregor.

#12: August b. June 1862 ,died Nov.,1936. Married Louise Schulen
berg and reared 7 children;Elizabeth Louise,Emma,Ernest,August
Jr.,Ida,Minnie and Heneritta. They lived in the Whitehall
community a few miles west of Moody,Texas.

#13:(Twin to August) Wilhelmena b. June 1862,died on Jan.13,1925.
Married Fritz Wehmeyer and reared 10 children;Carl,Charlie,
(who died), Charlie,Emma,August,Willian, Herbert,Fred Henry,
Bernie, and E. a. The family lived in Pandora,Texas and Port
Lavaca. Erna, the youngest child lives in San Antonio.

#14: Henriette Luise Caroline b. April 22,1864,bpt.May 5,1864.
died July 8,1946 in Perry,Texas.Married Emile Kluck and reared
6 children;Minnie,Charlie,Heneritta,and Willie,who lives in
Perry.

#15: Marie Wilhelmine Charlotte b. Oct.11,1865 bpt.Oct.22,1865
and died Jan.1,1867, in Germany.

C. Wiese et al

to

A. Wiese et al

(Instrument: Deed & Agmt.
(Dated: Nov.28,1902
(Filed: Mar.2,1903
(Recorded: Vol.49,pg.371
(Deed Records
(Washington County,Texas

(SYNOPSIS OF WILL)

On Feb.7,1883, Carl and Wilhelmina made their last will. Each conveyed to each other as survivor during life time. On death of both, the estate would pass to and be divided among their sons and daughters.

1. Wilhelmina died Dec.26,1896

2. Carl died Oct.12,1902

3. Gives Fred Wiese (Fritz) $100.00. Carl must pay Fred out of his share.

4. William Wiese $100.00. William had died, so money divided between his children,Bertha,Carl,Louise,Anna,William and Minna. Carl must pay out of his share.

5. Gave to their beloved son Henry Wiese $100. Carl must pay.

6. Gave to their beloved daughter Louise Grube $300.00. In case of her death, to be divided amony her children. This $300.00 to be paid out of share allotted to August. Louise died,Dec. 2,1884 leaving Bertha Gossler,Charles Loesch, Anna Burmeister and W.F.R. Grube.

7. Caroline Bohne to receive $500.00. Beloved daughter.Carl pays.

8. Minna Wehmeyer to receive $500.00 Beloved daughter.Carl pays.

9. Gave to their beloved daughter Henrietta Kluck the sum of $1,000.00 to be paid by August out of his share.

10. Gave to their beloved son Carl, the south half of their farm containing about 82 acres and 12½ acres of wood land.Must pay Fred,William and Henry within one year.

11. Gave to their beloved son August the North half of their farm containing about 82 acres and 12½ acres of wood land. Must pay Louise,and Henrietta within one year.

12. All personal property(except money) shall go to the child they were living with at time of death.(1)farming implements, (2)furniture and household goods,cattle,houses,corn and cotton.

All money and notes on hand used first to pay the doctor bills nursing and funeral expences,taxes and to purchase a tombstone and a fence for the graves.The remainder, if any, to be divided equally between the living children or their heirs.

13. All heirs be willing to honor parent's wishes to save the cost of probating their will and court cost and to make the settlement of the estate as cheap as possible.

14. All heirs were of age and agreed to the above.

15. Each note was to retain a lein on the land until paid. 8% after maturity.

16. Homestead and woodland described.

A: T.J.Alcorn dated Jan.31,1872 to Chas.Wiese for 72&7/10 acres (Book Y.p.405 Deed Records Wash.Co.Tx.)

B: Henry W. to C.Wiese for 12&7/10 acres dated Jan.31,1872 and recorded (Book Y.p.404)

C: John Focke and Henry Wilkens to C.Wiese 100 acres,Mar.6,1877 (Book 5,p.573)

D: Henry to Chas Wiese 66/100 acres (Book 7,p.183)

17. Listing of heirs:

(a) Carl-son (b)C.W.and Caroline Bohne-dau. (c)August-son (d) Chas.H.Loesch-grandson(e) W.C.Wiese-grandson(f) W.F.R. Grube-grandson(g)Wm.and Bertha Goessler-grandaughter(h)H.& Ann Burmeister-grandaughter(i)Fritz Wiese-son (j)John N.& Anna Thim-grandaughter (k)Emil and Heneriette Kluch-daughter(l)F.R.& Minna Wehmeyer-daughter(m)J.F.& Bertha Fehler -grandaughter (n)F.F. Wedeking & Louise -grandaughter(o)Henry-son,(p)William and (q)August-son.

HENRY OF WASHINGTON CO AND Wm.CARL WIESE OF MCLENNON CO.GIVES AUGUST OF WASHINGTON CO. POWER OF ATTORNEY TO SETTLE ESTATE OUT OF COURT.
(Vol.49,pg.370)

WAS GOTT ZUSAMMEN FÜGT, DAS SOLL DER MENSCH NICHT SCHEIDEN

VERHEIRATHET.

Karl Friedrich August Wiese geboren im Jahr 1820

Charlotte Wilhelmine Dorothea Wiese eine geborene

den 8 Mai

Meier, geboren 1822 den 30 November, wir sind

getraut im Jahr 1842 wir haben in unsrer Ehe

15 Kinder geboren, 8 Knaben und 7 Mädchen

Bible of A.F.Carl Wiese

Only one page has been saved that has information
on it. The Bible measures 8x12 inches. Leather bound
with the following inscription on the cover,"Holy
Script". The Bible is printed in German with the
following translation:

WHAT GOD HAD JOINED,LET NO MAN TAKE APART

Carl Friedrick August Wiese born in January 1820
Charlotte Wilhelmine Dorothy Meyer born November 30,1822
They were married in 1842
They had 15 children, 8 sons and 7 daughters.

A.F. Carl Wiese

Wilhelmina Meyer

1977
Lydia,Agnes,Clara,Ruby,Ernie, and Emma.Great,grandaughters.

A.F.Carl and Wilhelmina Meyer
ca 1900

Wiese-Quebe Homeplace (William Wiese)

St. John's Church on top of the hill

Prairie Hill, St. John's Church at end of road

x-e

St. John's Lutheran Cemetery

Land of A.F.Carl and Mina Wiese---now owned by Mr and Mrs. Glen Jeske

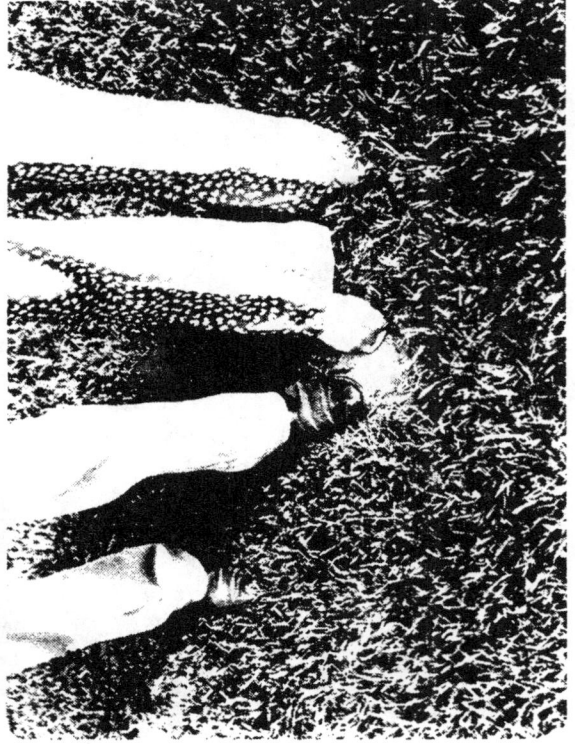

Oscar and Lydia on a cornerstone

Cornerstones of house

Glenn Jeske, Oscar Fuelberg and Lydia Hodel

A.F.Carl's well on homeplace

A.F.Carl's chair

1st born: Fritz

Wife: Caroline

CHILD #1: Hermann Friedrich Wilhelm,b.Feb.18,1843,Baptized Feb.26,
 1843,Register No.23,Wehdem,Germany. d. Aug.22,1929,married Feb.4,
 1861 (MB 2,p.125,Brenham,Tx.) to Caroline Brenning b.March 13,
 1839,d. June 3,1908. Both buried in Chappell Hill Quadrangle,
 Wiedeville Cemetery,Wiedeville,Community,near Brenham,Texas.

In 1859, Fritz immigrated from Germany on the ship IRIS, along
with his cousin "W.Meyer". Both were 16 years old. Brothers
William and Henry followed the next year.

Fritz married Caroline Branning Feb.4,1861 in Brenham,Texas.
Caroline's son Alonzo(Lonnie) was adopted by Fritz. At the
outbreak of the Civil War, Fritz served his new country and
returned to farm in the Post Oak Community, now known as the
Wiedeville Community. In 1871, eleven families in the community
felt need of their own church and pastor, and Fritz was one of
those present of the first congregational meeting in January,
1881.Others were,Heinrich Wiede, Christian Wiede,Christoph Schenkel,Johann Wiede,Ferd. Wiede,Carl Martins,Friedrich Martins, Frit
Fehler,Fritz Schulz,Johann Rann, Joachim Schulz,Friedrich Franke,
and H.Wellmann. They constructed the Immanuel Lutheran Church
that same year.

For many years Fritz,along with a friend,would ring out the old
year and the new year in by ringing the church bell. At the 50th
anniversary only 1 charter member, Fritz Wiese, was still living.

In 1889, Fritz and Caroline built their home. Today, it still
stands with many of their fine pieces of furniture still being
used by Bertha and Oscar Fuelberg.

After Caroline died Fritz went to Temple,Texas to visit his niece
Anna, whom he had reared. Anna was the child of his sister Louise.
He needed someone to care for him,so in 1909, Bertha returned to
his home and cared for him until he died in 1929. At that time,
Bertha was 18 years old and she later married Oscar Fuelberg. They
reared 10 children and today, Bertha along with her son Oscar Jr.,
still live on the "homeplace".

The 1880 census listed Fritz 37,Caroline 40,and Anna Loesch aged 4.
Anna was to become the mother of Bertha,Martha,Lillie and Herman
Burmeister.

CHILD #1: Alonzo(Lonnie) Wiese. born Morgan. b. Jan.19,1859 and
died March 7,1934. He married Rene Charlotte (Lottie) in Brenham,
Texas on Oct.16,1879(MB 6,p.393)Lottie b. Dec.1862 and died Nov.
26,1935. Both buried in the Brenham Quadrangle, Prairie Lea
Cemetery,Brenham,Tx.

William Alonzo(Lonnie) was the son of Caroline Branning who m.
Fritz Wiese. Fritz later adopted Lonnie.

Lonnie and Lottie had 9 children.

    a. Lorina (Lora) b. 1881 d. Feb.14,1969.Married Charlie Loesch
        b. 1881,son of Louise Wiese and Herman Loesch.Fritz Wiese
        had also reared Charlie. (Ref.to Child #6: Louise Wiese)
        (6 children)
    b. John b.Feb.1882 m.Bertha Schwartz(2 children)
        1. Robert (Buddy)
        2. Elizabeth m. Garfield Woods(1 child)
            a. Charlotte Beth
    c. Willie b. Oct.1884 m. Malinda Quebe (1 child)
            a. William Henry m. Josephine Ditta
    d. Roy b. July 1886 m. Rosa Roessler (1 child)
        1. . Roy Jr.m.Ellen Yarbrough (3 children)
            a.Walter
            b.Rose Mary
            c. Nancy
    e. Joseph b. July 1889 d. July 16,1944 m. Freida Schwettmann
    f. Lonnie b. Apr.30,1894cd.Nov.16,1977 m. Ada Beaumier b.June1,
        1918
    g. Thomas b. Feb.1897 m.Louise Dietz (2 children)
        1. Eloise m.Jack Routt (1 child)
            a. Jackson
        2. Marion Thomas
    h. James died in infancy on Nov.1899
    i. Guy m Edwena Meisner (1 child)
        1. Carolyn Sue m.Vernon Madden (2 children)
            a. Mitzi
            b. Mike

(Confederate.)

W | 16 | Texas.

F. Wiese

Pvt., Co. E, Flournoy's Reg't Texas Inf.

Appears on

Company Muster-in Roll

of the organization named above.

Roll dated

Not dated, 186 .

Muster-in to date Apr. 7, 1862.

Joined for duty and enrolled:

When Mch 18, 186 .

Where Brenham

By whom G. T. Marold

Period War

Remarks:

Field officers for the 16th (also known as the 7th and as Flournoy's) Regiment Texas Infantry were appointed in October, 1861, and the ten companies (A to K) were organized on various dates from November 20, 1861, to April 25, 1862, but they were nearly all below the minimum and merely squads, or skeleton companies, when mustered into the service of the Confederate States.

Book mark:

J. W. Love Copyist.

(666)

(Confederate.)

W | 16 | Texas.

F. Wiese

Pvt., Co. E, Flournoy's Reg't Texas Inf.

Age 20 years.

Appears on

Company Muster Roll

of the organization named above,

for May & June, 1862.

Joined for duty and enrolled:

When Mar 18, 186 .

Where Brenham

By whom G. T. Marold

Period During the war

Remarks:

Field officers for the 16th (also known as the 7th and as Flournoy's) Regiment Texas Infantry were appointed in October, 1861, and the ten companies (A to K) were organized on various dates from November 20, 1861, to April 25, 1862, but they were nearly all below the minimum and merely squads, or skeleton companies, when mustered into the service of the Confederate States.

Book mark:

J. W. Love Copyist.

(642)

(Confederate.)

W | 16 | Texas.

F. Wiese

Pvt., Co. E, Flournoy's Reg't Texas Inf.

Appears on

Company Muster Roll

of the organization named above,

for July 1 to Aug 31, 1862.

Enlisted:

When Mar 18, 186 .

Where Brenham

By whom G. T. Marold

Period War

Last paid:

By whom A. Kemp

To what time July 31, 186 .

Present or absent Present

Remarks:

Field officers for the 16th (also known as the 7th and as Flournoy's) Regiment Texas Infantry were appointed in October, 1861, and the ten companies (A to K) were organized on various dates from November 20, 1861, to April 25, 1862, but they were nearly all below the minimum and merely squads, or skeleton companies, when mustered into the service of the Confederate States.

Book mark:

J. W. Love Copyist.

(643)

2a

The undersigned Royal Government certifies therein, that Herman
Friedrich Wilhelm Wiese, born February 18, 1843, in Wehdem, Lubbecke
County, ith his fathers permission, had his request to emigrate
to Texas granted and is thereby discharged as a subject from
the assemblage of Prussia.
The discharge papers are only for the aforementioned person
from the time of delivery from the assemblage and afterward
he will no longer be a subject of Prussia.

Minden, March 7, 1859

Discharge Papers #386, Vol.1.   Royal Kingdom of Prussia

[Handwritten German text:]

Die unterzeichnete Königliche Regierung bescheinigt
hierdurch, daß dem Hermann Friedrich Wilhelm
Wiese, geboren den 18. Februar 1843 zu
Wehdem, Kreises Lübbecke, mit weiterer
... Genehmigung, auf sein Ansuchen und
... seiner Auswanderung nach Texas,

die Entlassung aus dem Preußischen Unterthanen-Ver-
bande bewilligt worden ist.
Diese Entlassungs-Urkunde bewirkt, jedoch nur für die
darin ausdrücklich genannte Person, mit dem Zeit-
punkte der Aushändigung den Verlust der Eigenschaft
als Preußischer Unterthan.

Minden, den 7ten Maerz 1859.

Königlich Preußische Regierung.

Villers

Entlassungs-Urkunde
№ 586. C. I.

United States of America,
STATE OF TEXAS.

Original No. _____

REGISTER'S OFFICE,

Washington County.

OATH.

"I, _Frederick Wiese_ do solemnly swear, or affirm, in the presence of Almighty God, that I am a citizen of the State of _Texas_, that I have resided in said State for _Eight Years_ months next preceding this day, and now reside in the County of _Washington_, or the parish of _____, in said State, as the case may be; that I am twenty-one years old; that I have not been disfranchised for participation in any rebellion or civil war against the United States, nor for felony committed against the laws of any of the United States; that I have never been a member of any State Legislature, nor held any executive or judicial office in any State, and afterwards engaged in insurrection or rebellion against the United States, and given aid or comfort to the enemies thereof; that I have never taken an oath as a member of Congress of the United States, or as an officer of the United States, or as a member of any State Legislature, or as an executive or judicial officer of any State, to support the Constitution of the United States, and afterwards engaged in insurrection and rebellion against the United States, or given aid or comfort to the enemies thereof; that I will faithfully support the Constitution and obey the laws of the United States; and will, to the best of my ability, encourage others so to do. So help me God."

F. Wiese

I do hereby certify that on this _24th_ day of _June_ 186_7_ appeared before me _Fred Wiese_ who subscribed to the foregoing oath.

Louis Emil Edward
Register.

ORIGINAL.

(Peter O'Donnell, Stationer, 16 Camp St., N O.)

Paper found in the belongings of Fritz Wiese in 1978 by Dora Fuelberg Steele, the daughter of Bertha and Oscar Fuelberg.

$600.00

On or before th first day of January 1874 2-d
I promise to pay to Wm Bohne the sum of
Six hundred Gold Dollars for value recieved—
This Note is to act as a lien on the Homested
tract of land deeded to Friedrick Wiese by
J.G.C. Moore and wife until fully liquidated
and this Note is to bear ten pr Cent intrest
from date until paid This date the 15 day
of December 1871.

Received on the within the sum
of $ 100.00 One hundred dollars
and $ 20.05 two dollars & five cents
as interest thereon.
March 1st 1873   Wm Bohne

John Green Brickley
8th   1872

Interessen bezahlt für
Jahr 72
Interessen bezahlt für
Jahr 73. Interessen
bezahlt für Jahr 1874

Recieved on the within
$ 50.00 fifty Dollars as interest
for 1875 :— also :($ 100.00)
One hundred Dollars on the
principal

Papers found in the belongings of Fritz Wiese in 1978 by Dora
Fuelberg Steele, the daughter of Bertha and Oscar Fuelberg.

No. 1557560

UNITED STATES OF AMERICA
CERTIFICATE OF CITIZENSHIP

Petition, Volume 5 ### Number 354

Description of holder: Age, 77 years; height, 5 feet, 7 inches; color, White ; complexion,
Light ; color of eyes, Blue ; color of hair, Light-grey ; visible distinguishing
marks.

Names, ages, and places of residence of wife (Dead)

Names, ages, and places of residence of minor children

ORIGINAL

S.S. _Fritz Wiese_
(Signature of holder)

The State of Texas,
County of Washington

Be it remembered, that Fritz Wiese,

now residing at number Brenham, R.F.D. #5

City or Town of Brenham, State Country of Texas,

District aged Twenty-One , who previously

his naturalization was as a subject of Germany First

citizen of the United States of America pursuant to law, etc., the 6th day of September,

County of Washington held at Brenham, Texas, on the 5th day of September,

in the year of our Lord nineteen hundred and Twenty-One

Clerk, District Court
Washington County, Texas,
(official character; if attestor.)

In testimony whereof the seal of said court is hereunto affixed on the 5th day of September,
in the year of our Lord nineteen hundred and twenty-One and of our Independence the
one hundred and Forty-Sixth.

Fritz and Caroline Branning
Wedding Certificate , Brenham, Texas

State of Texas, to wit: Washington County, S. S.

To all who shall see these Presents, Greeting:

Know Ye, That any person legally authorized to celebrate the Rights of Matrimony, is hereby Licensed to Join in Marriage, as Husband and Wife Frederick Wiese and Caroline Branning and for so doing, this shall be your authority.

In testimony whereof, I, S. S. Hosea, Clerk of the County Court, hereunto subscribe my name and affix the seal of said Court, the 4th day of February, 1861.

S. S. Hosea Clerk

STATE OF TEXAS. TO WIT: WASHINGTON COUNTY,

This Certifies That I Joined in Marriage as husband and wife, Frederick Wiese and Caroline Branning on the _____ day of February, 1861

Geo. H. Herder
J. P. W. C.

Fritz and Caroline's beds

Wood water cistern

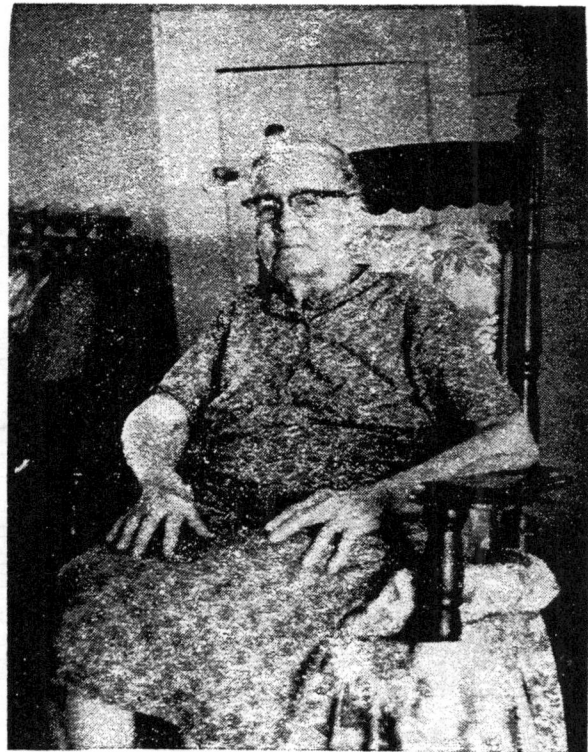

Bertha Fuelberg in her Great,
Grandfather's chair

Oscar holding Fritz's "Long Tom". Note the year 1889 over the door. (1978)

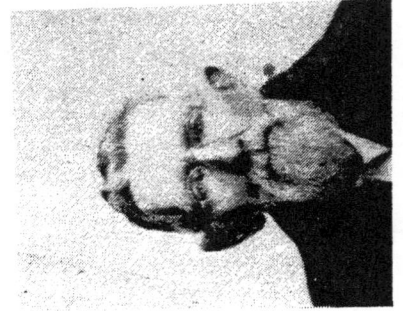

Fritz

Fritz and Caroline built home in 1889

Fritz and Caroline :Weideville Cemetery

PARENTS: A.F.CARL WIESE AND CHARLOTTE WILHELMINE D. MEYER
CHILD #2: JOHANN FRIEDRICH WILHELM b. Aug.14,1844,Bpt. Aug.20
d.Aug.28,1883. Married   July 11,1869 in Brenham,Tx. by
J.G. Lieb.M.G. to Mina Maier.They owned a beautiful farm
adjacent to his father,Carl. William died at the age of 38
and is buried in the St.John's Lutheran Cemetery at Prairie
Hill, about five and one half miles out of Brenham. Two years
after his death Mina married William Quebe and one daughter,
Malinda, was born. Two years passed and Mina died. She is
buried in the same cemetery as William, but buried as a
Quebe and not as a Wiese. His grave is under a lone tree
that grows in the center of the Cemetery and she is back
in the far corner. The farm is known today as the Wiese-
Quebe Place.(6 children)
    Bertha,Carl,Louise,Annie,and William. One child died.

The State of Texas, to-wit: Washington County, S. S.

TO ALL WHO SHALL SEE THESE PRESENTS, GREETING:

Know Ye,

That any person legally authorised to celebrate the RITES OF MATRIMONY,

is hereby Licensed to join in Marriage as Husband and Wife.

William Wiese and _Mina Maier_

and for so doing, this shall be your authority.

In Testimony Whereof, I, JOHN WELCH, Clerk of the County

Court, hereunto subscribe my name, and offix the seal of said

Court, the ____10____ day of ____July____ 1869

Jno Welch C. C. W. C.

The State of Texas, to-wit: Washington County, S. S.

THIS CERTIFIES that I joined in Marriage as Husband and Wife _William Wiese_

and Mina Meyer, on the 11th July 1869

J.G. Lieb, M.G.

William

Wilhelmien

Wilhelmien's tomb.

Wilhelmien Meyer (Wiese) Quebe
Grandaughter, Lydia Hodel

Wilhelm Wiese
Grandaughters Lydia and Ruby,1978

Charles

Louise and Fritz Wedeking

Annie Wiese Thim

Anita and Adolph Boedeker

Malinda Quebe & William Enox

Louise Wiese Wedeking

Wiese Children
Bertha Fehler, Annie Thim, Charles Wiese,& William

PARENTS: A.F.CARL WIESE AND CHARLOTTE WILHELMINE D. MEYER

CHILD #2:JOHANN FRIEDRICH WILHELM AND WILHELMENE MEIER WIESE

CHILD # 1: BERTHA

Bertha Wilhelmine Louise Wiese b. May 13,1870 in Prairie Hill, Texas, died August 8,1956 in McGregor,Texas. Married March 10,1888 to Fritz Fehler who was born Sept.24,1868 in Germany. The journey from Germany took three months for Fritz to arrive in the United States. He was a farmer all his life and when he died on March 29,1959 at the age of 91, he was the proud owner of 700 acres of land in McGregor,Texas. Both Bertha and Fritz were charter members of the Zion Lutheran Church in McGregor and are buried in the McGregor City Cemetery.

They were parents of eight children.

1. Carl William b. June 1,1888 m.Nov.26,1916 to Dora Folterman.

2. Henrietta Frieda b. June 16,1890 m. Jan.13,1911 to Lorence Sanders.

3. Charles Henry b. Oct.23,1892 m. Dec.22,1914 to Emma Louise Becker. Charles twin to Fred Henry.

4. Fred Henry b. Oct.23,1892 m. Nov.22,1917 to Erna Augusta Hackfeld

5. Anna Friedricka b. Sept.7,1898 m. July 21,1896 to Charlie Jeske.

6. Baby Son b. Feb.13,1897

7. Hedwig Louise Emilie b. March 3,1895

8. Bertha b. Feb.9,1916 m. March 27,1941 to F.C. Luedtke

August Friedrick Carl Wiese &
Charlotte Wilhelmine D. Meyer

William,their 2nd born with his
1st born,Bertha

Bertha m.March 18,1888 to Fritz
Fehler

Bertha and Fritz with their 1st born,
Carl

Bertha, born 18 years after
Annie

The Fehler Family
Fred, Will, Henneritta, Charlie
Bertha, Annie and Fritz

Bertha and Fritz
March 10, 1956

Bertha, Charlie, Fred, Annie
Willie, Bertha, Fritz and Henneritta

PARENTS: BERTHA AND FRITZ FEHLER
Child #1:<u>Carl William</u> b. June 1,1888 Prairie Hill, Tx. m.Nov.26,1916
in Gay Hill, Tx. to Dora Folterman b. May 2,1897,dau. of Heinrich(Henry)
Folterman and Sophie Wendt.(5 children)
- a. Alfred b. Nov. 21,1917 McGregor,Tx. d. Jan.19,1919 buried in
  McGregor Cemetery.
- b. Melita Sophia b. Oct. 20,1919 at McGregor,Tx. m. Oct.16,1944
  in Temple,Tx. to Vernon Beldon Parker b. Oct.22,1917 Shelley,Idaho,
  son of Audrey James Parker and Emma Parker. Vernon died Jan.1,1957
  in Barbara,Calif. and is buried in Logan,Utah in the Logan Cemetery
  (4 children)
  1. Patricia Ann b. June 27,1945 Temple,Tx.
  2. Norma Jean b. July 15,1947 in Logan,Utah. m.Aug.25,1965 to Nolan
     Dill Fergus b. Mar.14,1917.(4 children)
     a. Perry b. Mar.14,1966 Opi,Calif.
     b. Cindy b. Nov.1,19   Seattle,Wash.
     c. Julie b. Apr.4,19   Seattle,Wash.
     d. Gary b. May 1,1975 Seattle,Wash.
  3. William Vernon b. Jan.8,1949 Logan,Utah m. Sept.9,1971 to
     Beverly Dee Lafgen b. Feb. 25,1953,
     a. Brendon b. Aug.21,1974 Vanderberg A.T.B. Calif.
     b. Jeremy b. Nov.18,1975 Vanderberg A.T.B. Calif.
  4. James Beldon b. Sept.29,1950 Logan Utah.m.May 4,1974 to Katherine
     Rose Eum b. Apr.28,Tacoma,Wash.(1 child)
     a. James Daniel b. Dec.3,1975 Biloxi,Miss.
  5. John Frederick b. Mar.7,1952 Logan,Utah m. May 21,1971 to
     Charlyn Marz b. Mar.25,1953.(2 children)
     a. Kimberly b. Jan.2,1972 Opi,Calif.
     b. Wendy b.Mar.9,1974 Minot A.F.B. North Dakota

- c. Luther Gustav b. Feb.9,1921 McGregor,Tx. m.Dec.25,1945 to Mary
  Margaret Baumann Elliott b. Feb.13,1923 (3 children)
  1. Ronald Carl b. Jan.6,1947 Dallas,Tx. m. Mar.12,1971 to Marlene
     Kay Hewett b. Apr.1948 Dallas,Tx. (2 children)
     a. Shelly Lynn b. Oct.25,1974 Irving,Tx.
     b. James Dougles b. Apr.9,1977 Dallas,Tx.
  2. Naioma Daune b. May 2,1949 Dallas,Tx. m. June 29,1968 to Richard
     Jay Boehringer b. Mar.10,1947 Buffalo,N.Y. (2 children)
     a. Shannon Marie b. Mar.21,1970 Ft.Worth,Tx.
     b. Shawn Marie b. Sept.15,1973 Houston,Tx.
  3. Mary Evelyn b. Apr.13,1951 Dallas,Tx.
  4. William Ray Elliott b. May 26,1943 m. Aug.4,1962 to Mary
     Antonnette Freeman b. Sept.9,1943 .
     William is the son of Mary Margaret (Baumann) Elliott

- d. Corine Fehler b. Mar.25,1923 McGregor,Tx. m.Nor.15,1945 in Pampa,
  Tx. to Ralph Lewis Walker b. May 3,1919 and died Apr.30,1977
  (1 child)
  1. Theodore Walker b. Aug.7,1948 Dallas,Tx.

- e. Otto b. May 26,1925 McGregor,Tx. m. May 11,1954 to Sue Ann Mick
  (4 children)
  1. Daniel   2. Brian   3. Keith   4. Tonja

6

PARENTS: BERTHA AND FRITZ FEHLER
Child #2: <u>Henrietta Frieda</u> b. June 16,1890 in Brenham,Tx.M.Jan.13,1911
(or 12) , to Lorence Sanders b. July 10,1889 Prairie Hill, Tx. son of
William Sanders and Minnie Vahrenkamp. Lorence died Nov.20,1937 at
McGregor and is buried in the city cemetery.(5 children)

   a. Robert Fred b. Oct.10,1914 McGregor m. Apr.3,1941 to Irene Miller
     b. Nov. 15,1915 in Mart,Tx.,dau. of Tom Lee Miller and Gesena
     Schroder (4 children)
     1. Ron Warren b. July 4,1945 Waco m. Aug.26,1966 Marlin,Tx.to
       Martha Perkins b. Jan.23,1946 in Cleveland, Ohio,dau. of Neil
       Perkins and Margaret Graham (1 child)
       a. Julie Ann Sanders b. Dec.29,1970
     2. Stanley Gene b. July 19,1950 Waco m. March 25,1972 in Moore,Okla.
       to Gloria Hoile b. Oct.10,(divorced) Gloria dau. of Jacki Hoile.
       (2 children)
       a. Tracy b. Aug.20,1972
       b. Stacey b. Aug.20,1972 TWIN TO TRACY
     3. Randell Robert b. Jan 30,1954
     4. Richard Lawrence b. Jan. 30,1954 TWIN TO RANDELL ROBERT

   B. Nora Bertha b. Sept.17,1918 McGregor m. Nov.22,1950 in Lutheran
     Church at Crawford,Tx. to Paul Crawford b. Sept.6,(he will not tell)
   c. Elsie Anna b. Oct.10,1920 McGregor, d. Dec. 18,1922, buried in
     McGregor Cemetery.
   d. Buster (Lonnie) b. Mar.15,1922 in McGregor,Tx.
   e. Margie Myrtle b. Jan.8,1930 McGregor,Tx. m. Sept.9,1950 in
     Crawford to Robert Edwin Stuth b.Nov.3,1928 Crawford, son of Ed
     Stuth and Ester Mattlage (2 children)
     1. Pamela Dianne b. Mar. 18,1954 Clifton,Tx. m.Sept.11,1976 to Joe
       Paul Cook b. Mar.30,1953, son of Elmer Joe Cook and Bobbie Gene
       Smith.
     2. Robert Deryle b. Oct.10,1964 in Clifton,Tx.

Child #3: <u>Charles Henry Fehler</u> (TWIN TO FRED) b. Oct.23,1892 in
McGregor,Tx. m. Dec.22,1914 to Emma Louise Becker b. Oct.25,1890 in
Riesel,Tx.,dau. of Wm. Becker and Louise Stammeier.   Charles
died June 18,1969 in Clifton, Texas.(4children)

   a. Clara Louise Bertha b. Apr.20,1916 m. Nov. 27, 1938 in Clifton,Tx.
     in the Immanuel Lutheran Church in Clifton to Walter Henry Wiede
     b. Mar.4,1910, d. Aug.16,1972, son of Adolph Wiede and Martha
     Wagner of Clifton,Tx.(3 children)
     1. Alice Fay b. Dec. 18,1940 m. July 15,1967 to James Emery Rude
       b. June 9,1944 , son of Joseph Emery Rude . Alice married in McAllen
       Tx. (1 child)
       a. David b. Sept.17,1972 in Ohio
     2. Linda Mae b. Feb. 21,1950 m. Nov.1,1974 at Redeemer Luthern
       Church in Dallas,Tx. to Dudley Cottle b. Sept.30,1953,son of
       Mr. Temple and Glenda Cottle Temple of Eules,Tx.
     3. James Ray b. Dec.17,1951
   b. Walter William b. July 29,1920 Clifton,Tx. m. Oct 27,1946 to
     Pauline Louise Helms b. Aug.22,1921 in Clifton,Tx.,dau. of John
     Emil Helms and Bertha Ottilie Conrad(Courad?) (3 children)
     1. Bobby John b. Jan.18,1948 Clifton,Tx.
     2. Michael Paul b. Oct.17,1951 Clifton, Tx. m. Apr.6,1973 Ft.Worth
       to Beverly June Burnett b. June 29,1954 at Hillsboro,Tx. , dau

Charles Henry Fehler cont. .

        of Jim Sidney and Ruthy Faye Mosely Burnett (2 children)
    3. Judy Ruth b. Nov.18,1959 Ft. Worth,Tx.

  c. Willie Mae b. Nov. 17,1924 Clifton,Tx. m. Dec.1,1946 Clifton,Tx.
    to William Paul Wiethorn b. Jan.25,1920 in Crawford,Tx.,son of
    Mr.& Mrs. Henry Wiethorn (2 children)
    1. Donald Dale b. Sept.21,1951 Ft. Worth,Tx. m. Feb.14,1976 to
      Louise Carol Poucher b. Dec.2,1953 ft.Wayne,Indiana,dau. of
      Donald Earl and Joe Ann Bell Poucher (2 children)
      a. Michael Dwain Seeton(step-child)
      b. Alan Paul Wiethorn b. Oct.4,1977
    2. Glenn Paul b. June 29,1953 in Ft. Worth

  d. Charles William Fehler Jr. b. Nov.7,1927 in Clifton,Tx. m. July
    20,1948 Clifton,Tx. to Regina Ruth Helms b. Feb.10,1929 Clifton,
    Tx.,dau. of John E. Helms and Bertha Conrad Helms. (4 children)
    1. David Anthony b. Feb. 18,1951 Clifton, m. Dec.29,1971 to Jeanne
      Marie Staudt. b.Jan.8,1951 in Richardson,Tx.dau. of Ruben
      Staudt and Cora Dirks Staudt (2 children)
      a. Heather Leigh b.Dec.17,1972
      b. John Charles b. Mar.19,1977
    2. Deborah Kay b. July 31,1953 Fredericksburg,Tx. m. Aug.17,1974
      to James Allen Canuteson b. Jan.31,1953,son of Oren Canuteson
      and Barbara McGehee.
    3. Douglas Ray b. Nov.17,1954 m. Jan.11,1974 to Kristye Brynie
      b. Jan.11,1956 ,dau. of Henry & Josephine Oswald Brynie
      (1 child)
      a. Karie Shea b. Nov.30,1976
    4. Doyle Charles b. Dec.30,1961

Child #4.Fred Henry (TWIN TO CHARLES) b. Oct.23,1892 d. Nov.26,1973 m.
Nov.22,1917 to Erna Augusta Hackfeld b. Jan.7,1898 in Garfield,Tx.
dau. of John Henry Hackfeld & Bertha Matilda Schroder (2 children)
    1. Evelyn Margaret b. Jan.17,1921 Clifton m. July 21,1945 in
      Clifton to Lonnie Louis Lammert b. Mar.15,1917 in Crawford, son
      of Wm. Lammert & Annie Weithorn (3 children)
      a. Carolyn Ann b. June 1,1946 Clifton m. Nov.28, 1970 Crawford
      to Wm.Randel Lee b. Aug.11,1940 Luling,Tx., son of Curtis
      Eugene Lee and Annie Shoemacher (2 children)
        1. Rhonda D'Ann b. Aug.29,1971 in Sinton,Tx.
        2. Taunia Denise b. May 8,1973 in Sinton,Tx.
        3. Curtis Eugene b. June 23,1976 in Sinton,Tx.
      b. Wayne Fredrich Lammert b. Jan.10,1949 Clifton
      c. Jerry Don Lammert b. Dec.8,1952 Clifton m. Aug.10,1974 in
      McGregor to Donna Kay Stienke b. Mar.9,1952 Clifton, dau. of
      Henry Alfred Stienke & Dorothy Louise Hoehn (1 child)
        1. Erika Allison b. Sept.30,1975 Clifton
    2. Harold Elmer b. Nov.27,1927 Clifton m. Nov.6,1954 to Marie
      Prinz b. Oct.27,1932 Riceville,Iowa,dau.of August &Sophie Prinz.
      (2 children)
      a. Janice Colleen b. Mar.12,1956 Fredericksburg,Tx. m.Nov.30,
      1974 New Ulm,Tx. to Larry Dale Werland b. Columbus,Tx.,son of
      Clyde & Dora Werland
      b. Steven Harold b. Jan 6,1959 in Georgetown,Tx.

8

Child # 5: <u>Anna Friedricka Fehler</u> b. Sept.7,1898 McGregor m.
to Charlie Jeske b. July 21,1 96 at Gay Hill,Tx.(3 children)
    a. Helen b. Jan.13,1922 McGregor,Tx. m.Feb.26,1946 McGregor to Aurthur
       Hamilton (2 children)
         1. Kathyleen b. Mar.19,1955 Waco
         2. Charles Aurthur b. Dec.24,1958 Waco.
    b. Hildegard Gertrude b. Dec. 18,1924 McGregor m. to Eldon
       Schmalriede b. Nov.29,1922 McGregor (1 child)
         1. Mary Ann b. Mar.19,1951 Waco m. Apr.1975 Crawford to Roy C.
           Novasas son of John & Mary Novasad.
    c. Anna Mae b. June 8,1929 McGregor m. Aug.31,1951 in Crawford to
       James F. Rogers, son of Bill Rogers and Winnie Trammel (3 children)
         1. Janet May b. Dec.16,1952 Clifton m. Sept.20,1974 to Danny
           Knox, son of Billie Knox and Erlene Hamilton.
         2. Martha Lynn b. Jan 12,1956 Clifton m. Feb. 8,1975 McGregor,
           Tx. to Stephen Gerald Reese, son of Robert Reese and Minnie
           Sue Wright.
         3. Karl Patton b. Apr.7,1961 in Clifton,Tx.

Child # 6: <u>Baby Son</u> b. Feb.13,1897 died same day

Child # 7: <u>Hedwig Louise Emilie</u> b. Mar.3,1895 d. Oct.23,1898

Child #8: <u>Bertha</u> b. Feb.9,1916 m. Mar.27,1941 in McGregor to F.C.Luedtke
(Fredrick Charles) b. Feb. 26,1919,son of Ernest and Christine Witte
Luedtke (2 children)
    a. Donna Kay b. Oct.19,1944 m. Oct.26,1974 in McGregor to Richard
       Hylton Sutton b. Sept.17,1941 in Dallas,Tx.,son of Hylton and Betty
       Sutton.
    b. Betty Ann b. Nov. 26, 1948 m. June 22,1974 in McGregor to Joe
       Crawford Marshall b. Sept.16,1942, son of Joe and Maryanna Marshall
       (1 child)
         1. Allison Kay b. Sept.16,1977 in Houston,Tx.

PARENTS: A.F.CARL AND CHARLOTTE WILHELMINE D. MEYER WIESE
PARENTS: WILLIAM AND MINNA MAIER WIESE

CHILD # 2: <u>Wilhelm Carl Wiese</u> (Red Charlie, as many people knew him)
  b. Mar.28,1872 d. March 1.1959 m. Married Mithilda Charlotte
  Klostermann on Nov.19,1896 by L.C.Zettner,Lutheran Minister
  in Brenham,Tex.Mithilda b. Aug.6,1877 d. Oct.16,1962.Both buried
  in Cranfills Gap,Tex. in Rock Church Cemetery. Both lived to
  celebrate their 62nd. anniversary(13 children)
  Heneritta Louise, William, Lydia,Ella,Lonnie,Emma,Charley,Henry,
  Agnes,Minnie,Ruby,Ernie and Clara.

Golden Anniversary
November 19,1956
Left to right: Ella,Emma,Ruby,Clara,Lonnie,Ernie,Henry,Agnes,Charlie,
Lydie,Minnie. Seated: Heneritta,Papa,Mama, and Willie.

  1.<u>Heneritta Louise</u>: b.Dec.14,1897 Brenham.m.1st.Oct.19,1924
    Cranfills Gap to Arcy Frank Lassiter(3children)m. 2nd.July 8,
    1960 to Oscar Chris Grimland.
        a. Emma Mae Lassiter b. Dec.17,1925 Iredell,Tex. m.Apr.19,
          1941 to Alvin Pruitt(1 child)
           1. Elenor Gail b. Feb.26,1942 Los Angles,Calif.m.Apr.
             25,1965 Dallas to James Douglas Kilcrease(3 children)
                a. Cynthia Gail b.Nov.18,1966 Killeen,Tx.
                b. Gary Douglas b. May 14,1967 Dallas
                c. Randy James b. May 16,1974 Cleburne

        b. Earline b. Oct.14,1927 Iredell,Tx.m.June 1,1947 Cranfills
          Gap to Milton Salberg Jr. of "Norse"(2 children)

1. Gerald Ray b. Apr.25,1948 Clifton m.Aug.5,1967
   to Mrs. Carla Gail Beavers of Snyder,Tx.(2 children)
       a. Robert Carl (adopted son) b.Nov.25,1965
          in Snyder,Tx.
       b. Randy Keith b.Feb.14,1969 Clifton.
2. Deloras Kay b. May 22,1950 Clifton m.1st June 29,
   1968 to Jerry Olin Odle(1 child)
       a. Barry Clint b. Jan.29,1970
   Deloras married 2nd. to Jimmy Carroll Johnson on
   July 4,1974 (1 child)
       b. Kim Annette b. June 27,1975
c. Hugh Frank b. Mar.19,1933 Iredell m.1st June 17,1958
   to Mrs.Janie Duvall who had 2 children,David and Rebecca.
       1.David Jay b.Sept.13,1954 Mineral Wells,Tx.
       2. Rebecca Ann b. Nov.14,1956 Meridian.
   Janie and Hugh had 3 children
       3. Daniel Ray b.Feb.2,1959 Cleburne
       4. Rhonda Deleon b. Aug.10,1965
       5. James Michael b. Nov.7,1970
   Hugh married 2nd. to Mrs.Dorothy Lucyle Rowe Aug.1,1975
   in Cleburne where they make their home.

Child #2: William (Willie)b. May 27,1900 Brenham m.Mar.9,1931 in
   Cranfills Gap,Tx. to Emma Louise Muegge b.Apr.11,1911 McGregor,
   dau. of August Muegge and Henerietta Holtkamp(6 children)
       a. Laura Bell b. July 6,1933 Iredell m.July 1,1951 to Albert
          Kelm b.July 23,1924,son of Otto Kelm and Velaska Gottchalk
          (4 children)
              1. Cynthia Ann b. Oct.2,1953
              2. Marcus Dwain b.Oct.3,1955
              3. Daryl Ross b. Aug.6,1965
              4. Lori Michelle b. Mar.2,1969
       b. Gertrude b. Aug.7,1935 Fairy Tx.m.Jan.28,1957 to Maurice
          Gunn b. May 3,1931(2 children)
              1. Steven Maurice b. Nov.29,1958(9)
              2. Bradley Stuart b.July 24,1964
       c. Ora Marie b. March 4,1938 Cranfills Gap.m.June 2,1956
          Clifton to Henry Sanders b. Sept.23,1927 Crawford,son of
          Otto Sanders and Betty Sicks(8 children)
              1. Wm.Wayne
              2. Janet Diane
              3. David Glen
              4. Lisa Dawn
              5. Betty Louise
              6. Virginia Marie
              7. Johnnie Edward
              8. Christopher James
       d. Billy James b. Jan.16,1943 Cranfills Gap m.May 24,1973
          in Beaumont to Lela Carrol b.Feb.18,1950 Monroe,La.dau of
          Clarence and Levina Ingram Carrol(3 children)

To any Regularly Licensed or Ordained Minister of the Gospel, Jewish Rabbi, Judge District or County Court, or any Justice Peace Greeting:

You are hereby Authorized to Solemnize the

RITES OF MATRIMONY

Between Mr. *W. C. Wiese* and *Mathilde Klostermann*

and make due return to the Clerk of the County Court of said county, within sixty days thereafter, certifying your action under this License.

Witness my official signature and seal of office, at office in Brenham, the 17 day of November 1876

O. H. Seward
CLERK COUNTY COURT WASHINGTON COUNTY
By R. V. Hoffmann Deputy

I, S. C. Fellner, hereby certify that on the 17 day of Nov. 1876 I united in Marriage *W. C. Wiese*

and *Mathilde Klostermann* the parties above named.

Witness my hand this 17 day of Nov. 1876

S. C. Fellner
Luth. Pastor

Returned and filed for record the 26 day of Feby 1877 and recorded the ___ day of _____ 187_

_____ Deputy

O. H. Seward
CLERK COUNTY COURT WASHINGTON COUNTY

Christian Carl Wilhelm Wiese aus _____
Sohn des Herrn Johann Friedrich Wilhelm Wiese
und _____ Elisabeth Wilhelmine ___ geborene _____
geboren den 28ten März 1872 ist am
13ten April 1873 im Beisein der Zeugen

1. August Friedrich Carl Wiese
2. Christian Meyer
3. Dorote a. Wilhelmine Holle

im Namen des

Dreieinigen Gottes

getauft worden, welches hierdurch
glaubwürdig bescheinigt wird

F. Klinworth
ev. luth. Pastor bei Brenham
Texas

Wilhelm Carl Wiese and
Charlotte Klasterman

1955
59th anniversary

"Papa"
Agnes, Ruby, Minnie & Ernie

50th anniversary

William and Mina Wiese

Charles, the first son

Charles (W.C.) Wiese and Mithilde Klostermann

                1. Tammy Lee
                2. Barbara Lynn
                3. James Howard b. Feb.1977
           e. Emma Matilda b. Aug.5,1945 Cranfills Gap,Tx.
           f. Kenneth Edward b. Oct.3,1947 Cranfills Gap.m.June 1,
              1968 to Audra Stockton b. July 25,1950 Meridian.dau.of
              Audrey Stockton and Ruby Connors(1 child)
                1. Kenney Allen b. Feb.1969

Child #3: <u>Lydia Louise</u> b. Nov.20,1901 Brenham,Tx.m. June 21,1930
    in Durant,Okla. to Herman B.Hodel b. July 21,1895 d. March 9,
    1950,son of John Hodel and Lucy Jackley. Herman was born and
    died on the family farm in Coryell City which Lydia still owns.
    She lives in Waco now after retiring from years of nursing at
    the Hillcrest Hospital. She and her sisters cared for their mother
    until her death in Lydia's home. Without Lydia's help, this book
    could not have been compiled as she was my "co-pilot" on many
    trips to Brenham and surrounding areas. It is impossible to know
    how many telephone calls she has made and received to make my
    work easier.

Lydia and Herman Hodel,1928

Child #4: <u>Ella Annie</u> b. Apr. 12,1903 d. Mar. 10,1975 m. Oct. 29,1923 to
Johnny Grimes b. July 1,1899 d. Feb. 12,1971 Son of Beatrice Adaline
Tellis and Malcom DeKalb Grimes.(3 children)
    a. James Edward b. Mar.29,1925 m. Sept.23,1951 Seguin Tx. to Helen
      Martha Hahn b. Dec. 12,1929 dau. of August Bernhardt Hahn and Martha
      Elisa Koopman.(2 children)
        1. Marla Yvette Grimes. b.Nov.8,1955
        2. Kirk Vaughn Grimes b. Nov.15,1957
    b. Ernest Carl b.Nov.19,1928 d. Dec. 2,1928
    c. Norma Ruth b. May 26,1930 m. Ft. Worth to Thomas Howard Finch
      b. May 19,1924 d. 1962 (3 children)
        1. Renda Gayle b. Nov.26,1955
        2. Teresa Nell b. Apr. 16,1957
        3. Renita K. b.Aug.28,1961

Child #5: <u>Lonnie William</u> b. Oct.6,1905 Brenham d. Aug.1,1965 m.1930 to
Helma Gladys Jorgenson b. Dec.3,1909 Dau.of Andrew Jorgenson and Losma
Hastings.(4 children)
    a. Lucille b. Apr.7,1931 d. Apr.12,1931
    b. Jessie Wayne b. Aug.4,1937 m.Oct.1958 to Tricia M.Boyd b.June 9,
      1938 Dau. of Luella Collins and Mr. Boyd.
    c. Lonnie Wm.Jr. b. Feb. 10,1941 d. July 29,1941
    d. Lois N. b.Oct. 26,1943 m.Apr.5,1964 to Jimmie C.Brown b. Apr.21,
      1944. Son of Laverne Davis and Mr. Brown.(2 children)
        1. Lori Justine b. Sept.26,1964
        2. Dina Page b. Aug.3,1967

Child #6: <u>Emma Louise</u> b. May 7,1906 Moody Tx. m.March 11,1928 in
Cranvilles Gap to Albert Muegge b.June 14,1901 in Brenham d. Aug.23,
1972. Son of August Muegge and Henrietta Halcamp.(2 children)
    a. Bernice b. May 10,1933 m. May 20,   to Richard Kelm b. Nov.29,
      1925 at McGregor.(2 children) Richard son of Mr. & Mrs. Otto Kelm
        1. Rodney b. June 23,1952
        2. Sharon Kay b. May 20,1955 m. Aug. 3,1974 to Dennis Robert
          Kraemer b. Nov. 11,1949
    b. Roy b. Apr.19,1936 m. May 4,1959 to Pethrica Linnard of Tyler,Tx.
      dau. of E.A.Linnard (3 children)
        1. Mike b. Mar 9,1961
        2. Judy b. Jan. 17,1963
        3. Sharon Kay b. June 19,1969

Child #7: <u>Charley William</u> b. June 20,1908 m.1st. Sept.30,1928 in Iredell,
Tx. to Lorene Pierce b. Apr.9,1911 d. Aug. 20,1958 Dau. of Wm. Pierce of
Pala Pinto Co. (2 children)
    a. Wm. Carl b. Oct. 14,1930 m. Pansy Lie Prator Sep.17,1951. Pansy
      b. Nov.3,1929 (2 children)
        1. Terry Wayne b. Apr.28,1954
        2. Pamla Ann b. June 23,1957 d. May 13,1965
    b. Jerry Jeffery b. Feb. 11,1943 m. June 3,1964 Donna Kay Tidwell
      b. May 20,1946 (3 children)
        1. Jerry Jeffery Jr. June 3,1964
        2. Steven Wade b. Nov. 14,1966
        3. David Lee b. July 18,1970
Married 2nd: Oct.1,1960 to Lorener Wilson b.   d. 1967

Child #8: <u>Henry Louis</u> b. Mar. 21,1910 m. Oct. 25, 1931 to Selma Pauline
Finson b. June 16,1910 Hamilton Co. Dau. of Sam and Emilie Finson.(3 children)
   a. Thelma Louise b. Oct 2,1933 m. Jan.3,1952 in Clifton to Raleigh
      Dunlap b. Jan. 21,1934 in Hubbard Tx. Son of Bill and Rena Dunlap
      (2 children)
      1. Ronnie Wayne
      2. Deborah Lynn
   b. Margie Estelle b. May 23,1936 Cranfills Gap m. Sept.23,1955 in
      Stephen,Tx. to Duane Mooney b. Mar.2,1935.Son of Bill and Opal
      Mooney (4 children)
      1. Audry Dale
      2. David Neal
      3. Hershal Wayne
      4. Opal Laura
   c. Harold Sidney b. Sept. 14,1944 in Iredell m. Dec. 17,1965 to Preshie
      Estelle Johnson b. Mar. 10,1948 Dau. of Henry and Dolly Johnson
      (2 children)
      1. Henry Russell
      2. Harold Joseph

Child #9: <u>Agnes Annie</u> b. June 30,1912 in Moody, Tex. Agnes lives in Waco.

Child #10: <u>Minnie Louise</u> b. Jan. 17,1914 in Iredell m. Jan.6,1935 to
Marion A. Sorenson , son of Conrad and Lula Meckleson Sorenson. Both
Norvegian pioneers. (5 children) Marion died Oct.9,1978
   a. Mina Fay b. May 9,1936 in Jonesboro, Tx. m. David Bergman, son of
      Meltion and Clarice Peterson Bergman.(4 children)
      1. James Melvin b. Oct. 8,1963 m. Oct.26,1974 to Lisa Shank of Houston.
      2. Danny b. Dec.9,1955
      3. James b. Oct.3,1957
      4. Marion b. Oct.19,1963
   b. James Marion b. Sept.8,1937 m. Helen Young, dau of Oliver and Estell
      Stewart Young of Walnut Springs (2 children)
      1. Kathey b. Jan.28,1960
      2. Karen b. Apr.3,1963
   c. Troy b. Mar.7,1940 m. Linda Ratliff of Lomita ,dau. of Lee and Ethel
      Donnheian Ratliff (3 children)
      1. Troy Don b. Sept.14,1967
      2. Tad Marion b. Oct.1968
      3. Lane K. b. Dec.12,1970
   d. Leroy b. Mar.16,1941 m. Donna Gray of Tusco,Arizona,dau. of Walter
      Gray (4 children)
      1. Dennise b. May 28,1963
      2. Debbie b. Oct.6,1965
      3. Bryan b. Feb.15,1969
      4. De Ann b. Feb.15,1969 TWIN TO BRYAN, lived only a short while.
   e. Marynell b. May 8,1944 m. Clinton Murphee of Burrelson,son of Cloves
      and Fern Rahne Murphee (2 children)
      1. La Renda b. Feb.12,1964
      2. Angela b. May 13,1965

Child #11: <u>Ruby</u> b. Aug.16,1916 m. Feb.17,1934 to Ed.McCherry b. Feb.22,1913
(4 children)
   a. Bobby Ray b. May 8,1935 m. May 1,1964 to Nettie Ruth Bush b. Apr.10,
      1923 (3 step-children)

14

    1. Janette Lundy b. April 23,1941 m. Earnest Mosley b. Feb. 12,1936
    2. Charles Lundy b. July 30, 1943 m. Jill b. Feb. 2,1948
    3. Nadene b. Feb. 20,1949 m. Jim Watson b. Oct.14,1941
  b. Betty Ann b. Iredell Sept.23,1938 m. Mar. 10,1969 to Henry Rathliff
    b. Mar. 7,1930 (1 child)
    1. Dehn Marline b. Aug. 8,1970 San Antonio
  c. Peggy Joyce b. Jan 17,1942 Clifton m. Jan. 8,1965 to Jack Ray Foster
    of Stevenville, Tx. (2 children)
    1. Sherry Lynn b. Jan. 28,1967 in Frienswood, Tx.
    2. Malaine Ann b. May 11, 1969
  c. Pauline b. Sept.24,1946 Waco.

ALL DAUGHTERS ARE L.V.N. 's

Child #12: Ernie Louise b. May 16,1918 in Iredell. m.1st: Elmo Hovend,
  son of Charlie Hovend. Elmo died in WWII.
  Ernie married 2nd: Cecil Samuelson, son of Otto Samuelson.

Child #13: Clara Mathilda b. Oct. 6,1921 in Iredell m. June 15,1946 to
  Alvin Samuelson b. Dec. 21,1916 d. Oct. 20, 1970 , son of Otto
  Samuelson (2 children)
  a. Shelia Laverne b. Apr. 10,1946 m. Jan. 13, 1971 to Thomas Lee
    Robertson b. Dec.14,1945, son of Lee Robertson Jr. (1 child)
    1. Justian Lee b. Jan. 24,1976
  b. Michael Dwayne b. Sept. 11,1951

In August,1978, the husband of Minnie Louise,Marion Sorenson was
the second patient to use a new type of machine, the first of its
kind in central Texas.The Hillcrest opened a new cancer center and
treated Marion's tumor with this machine which has the ability to
penetrate any part of the body and dry up the tumor without affecting
any surrounding area.

PARENTS: WILLIAM AND MINNA MAIER WIESE
CHILD #3: LOUISE AND FRED WEDEKING

Child #3: <u>Louise</u> b. May 13,1874 d. May 4,1918 . m. Aug. 1897 to Fred
   Frank Wedeking b. May 17,1867 Germany. d. Sept. 8,1956, son of William
   Wedeking and Dorthea Meier. Parents stayed in Germany. (10 children)

   Child #1: <u>Rosa</u> b. May 27,1898 d. Aug. 12, 1910 of typhoid fever.
   Child #2: <u>Willie Fritz</u>: b. July 21,1899 d. Jan. 21,1976 . m. Dec. 14,
      in Wese, Texas to Eliza Zahn b. July 20,1896 d. Sept. 20,1977
      dau. of Henry Zahn and Rosa Benkendofer.(6 children)
      1. Reinhart b. Nov. 17,1922 in Waco. m. Sept. 4,1943 to Dorothy
         Thomas b. Dec. 3,1925, dau. of James W. Thomas and Sophie
         Schiller. (6 children)
            a. Betty Jean b. Sept.11,1944. m. July 15,1967 to Pete Wese of
               Douglas, Ga.
            b. Joyce Marie b. Nov. 17,1947 d. Nov. 19,1947
            c. Reinhardt Jr. b. March 7,1949 d. June 23,1949
            d. John Wayne b. Sept. 25,1950
            e. Richard Lee b. May 7,1954
            f. Danny Ray b. Feb. 17,1961
      2. Wilfred b. Oct. 18,1924 d. Nov. 26,1973 m. April 11,1946 to Naome
         Thomas b. Sept. 3,1924, dau. of William Thomas and Dora Thomas.
         Wilfred buried in Greenwood Cemetery, Ft. Worth. (4 children)

            a. William Wedeking b. June 17,1947
            b. Henry Z.Wedeking b. Jan. 1,1949
            c. John T. Wedeking b. Aug. 25,1950
            d. Elisa Jo.Wedeking b. June 20,1953
      3. Paulita b. July 14,1926. m. Oct. 1,1949 to Leo Robins b. Oct. 21,
         1924 son of Charles R.Robins and Lilie May Collins. (3 children)
            a. Sandra Jean b. Feb. 7,1951 m. April 29, 1971 to Garland Craig
               Row b. May 22, 1951, son of Seymore Row and Faye Stallard.
               (3 children)
                  1. Melanie Lynn b. Jan. 19,1972
                  2. Rebecca Lee b. June 26,1974
                  3. Tara Ann b. Dec. 15,1977
            b. Carla Sue b. Nov. 8, 1956 m. Jan.3,1976 to Russell Allen
               Benfer b. Aug. 20,1955, son of Jerry Benfer and Dorothy
               Anz. (1 child)
                  1. Nathan Allen b. May 29,1976
            c. Robin Lea Robins b. March 26,1966
      4. Jeanette b. July 9,1928 m. June 4,1946 to John Reichle b. Aug.3,
         1924, son of Clarence Reichle and Rosie Schumacher (2 children)
            a. Jan b. July 16, 1953 m. May 19,1973 to Randall Possey of
               Dallas.
            b. Joh Carl b. Oct. 13,1958
      5. Betty Jean b. June 1932
      6. Billy Gene b. June 1932 TWIN TO BETTY JEAN. Both buried in the
         Clausner Cemetery in West, Tx. (Zahn Plot)

Child #3: <u>Matilda</u> b. April 13,1901 m. Ross, Tx. Dec.11,1924 to Otto
Brinkman b. Feb.1,1996 d. Nov. 29,1954. Son of August Brinkman and
Johanna Brands. (4 children)
1. Louise b. Nov. 3,1925 m. April 24,1944 West, Tex. to Jerry (Jerome)
Hutyra, b.Dec. 17,1911 d. Oct. 17,1949, son of Vince Hutyra and
Christine Ondrej.(3 children)
    a. Doris Louise b. Jan.8,1945 m. Oct.2,1965 to Ronald Edmund Rauch
      b.Sept.10,1940 ,son of Victor Max Rauch and Alice Louise Knapp.
      (3 children)
        1. Michael Edmund b. Feb. 15,1966
        2. Patricia Marie b. May 17,1968
        3. Daniel Edward b. May 17,1971
    b. Martha Ann b. Feb.18,1946 m. June 26, 1966 to William John
      Edward Quicke b. March 20,1946 and divorced 1971.(1 child)
        1.Timothy John Edward b. March 8,1967
      Martha married 2nd: Sept.4,1972 to Frederick Michael Trolinger
      b. Oct. 5,1948 , son of Wayne Eugene Trolinger and Evelyn
      Hutchcraft. (2 children)
        2. Christopher Michael Trolinger b. Dec.3,1975
        3. Amy Michelle Trolinger b. March 3, 1977
    c. Geraldine b. Feb. 23,1948 m. August 31,1968 to Raymond Edward
      Barton b. Nov. 15,1944, son of William Frank Barton and Albina
      Leona Kadubar. (2 children)
        1. Raymond Edward b. Sept. 4,1969
        2. Karen Rena b. Dec. 13,1974
Louise 2nd marriage July 9,1951 West,Tx. to Daniel John Ondrej
b.July 11,1913 , son of John Ondrej and Anna Kaska.(3 children)
    d. John Daniel b. Nov. 13,1951 m. Mar. 27,1976 to Marilyn Kay Crow
      dau. of Gerald Ray Crow and Mary Katherine Gray.
    e. Elizabeth Anna b. June 19,1953 m. Mar. 4,1972 to Ronald Charles
      Sulak, b. Oct.4,1951 son of Albert Paul Sulak II and Caroline
      Kaska. (2 children)
        1. Audra Elizabeth b. Apr.28,1973
        2. Darrell Ronald b. Aug. 16,1974
    f. Mary Barbara b. Feb. 23,1955 m. July 4,1973 to Danny Lynn
      Shelton,b. Apr.3,1955, son of Burl Harrison Shelton and Edelene
      Danford.(2 children)
        1. Bobby Lynn b. Mar.24,1974 d. Mar.24,1974
        2. Shephanie Ann Shelton b. Sept.30,1975
2. Lennora b. Oct. 18,1927 Waco m. Nov.9,1946 to Lornze Kluck b. Feb.27,
  1923,son of Otto and Elsie Kluck.(3 children)
    a. Otto b. July 19,1947 m. Shirley Ann Leuschner June 15,1968. Shirley
      b. Oct.14,1947 dau. of Julius and Lucille Leuschner of Waco.
      (2 children)
        1. Shelly Ann b. Jan. 19,1970
        2. Kraig Scott b. Dec. 5,1974
    b. Rose Ellen b. Aug. 9,1949 m. April 12,1969 to Clifton Emerson
      Jenkins b. Oct. 30,1942. Son of Pete and Bells Jenkins of
      Dahlgren,Va.(2 children)
        1. Clifton Emerson Jr. b. July 2,1970
        2. Christine Danyal b. July 11,1972

      c. Mildred Ann b. Aug.18,1951. m. Feb.22,1969 to Stanley J.
         Leuschner b. Nov.24,1942, son of Julius and Lucille Leuschner
         of Waco. (2 children)
            1. Lance Allen b. June 19,1974
            2. Laurie Ann b. Aug. 11,1976

    3. Esther Brinkmann b. July 21,1931. M.Nov.24,1956 to James L. Alsup
      born Feb.21,1933,son of James B.and Dorothy L. Alsup.(2 children)
        a. Karen Ann b. June 4,1960
        b. James Arthur b. March 24,1962
    4. Helen b. Apr.22,1936 m. June 14,1956 to Harold Willhite b. Dec.31,
      1932,son of Clara Ann Ulrich and Lester Louis Willhite.(4 children)
        a. Donna Marie b. Apr.2,1957
        b. Gloria Ann b. Nov.9,1958
        c. Harold Wayne b. Sept.10,1962
        d. Darrel Layne b. Sept.10,1962 TWINS

Child #4: <u>Fritz W.</u> b. Aug.15,1903 Crawford Tx. d. Aug.13,1973 m. Nov.
    28,1928 to Minnie Hessel b. Sept.20,1909, d. July 3,1973, dau. of
    F.H. and Henrietta Hessel (3 children)
    1. Donald Wayne b. Oct.9,1939 Waco. M. May 25,1968 to Doris Richter
      b. Apr.6,1947. Dau. of Helmut and Mrs. Richter.
    2. Charles b. Sept.1,1941 Waco m. Nov. 11,1967 to Estelle Matus
      b. Jan.28,1939, dau. of Louis and Mary Matus.(2 children)
        a. Eric b. Sept.11,1968
        b. Darren Lane b. April 23,1976
    3. Jo Ann b. Oct.26,1948 m. Mar. 30,1968 to Joe Wacht b. Mar.30,1941,
      son of Michael and Louise Wacht.

Child #5: <u>Malinda Louise</u> b. Sept. 2,1905 in Crawford, Tex. She m.
    Nov. 7,1929 in West, Tex. to Ewald Adolf Pfeffer b. June 17,1905
    in Bellville, Tx. Ewald's grandfather, Karl Pfeffer came to America
    from Germany to Austin County , near Bellville. He and his wife
    (maiden name,Ueckue) had 12 children,3 boys and 9 girls. It was there
    that Ewald's father , Frank F. was born on July 30,1972 . He died
    Feb. 24,1959 . He married Augusta Harms, dau. of John F. Harms and
    Johanna Jansen. Augusta b. Austin Co. Aug. 15,1873 d. July 14,1960.
    Her father , John was born in Germany on Nov. 17,1945 and died Jan.
    18,1936. Johanna b. May 11, 1836 and died in 1902.

John F. Harms as a young man hauled cable for the Brazos Suspension
Bridge from the Houston area to Waco with a oxen tean and wagon.

Malinda and Ewald had 1 child.
    a. James Ernest b. Apr. 13,1947 in Ft.Worth m. West,Tex. June 17,
      1967 to Evelyn Louise Carpenter b. July 31,1949 Waco. (2 children)
        1. Judy Louise b. Dec. 30,1968
        2. Elizabeth Marie b. Feb. 25,1975

Child #6: <u>Anna Henrietta</u>. b. Oct. 31,1907 Crawford d. Dec. 15,1968
She m. <u>Nov. 14,1928</u> to Willie (Bill) Hessel. b. Apr.25,1899 d. Jan.
28,1969. Both buried in Riesel,Tex. Annie and Bill died six weeks
apart. The had shared a double wedding ceremony with Fritz and Minnie.
(5 children)

    a. Lonnie Harold b. Feb. 12,1930 Aquilla Tx. m. Sept. 14,
       1957 Grossbeck to Mona Sue Reagan of Groesbeck. b. Oct. 23,
       1934. Dau of Mr. & Mrs. Reagan.

    b. Billy Gene b. Feb. 6,1935 Ross, Tx. m. July 3,1958 to
       Shirley Ann Gilbert b. Aug. 20, 1938 Riesel,Tx. (2 children0
       1. Mark Alan b. Nov. 30,1959 Marlin
       2. Barry Glenn b. Sept.26,1962 Marlin.

    c. Dorothy Louise b. June 13,1936 Ross, Tx. m. Mar.1,1956
       Waco, to Thomas Marvin Federwisch b. July 12,1937. (4 children)
       1. Carol Elaine b. Apr.25,1959 Waco
       2. Teresa Lynne b. Feb. 18,1961 Temple,Tx.
       3. Patricia Diane b. Aug. 11,1962 Temple,Tx.
       4. Michael Weldon b. Mar. 9,1965 Temple,Tx.

    d. Geneva Ann b. Feb. 4,1941 Ross,Tx. m. Sept. 9,1965 in
       Houston to Ian Louis Landry of New Orleans,La. b. Sept.13,
       1926. (3 children)
       1. Michael Ann b. Nov. 8,1969 Dallas
       2. Meridith Leone b. Dec. 28,1971 Tulsa,Okla.
       3. Margo Renee b. Sept.5,1976 Tulsa,Okla.

    e. Violet Laverne b. Jan.12,1945 Waco.m. Aug.30,1963 Riesel,Tx.
       to Richard (Dickie) Lee Person of Mexia. b. Dec. 13,1941.
       (3 children)
       1. Melanie Dawn. b. Apr.19,1965 Sulphur Springs,Tx.
       2. Ronald David b. Aug.31,1967
       3. Baby girl born and died Apr.26,1970 in Corpus Christi,
         Tx.and buried in Riesel,Tx.

Child #7: <u>Charles Henry</u> b. Dec. 3,1909 Crawford,Tex.m. April 23, 1938
Waco,Tex. to Jeanette Wilson b. Dec. 4,1914 in Italy,Tex.Dau. of
Mr. & Mrs. Wilson (2 children)

    a. Charline b. May 23,1940 Turnerville,Tex.m. April 16,1956 to
       Frank Wavrusa b. Feb.2,1932 Alma,Tex. (4 children)
       1. Kathryn b. Nov. 20, 1957 Dallas,Tex.
       2. Frank b. June 8, 1959 Dallas,Tex.
       3. Bradley b. June 28,1961 Dallas ,Tex.
       4. Stevie b. Mar. 14,1969 Dallas, Tex.

    b. Yvonne b. Apr. 27,1944 m. July 1966 to Frank Johnson b. Nov.
       29,1939 ,son of Mr. & Mrs. Johnson.(2 children)
       1. Timmy b. Nov.10,1968 Keller,Tex.
       2. Lonnie b. Mar. 11,1974 Dallas,Tex.

Child # 8: <u>Henry Otto</u>.b. March 25,1912 m. Sept.5,1934 in
    Gerald,Tex. to Clara Efrieda Wilhelmina Lehmann b. Jan.1,1916
    Leroy,Tex. Dau. of Paul and Mary Blankenstein Lehmann. Paul
    b. May 23,1881 in Hamburg Germany,(a small town Newe Kirche).He
    came to America when he was nine years old and was a farmer all
    his life until his death on May 31,1962 in West,Texas. Paul's
    father was Ed Lehmann and his mother was Christina-both born in
    Germany. Ed b. Nov. 1853, d. Mar. 1931. Christina b. Oct. 1894
    d. Mar. 1921. They had 3 children, Paul, Pauline & Walter. Clara's
    mother Mary, was born Feb. 26, 1885 Waco. d. Aug.13,1968 Waco.
    Her parents: Gottfried & Christina Christinson Blankenstein. Both
    born in Germany, he in Barbi, Germany on June 18,1855 d. Mar.22,
    1921 Gerald,Tex. and she born May 10,1861 and d. Oct.20, 1924
    Gerald Tex. They were blessed with 7 children: Richard m. Ella
    Krenik, Mary m. Paul Lehmann, Elsie m. Carl Farkle, Alma m.
    Albert Banik, Paul m. Anna Hessel, Elfrieda m. Henry Bode, and
    Ziegfried m. Nona Mae English. Gottfried also had a sister, Mary
    and a brother Ernest, who came to America. Ernest m. Nannie_____
    and made their home in Temple. Mary Married a Mr. Baade and lived
    in Waco.

Henry Otto and Clara had (6 children)
    a. Rose Marie b. June 10,1935 West, Tex. m. Aug.17,1950
        to Rual(Blow) Dunn, b. Aug. 19,1927, son of Luther & Mattie
        Dunn. (5 children)
        1. Larry Wayne b. May 30,1952
        2. James David b. Aug. 20,1951 m. Aug. 24,1975 to Brenda
            Tedforn ,dau. of Mr.& Mrs. Ted Tedford.
        3. Bobby Gene b. Apr.22,1958 m. May 2, 1976 to Paula
            Seale b. 1958,dau. of John R. & Annie May Seale.
            (1 child)
                a. Boby Gene Jr. b. Jan.18,1978 St.Francis Colo.
        4. Charles Bradley b. Jan.15,1961
        5. Henry Luther b. Feb. 13,1963
    b. Ben Henry b. Jan.1,1937 Robinsonville, Tex. m. Sept. 4,1959
        to Betty Lemerle Griggs in Houston .Betty b. July 13,1938,
        dau. of Carl Joe & Arvie Griggs.(4 children)
        1. Timothy Ray Eugene b. April 11,1961 Houston
        2. Karl Edward b. June 18,1963 Houston
        3. Jon Paul b. Sept. 30,1970 Alba,Tex.
        4. Ben Josesh b. Aug. 5, 1976. Ben is a Dairyman.(the father)
    c. Daniel Carl b. Oct.29,1939 Ross, Tex. m. Dec. 15,1961, New
        York, N.Y. to Patricia Eileen Murphy b. Oct.24,1942 Bronx,
        N.Y.,dau. of Sidney and Pearl Murphy. Daniel is in the Air
        Force , now in Little Rock, Ark. (4 children)
        1. John Henry b. Mar. 22,1963 Staten Island, New York
        2. Daniel Carl b. May 11,1964 Denver, Colorado
        3. Kathleen b. Aug. 18,1966 Larado,Texas
        4. Cynthia Eileen b. Apr.3,1970 Altus, Oklahoma

      d. John Robert b. Mar. 10,1940 near Waco , a place called
         Beerjoints. M. Sept.2,1967 to Fabia Oldham Carlew b. Oct.
         22, 1947, dau of Melvin & Rena Beale Oldham.(4 children)
           1. Terry b. March 25, 1966. Terry's father had died and
              John legally adopted him.
           2. John Robert Jr. b. Feb. 1,1968 Houston
           3. Jeremy Lane b. May 17,1973 Houston
           4. Gregory Alan b. March 25,1975 Huffman
         John is a Houston Fireman
      e. Lynda Clare b. Aug. 9,1942 Waco,Tex. m. Nov.5,1960 to
         James Roy Crump b. Aug. 6,1940, son of James Roy & Virgie
         Swann Crump (4 children)
           1. Joni Lynn b. Sept.19,1963 Houston
           2. James Roy Jr. b. Dec. 18,1964 Houston
           3. Christina Marie b. Dec. 22,1970 Big Sandy,Tex.
        Lynda and Jimmy raise fryers.
      f. Paul Edward b. Dec. 9,1944 Houston m. April 23,1964 to
         Lucille Ostinelli b. Mar. 10,1945, dau. of Charles Ostinelli
         and Mary Ostinelli. (3 children)
           1. Paul Edward Jr. b. Oct. 5,1964 San Antonio
           2. Michael Lee b. Apr.18,1967 Sherman,Tex.
           3. Diana Clare b. Sept. 19,1976 Austin,Tex.
        Paul is in the Air Force at Bergstrom

Child 9: **Marie** b. Jan 28,1914 m. Nov. 20,1935 to Bohus J. Chupik
    b. Nov. 24,1907, son of Stepan and Mary Chupik. (6 children)
      a. Ruth Marie b. Jan. 20,1937 m. June 7, to Joe L. Owens
         b. Aug. 20,1934 son of Sam and Mildred Owens (3 children)
           1. Cynthia b. Sept. 29,1959
           2. Samuel Bohus b. Dec. 31,1961
           3. Earl b. March 2, 1963
      b. Bohus Jr. b. Sept. 29,1938 m. Feb. 1, to Diana Pierce
         b. Nov. 1944, dau of Roy Pierce (3 children)
           1. Doreen b. Dec. 30,1967
           2. Kevin b. Feb. 22,1968
           3. Jason b. March 2,1977
      c.   Betty Jean b. Oct 11, 1939
      d.   John C. b. Dec. 2,1941 m. Oct 20,1962 to Charlotte
         Drennan b. Nov. 7,1944 , dau of Mr&Mrs. Marvin Drennan
         (4 children)
           1. Robbie b. Aug. 5,1963
           2.Pamela b. Dec. 2,1965
           3. Troy b. May 10,1969
           4. Kimberly b. May 7,1970
      e. Stephen W. b. May 17,1943 m. Dec. 14,1968 to Elizabeth
        Lee b. Dec. 13,1951, dau of Mr.& Mrs. .D.Lee(2 children)
           1. Shawon b. Aug. 26, 1971
           2. Shelia b. Oct. 21,1975
      f. Jimmy A. b. June 25,1945 m. Jan. 12,1969 to Joan Black
        b. Nov. 3,1943, dau. of Mr & Mrs. Carl Lee (3 children)
           1. Yvonne Black b. Nov. 16,1959dau of Joan
           2. Ronald Black Chupik b. Nov. 19,1962 (adopted by
             Jim)

            3. Jimmy b. Feb.23,1972
        g. Carol Ann b. Sept.22,1947 m. Nov. 16,1962 to Ronald Pekar
           born Oct.25,1945, son of Mr. & Mrs. Joe Pekar (1 child)
            1. Kimberly b. May 2,1976

Child #10,<u>Ella(Ellen)</u> b. Dec. 8,1916 m. Oct. 15,1940 to Louis J.
    Kolar b. May 10,1916, son of Mr. & Mrs. Emil Kolar (3 children)
        a. Barbara b. May 30, 1942 m. June 13,1964 Waco to Ray Rodgers
           b. Mar. 15,1942, son of Mr & Mrs. Raymond Rodgers (1 child)
            1. Gregory Paul b. Jan. 15,1972
        b. Betty Louise b. Dec. 12,1945 m. Feb.8,1964 Waco to Charles
           Albert Hill b. Sept. 17,1942, son of Mr.& Mrs. Belvin Hill
           (3 children)
            1. Tina Rehna b. Dec. 9,1967
            2. Anthony Scott b. June 25,1971
            3. Kimberly Dawn b. Feb. 17,1973
        c. Marjorie b. April 9,1952 m. Dec. 16,1972 to Charles Conner,
           son of Mr. & Mrs. William Conner.

Child #4: <u>Annie</u> b. Oct. 31,1877 Washington Co. m. June 1899 Giddings
Tex. to John Thim b. Aug. 27, 1872, d. Apr. 4,1954. Buried in
Wiederville Cemetery. (6 children)
    a. Tracie (Theresa) b. Feb. 23,1899 Brenham, Tex. m. Aug.12,
       1919, to Emil Addicks b. 1891 Harris Co.Tex. , son of Gustav
       and Sophie Hoefelmeyer Addick(2 children)
          1. Esther Addicks b. Dec. 21,1919 m. Harry Roehling b. April
            14,1916 , son of Louie and Hattie Schatz (1 child)
              a. David Gene b. Dec. 14,1940 m. May 28,1961 to Doris
                 Wehmeyer b. Nov. 19,1941, dau. of Ernest and Dora
                 Finke Wehmeyer (3 children)
                    1. Debra Gail b. Dec. 16,1963
                    2. Dona Denise b. Mar. 9,1967
                    3. Doretta Ann b. May 11, 1972
          2. Nelson b. May 1,1942 m. Sept.3,1963 to Gloria Ann Draehn
            b. Oct. 14,1942, dau. of Alfred and Alma Draehn
            (2 children)
              a. Joel Thomas b. Dec. 18,1968
              b. Stacy Alan Roehling b. May 14,1973

    b. Roudolph b. Nov. 12,1900 m. Sept. 25,1930 to Hattie Breddin
       b. May 20,1932, son of Laura and Norbert Kramer(1 child)
          1. Linda Kay b. Apr. 1954 m. Dec. 29,1973 to Darrell Reimer
            b. Apr.3,1952, son of Evelyn and Otto Reimer(2 children)
              a. Donna Marie Kramer b. Mar. 6,1961
              b. Lisa Dawn Reimer b. May 5,1977
          2. John Weldon b. Oct. 6,1940 m. July 14,1962 to Faye
            Hildebrand b. Dec.7,1943, dau. of John and Lorine
            Hildebrand (2 children)
              a. Schelley Jean b.Nov.27,1964
              b. Raquel Leigh b. Oct. 14,1969

    c. Annie b. Feb. 17,1903 m. June 28,1929 to Alfred Emil Pfeffer
       b. July 23,1902, son of Frank and Augusta Harm Pfeffer (1 child)
          1. Bobby James Pfeffer b. April 6,1938 m. Dec. 22, 1973 to
            Joyce Colleen Berryman b. Sept.26,1943, dau of Arnold
            and Doris Berryman.

    d. Anita b. March 2, 1903 m. December 16, 1926 in Washington Co.
       to Adolph Boedeker b. May 1st, 1900, son of Theodore and Anne
       Boedeker.
       Without Anita and Adolph, this book could not have been written.
       They have always been available when I needed them. I can not
       thank them enough for their hospitality.

    e. Arnold b. June 16,1907 m. Feb.2,1933 to Elsie Herzog b. Aug.11,
       1906, dau. of August and Mitilda Weiss Herzog(2 children)
          1. Dorothy Ann b. Feb.17,1938 m. Jan.20,1960 to William
            Privette, son of Wm & Frances Privette. William was born
            June 2,1941(4 children)

          a. James b. Mar.29,1961
          b. Allen b. Jan.30,1963
          c. Scott b. Dec.9,1965
          d. Cathy b. Nov.23,1973

    2. James b. Sept.23,1940 m. June 15,1963 to Mary Easterling
       b. Sept.20,1944, dau of Carey and Burnice Easterling
       (3 children)
          a. Charlotte b. Sept.10,1964
          b. Sandy b May 7,1969
          c. Stacis b. June 1,1971
    f. Adele b. July 18,1910 m. Jan.22,1938 to Fred Wagener b. Sept.
       15,1914, son of August and Ida Wagener
Child #5: Mena, b. 1879 died as an infant

Tracie Thims and Emil Addicks

Child #6: <u>Hermann Carl Wilhelm</u> , known as William, spent his child-
   hood years in Washington County near Brenham, Tex. He was educated
   in the Brenham schools and attended nearby Blimm College. He later
   moved to the McGregor community where he worked as a farm hand,
   although his desire was to become a railroad engineer. He often
   played the accordian and the violin in a string band for the country
   dances. It was during these years that he met Anna Meiske, whom he
   married on Jan.1,1908, in McGregor. To this union were born eight
   children, four sons and four daughters.
      They spent most of their lives farming in the McGregor area, with
      the exception of a few years when they farmed in Carlsbad in Tom
      Green County and Osage in Coryell County, Texas. William and Anna
      retired from farming in 1948 and moved to Oglesby, Texas, and in
      1953 they moved to Waco, where they lived the remainder of their
      lives. Both buried in Waco Memorial Park.
William b. Feb.9, d. July 18,1957. M. Jan.1,1908 to Anna Meiske.
b. Nov. 16,1884, d. Sept. 21,1976, dau. of William Meiske and
Henriette Vahrenkamp. Her father, William was born in Westfalen,
Germany and her mother was also born in Germany. Both parents are
buried in the McGregor Cemetery,McGregor,Tex. (8 children)
      a. William (W.C.) b. Sept.7,1908 McGregor m. Jan.26,1941 to
         Lillie Herzoz b. Jan.5,1913 Burton,Tex., dau. of August Herzoz
         and Mithilda Weiss of Zionville.
      b. Bertha Henrietta b. June 20,1910 Carlsbad, Tom Green County,Tx.
      c. Walter Frederick b.April 30,1912 Carlsbad,Tex. m. Sept. 18,
         1948 to Norma Anne Hawes b. Aug. 14,1921 Parrsboro,Nova Scotia,
         Canada, dau. of William Irving Hawes and Annie Myrtle Yorke.
         (2 children)
            1. Roy Frederick b. Nov.4,1949 Hartford, Conn. m. July 17,
               1976 Wildwood, Illinois to Cynthia Dee Edwards b. Aug.5,
               1954 Chicago, Ill., dau. of Warren Milton Edwards and
               GlenDoris Eberle (1 child)
                  a. Craig Edwards b. Sept. 11, 1977 Schenedtady, N.Y.
            2. Brenda Vivian b. July 31,1952 Hartford, Conn. m. May 19,
               1973 Manchester, Conn. to Bruce Wright Ray b. Feb. 2,
               1953 Concord, New Hampshire, son of James A.Ray and Esther
               Wright (1 child)
                  a. Heather Anne b. May 18,1978
      d. Nora b. Oct.4,1915 Osage, Tx. m. Sept.1,1940 to J.P. Worley
         born Apr.6,1914 Axtell Tex.,son of John Phillip Worley and Eva
         Brackett (2 children)
            1. Margaret Elaine b. Mar. 4,1944 Victoria, Tx. m. Albert
               Leroy Childress b. Aug. 14,1943, son of Tate and Elrosa
               Childress. Margaret and Albert were married Apr. 16,
               1964 in Waco,Tx. (2 children)
                  a. Gary Phillip b. Dec. 10,1964 Waco,Tx.
                  b. Cathy Elaine b. Aug.31,1970 Tacoma,Washington

2. Charles Edward Worley b. Oct.28,1946 Bastrop,Tx. m. Feb.
16,1974 Kennebunkport,Maine, to Martha Barbara Young
b. May 4,1950, dau. of Mr.and Mrs. Norbert W. Young.

J.P. Worley died Sept. 30,1961 and Nora married Levi Sylvester
Cox Jr. b. Sept.1,1908 Waco,Tx., son of Levi Sylvester Cox Sr.
and Winnie Needham. Nora and Lee married Nov.4,1966 Waco.Tx.

e. Annie Louise b. July 10,1917 McGregor,Tx. m. Feb. 14,1946
Waco,Tx. to Anton John Cocek b. Aug.25,1914, Waco,Tx., son of
Anton and Julia Marie Mnar Cocek(1 child)
1. Kenneth John b. Nov.9,1955 Waco,Tx.

f. Heneritta Louise Lillie b. June 14,1919, McGregor, d.Nov.20,
1920 of diptheria.

g. Lonnie Henry Carl b. March 31,1921 McGregor,Tx. m. Mary Jane
Ross b. November 8, 1923 Rockwell City, Iowa, m. March 4,1944 in
Los Angeles, Calif. Divorced April 1964 in Miami, Fla.
(2 children)
1. Wayne Eric b. July 17,1947 Fort Dodge,Iowa m. to Mary
Ellen Hay b. Jan.19,1947 Boston,Mass.(1 child)
a. Keith b. April 17,1969 Miami,Fla.
2. Anne Lynn b. Nov.28,1956 Coral Gables,Fla.

h. Carl Henry John b. Aug.31,1924 McGregor,Tx. m. July 6, 1946 to
Ornel Lydia Geltmeyer b. July 12,1930 Crawford,Tx., dau. of
Fred and Emma Hedt Geltmeyer.(2 children)
1. Mary Diane Wiese b. Feb.22,1947 Waco,Tex.
2. Jerry Ray Wiese b. Jan.31,1948 Waco,Tex. m. Oct.6,1972
to Sue Ann Morrison Jordan b. July 31,1943, dau. of C.E.
and Helen Morrison.(2 children)
a. Chantelle Lee Ann Jordan b. June 19,1970 Dallas,
Tx.,adopted by Jerry on June 6,1977.
b. Tasha Renea Wiese b. Sept.6,1974 Okinawa, Japan.

William Wiese died Aug.28, 1883 at the age of 38 and is buried in the St.John's Lutheran Cemetery at Prairie Hill, Texas under a lone tree that grows in the center of the Cemetery. Two years after his death Mina married William Quebe and one daughter, Malinda, was born on July 3,1887. Two years passed and Mina died and was also buried in the same cemetery-back in the far corner - as Wilhelmine,Born Meier, Quebe.

Malinda was reared by her father, William Quebe and his second wife, Henriette Hodde,b. Sept.16,1869 d. Jan.9,1932.

Child #7: Malinda b. July 3,1887 m. William Enax and lived on a farm
    near Brenham (3 children) m.Oct.20,1912 M.B.17,p.295,Brenham.
    1. Raymond William Enax b. April 27,1914 m. Sybil Ener in Houston.
       Sybil b. Sept.18,1926 (2 children)
          a. Norma Jean b. Feb.13,1946 m. Glenn Poindexter Mar.26,1966.
          Glenn b. Aug.3,1944 in Phonex Arizona(4 children)
             1. Glenn Dean Jr. b. Mar.31,1967
             2. Frank Ray b. Mar.12,1969
             3. Homer Allen b. Apr.27,1973
             4. Malinda Nell Marlene b. July 23,1975
          b. Ruth Evelyn b. Apr.6,1947 m. Tommie Null b. Dec.28,1945
          in Houston,Tex., son of Tommie and Esther Null (2 children)
             1. William Monroe b. July 10,1960
             2. Wesley Dell b. Sept.17,1975
   2. Marvin Charlie b. Feb.7,1918 Brenham m. Mabel Ener on June 19,
      1954 in Houston. Mabel's first husband, Mr. Harper had died
      leaving her three children.
          a. Laverne Harper b. Feb.27,1948
          b. Jimmy Harper b. July 5,1951
          c. Mabel Marie Harper b. Dec. 1949
          d. Marvin Enax Jr. b. Feb. 16,1955 (Marvin and Mabel's child)
   3. Norma Enax b. 1928 and lives in Houston

Malinda Quebe(left bottom) with her half-sisters
on the steps of the Wiese-Quebe home

The Quebe Family
Malinda in striped dress and Bill Enox to the left of steps

Vol.2, p.396

Henry Wiese OT

No 3 marriage license

Sophia Holle

Issued Jany 12ᵗ 1867

Filed Jany 19ᵗ 1867

S. S. Hosea Clerk WC

The State of Texas, to wit: Washington County, S. S.

TO ALL WHO SHALL SEE THESE PRESENTS, GREETING:

Know Ye, That any person legally authorized to celebrate the Rites of Matrimony, is hereby Licensed to join in Marriage as Husband and Wife, Henry Wiese and Sophia Holle and for so doing, this shall be your authority.

In testimony Whereof, I, S. S. Hosea, Clerk of the County Court, hereunto subscribe my name and affix the seal of said Court, the 12ᵗ day of January 1867

S. S. Hosea C.C.W.C.

The State of Texas, to wit: Washington County.

This certifies that I joined in Marriage as Husband and Wife, Henry Wiese and Sophie Holle on the 18ᵗ day of January 1867

G. G. Diek, Minister of the Gospel.

Henry and Sophie Holle Wiese

"New Homeplace"

Phillipsburg Cemetery

"Old Homeplace"

Sophie with grandchildren

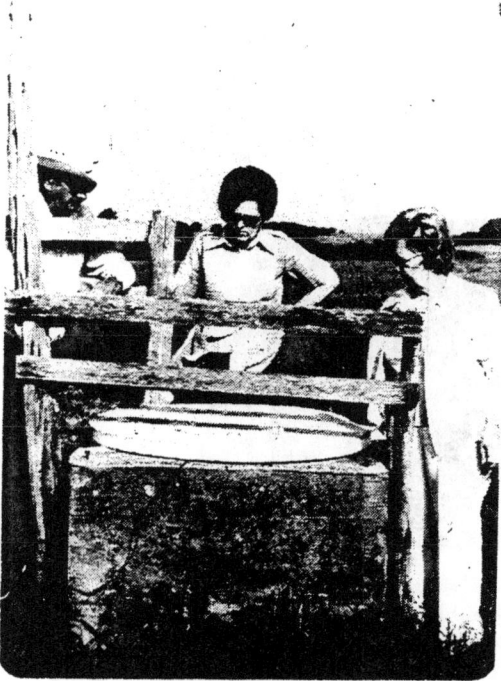

"House well"
Ed Korth,Annie Korth,& Lydie Hodel

Spring-fed well

Countryside

Cornerstones of house
Edwin, Annie, and Lydia

Ed's boots resting on "History"

WIESE FAMILY HOLDS REUNION *1950*

Descendants of the family o' the late Sophie and Henry Wiese met Sunday, July 23, at Cameron Park in Cameron for a family reunion. The day was spent getting re-acquainted as this reunion was the first one to be held in many years.

A delicious chicken dinner was served and late in the afternoon. a buffet supper was served.

The committee elected to serve for next year's reunion to be held the fourth Sunday in July at the same place were: Carl H. Wiese. Brenham, Chairman; Mrs. Fritz Beerwinkel, Secretary, Moody; Miss Lillie Brockermeyer, Treasurer, McGregor; Henry Wiese. Giddings; Walter Weise. Moody; Ronald Glaser, Ganado; Edwin Wiese. Ganado; and Mrs. Otto Weidner, Navasota.

Those attending the reunion were: Miss Lillie Brockermeyer; Mr. R. M. Brockermeyer; Mr. and Mrs. Vernon Schmidt; Mr. and Mrs. Walter Wiese, Walter Jr. and Linda; Mr. and Mrs. Gus Adler and Louise; Mrs. Hulda Wiese; Gus Adler Sr.. all of McGregor; F. W. Brockermeyer; Miss Clau-

da Mae Brockermeyer, all of Typer; Mr. and Mrs. Carl H. Wiese and Ruth and Miss Janelle Kruse; Mr. and Mrs. Henry Wiese and Janice; Mr. and Mrs. Willie Kelling; Mr. and Mrs. Charles W. Lemm and Ronnie, all of Brenham; Mr. and Mrs. Gilbert Wiese, Donnie and Gary; Mr. and Mrs. Herbert L. Kattner; Mr. and Mrs. George Beimer and Carolyn, all of Temple; Mr. and Mrs. Walter Wiese and Frances;

Mr. and Mrs. Arvell Schmidt; Mr. and Mrs. Chas. Wiese; Mr. and Mrs. O. A. Winkler and Lawrence; Mr. and Mrs. Fred Beerwinkel and Shirley; Mr. and Mrs. John Stuth; Mr. and Mrs. E. Schmidt Edward and Doyle; Mr. and Mrs. Will Wiese Connie and Ann; Mr. and Mrs. Wm. Haas, Gene and Margie; Mr. and Mrs. Jim Comer and Jo Evelyn; Rev. W. E. Harrell; Mr. and Mrs. Louis Schmidt, Ruby and Frieda Mae; Mr. and Mrs. Walter Schmidt and Weldon; Mr. and Mrs. Raymond Eakin and Dolores, all of Moody; Mr. and Mrs. Willie Schmidt; Mr. and Mrs. Henry Schmidt, Daisy Nell, Linda Lou, and Carol Sue; Mrs. Malinda Schmidt, all of Troy; Eldon Wiese; Mr. and Mrs. Fred Wellman; Miss Jo Ann Williams; Mr. and Mrs. Ervin Wiese, all of Houston; Mr. and Mrs. W. H. Moeller of Cleburne; Mr. and Mrs. Paul Glaser and Ronald; Mr. and Mrs. Bernard Kuretsch; Mr. and Mrs. Ed Wiese, of Ganado; Mr. and Mrs. Elmer Stuth and Jerry of Waco; Mr. and Mrs. F. C. Goessler, Hilbert and Ruby of Washington; Mr. and Mrs. Henry Wiese; Leroy Wiese; Miss Estelle Carmean of Giddings; Mr. and Mrs. Paul Schmidt; Mr. and Mrs. H. F. Beerwinkel of Pendleton; Mr. and Mrs. Ruben Beerwinkel and family of Belton;. Mr. and Mrs. Preston Nelson of Eddy; Mr. and Mrs. Ervin Henske and family; Chris Wiese of Kenney; Rev. and Mrs. E. C. Schmidt of Genoa; Mrs. Leona Luhn, Sugarland.

First reunion of Henry Wiese Family in Cameron, Texas. 1950

Henry, Willie, Charley, Chris
Sophie, Emma, Betty, Minna, and Melinda

Wiese Reunion Held Recently 1951

Descendants of the family of the late Sophie and Henry Wiese who came to this country from Germany in 1857 met Sunday, July 22, 1951 at Cameron City Park in Cameron, Texas.

Out of 13 children of Sophie and Henry Wiese, 9 are living and all were present for their reunion and they range in ages from 63 years to 82 years. They were Mrs Malinda Schmidt of Moody, Mrs Minnie Brockermeyer of McGregor, Mrs Sophie Glaser of Ganado, Mrs Emma Pfeffer of Chapel Hill, Mrs Betty Koerth of Brenham, Chas Wiese of Moody, Will Wiese of Chapel Hill, Chris Wiese of Kinney and Henry Wiese of Ganado. Of this group there was one set of twins, Mrs Betty Koerth of Brenham and Chas Wiese of Moody.

A delicous chicken dinner was served at noon and late in the afternoon a buffet supper was served.

This was the second reunion of this kind and was well attended with about 160 present coming from Navasota, Brookshire, Lolita, Copperas Cove, Belton, Chapel Hill, Kinney, Sugar Land, El Campo, Ganado, Washington, Giddings, Troy, Pendleton, McGregor, Temple, Houston, Caldwell, Deanville, Cleburne, Waco, Riesel, Brenham and Moody.

The committee elected to serve for next year's reunion to be held the fourth Sunday in July at Firemans Park, Giddings, Texas were Carl Wiese, Brenham, Miss Lillie Brockermeyer, McGregor, Mrs Fred Beerwinkle, Moody, Henry Wiese, Giddings, Irvin Glaser, Ganado, Mrs Raymond Eakin, Moody, Walter Koerth, Brenham, and Mrs Bernard Kuretsch of Lolita.

1975 Reunion in Brenham, Texas

1975 Brenham

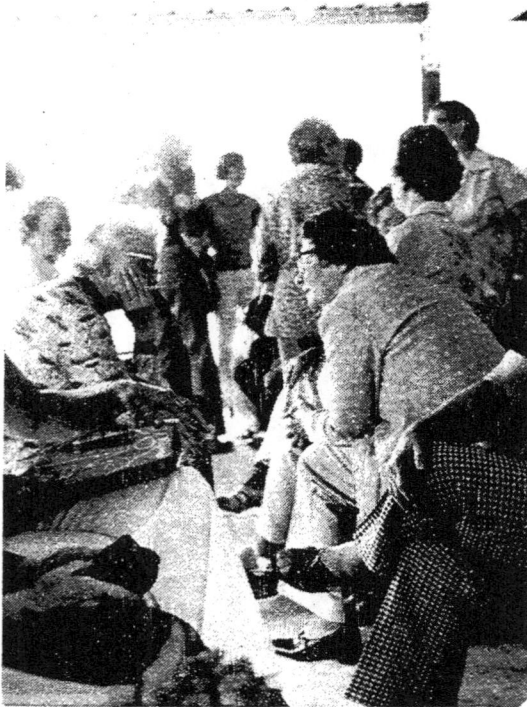 

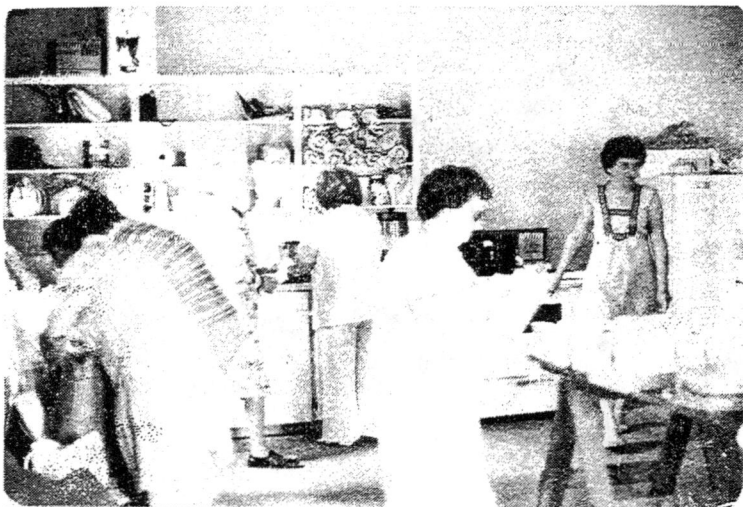

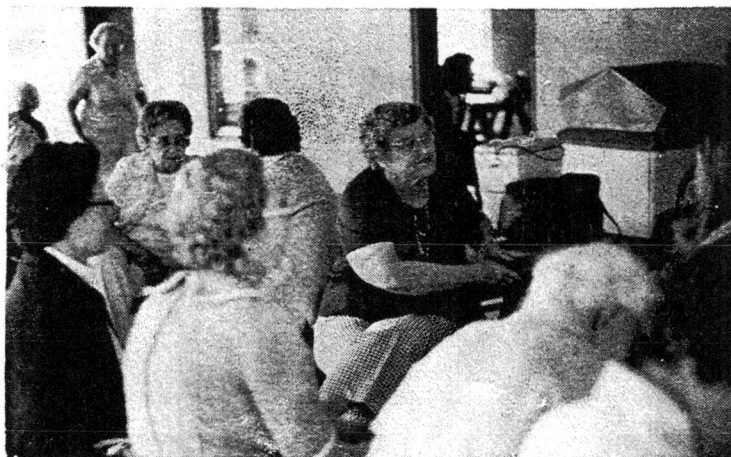

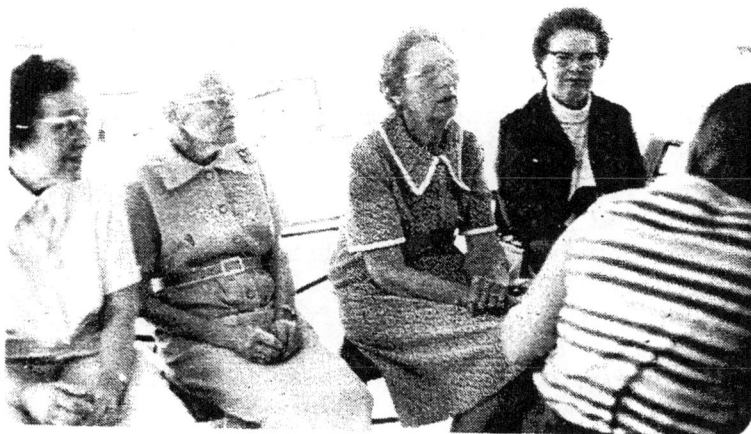

PARENTS: A.F.CARL WIESE AND CHARLOTTE WILHELMINE D. MEYER
CHILD #3: <u>HENRY FREDRICK</u> b. Nov.22,1845 d. Aug.20,1922 (77yrs.)
   Married Sophie Holle Jan.12,1867(M.B.2,p.396,Brenham,Tx.)
   b.Feb.11,1845 d. June 23,1932(87yrs). Both born in Germany.
   Henry arrived on the ship WESER in 1860 along with his brother
   William . His brother Fritz had arrived on the ship IRIS the
   year before. Sophie immigrated from Germany to Texas in 1855
   (See seperate material on the Holle Family)

Sophie and Henry lived for several years at Prairie Hill,a
community a few miles north east of Brenham,Texas. In 1875,
Henry, along with Sophie's brother William Holle, signed a
deed for 10 acres of land as trustees of St.John's Evangelical
Lutheran Church for $100.00 in gold.After 1903, the family
moved to Kenny,Texas in the community of Phillipsburg in Austin,
Co.,where they are buried in the Phillipsburg Cemetery between
Brenham and Kenny.

Henry was a lover of music and it was told by Ben Wiese, his
nephew, that Henry had played a choral on his organ the night
before his death. Many remember him sitting under the shade
trees smoking his water pipe. Sophie was a gentle and loving
person and is remembered with great fondness.

Henry and Sophie were parents of 13 children(3 sets of twins)

1. Fred b. April 8,1867 m. Hulda Neumann
2. Melinda b. Sept.10,1896 m.Louis Schmidt
3. Wilhelmine(Minna) b. July 27,1871
4. Unnamed child
5. Charlie b. Jan.1876 m.Lena Wellman
6. Bertha(Betty) TWIN TO CHARLIE m.Fritz Korth
7. Lidia b. Feb.1877 died
8. Chris TWIN TO LIDIA m. Augusta Wenzel
9. Henry b. June 3,1880 m. Agnes Glaser
10. Willie b. Oct.5,1882
11. Lydia TWIN TO WILLIE m. Otto Koeppen
12. Emma b. 1885 m. Herman Pfeffer
13. Sophie b. Feb.13,1887 m. Paul Glaser

PARENTS: A.F.CARL WIESE AND CHARLOTTE WILHELMINE D. MEYER
CHILD #3:HENRY FRIEDRICK AND SOPHIE HOLLE WIESE

Child #1: Henry Friedrick(Fritzb. April 8,1867 Washington Co.Tx.
d. August 20,1940 Crawford,Tx.m.Oct.22,1891 to Hulda Neumann
b. Aug.5,1871,Austin Co. d.Oct.5,1964 Travis Co.dau. of Sigmund
Neumann and Fredrika Janke Neumann.Henry (Fritz) and Hulda
were married by Charles Henry Kniker,Minister of the Gospel.

They were the parents of 12 children,one set of twins;Hulda
and Zelma. Zelma died as an infant and all 11 of the children
married.All were born in Washington Co. except the youngest,
Lillie who was born in McLennon Co.

Fritz and Hulda moved to the Buckhorn community in 1914, a few
miles from Moody,Texas. There they farmed until 1937 when
the family moved to the Crawford area.

At Fritz's death, he was buried in McGregor Cemetery,
McGregor Texas. Hulda spent her last days in the Lutheran
Nursing Home in Round Rock and was buried beside her dear
husband.(12 children)

1. Fred m.Lillie Edwards
2. Otto m.Ella Stuth
3. William m. Lydia Stuth(sister of Ella)
4. Henry m. Frieda Krueger
5. Lydia m. John Stuth(brother to Ella and Lydia)
6. Hulda m. Fritz Goessler
7. Zelma died
8. Carl m. Ettie Krueger(sister to Frieda)
9. Malinda m. Walter VonRuff
10.Robert m. Nellie Cox
11. Walter m. Emma Goessler (sister to Fritz Goessler)
12. Lillie m. Gus Adler Jr.

Child #1: Fredrick Sigmund b. Nov.15,1892 Brenham, Texas. d. Apr.3,
    1963 and is buried in the Waco Memorial Park. m. Nov. 19,1917
    Bell, Co.to Lillie Edwards b. Dec.31,1896 Moody,Tex. dau. of Louis
    and Mary Smith Edwards. Louis and Mary had 12 children and Lillie
    was the only one born in Texas. They lived for many years in the
    Buckhorn Community near Moody,Tex. (5 children)
    a. Joe Henry b. Nov.2,1918 Buckhorn Community, m. Feb.10,1940
        Moody to Mildred Marie Elliott b. Feb.20,1922,dau. of Robert
        Leonard Elliott & Minnie Glenn (4 children)
            1. Robert Joe b. Oct.14,1943 m. Jan. 1975 Belton, to
                Patricia Moore b. Mar. 17,1955 , dau. of Ben Moore &
                Mrs. Lola Cornet. (1 child)
                    a. Barbara Danielle b. June 18,1976
            2. Brenda Joyce b. Jan 11,1950 m. Dec. 19,1969 to Larry
                Nichols son of C.L. and Jeane Nichols. Divorced Mar.
                1976. (2 children) m.June 16,1978 Bobby Storm b.Nov.29,'48
                    a. Larry Michael b. Sept.5,1971
                    b. Aimee Denise b. June 15,1976
            3. Carol Anne b. Oct.14,1953
            4. Darrell Dean b. Oct.14, 1953 TWIN TO CAROL ANNE
                m. Aug.22,1975 Waco, to Cynthia Brown b. Dec.6,1957
                dau. of Gail and Charles Brown of Waco.
    b. Ernest Ray b. Aug. 13,1920 Buckhorn Community, Moody, Tex.
        m. Feb.22,1944 Baton Rouge, La. to O'Levia Neil Wilson. b.
        March 1, 1928, Bared,Miss. dau. of Roger O'Neal and Mittie
        Scott Wilson. Roger b. Kemper Co. Miss, and Mittie b.
        Wilkerson Co. Miss. They moved to Texas in 1952 to live near
        Ray and Neil. They brought their other five children to Texas
        where each married and settled there. Katherine m. Paul Kemp,
        Neil m. Ray Wiese, Robert, Roger B. m. LoeNell Dugger, Agnes,
        and Marie m. Jack Crawford. Ray and Neil have 2 children.
            1. Vivian Louise b. June 6,1946 Waco.m. Dec.20,1968 Austin,
                Tex. to Gary Kim Dodgen b. Sept.4,1946, Waco, son of
                Bill and Ginger Murray Dodgen of Waco.
            2. Sidney Ray b. Mar.21,1953 Waco,m.July 12,1975 Dallas,Tx.
                to Colleen Beth Finklea b. June 22,1954 Dallas, dau. of
                Carol and Helen Finklea.(1 child)
                    a.Megan Noel b. Oct.11,1978 Dallas,Tx.
    c. Roy Fred b. Feb.14,1922 Buckhorn Community, Moody,m. 1st,
        Effigene (Jean) Rose on Aug.1947. (1 child)
            1. Luanne b. Oct.18,1952 Waco m. 1st: Hughey Peeples
                (1 child) Divorced.
                    a. Christe b. Dec. 1971
                Luanne m. 2nd to Tom Dunlap
    Roy married 2nd to Charlotte Nannette Eskew b. Jan.11,1934
    dau. of Cecil Eugene and Agnes Margaret Vana Eskew.
    (4 children)
            2. Donna Katheleen b. Mar.10,1952 adopted by Roy.
            3. Joy Nell b. Aug.11,1958 Waco
            4. Roy Fred TWIN TO JOY NELL d. Aug.20,1958
            5. Suanne b. Aug.30,1959 Waco.

31

c. Viola Mae b. Nov.30,1924 Moody m. Jan.20,1945 to Aubrey Lee
Lightfoot b. Apr.22,1921, son of E.L & Nettie Killion Lightfoot. (3 children)
   1. Larry Lee b. Feb. 1,1949 m.1st Stevenville,Tex. to
      Donna Beth Stone on June 6,1970(1 child)
        a. Angela Kae b. Sep.14,1971
      Larry married 2nd to Cynthia Ann Coon b. Sept.28,1951
      dau. of Dean Coone.
   2. Gary Lynn b. Feb.1,1949 TWIN TO LARRY
   3. David Paul b. and d. Dec. 18,1958. Buried in the Moody
      Cemetery.
d. Helen Christine b. July 5,1930 m. Billie Francis Howell b. Sept.
6,1928, son os Lawrence & Lucille Howell(3 children)
   1. Donna Sue b. Apr.15,1951 m. to Stanley Glen Byrd b. Mar.
      3,1949 (2 children)
        a. Cheryl Annette b. Nov.29,1972
        b. Christian Diane TWIN TO CHERYL
   2. Debra Kay b. Mar.7,1955 m. Harry Steven Thompson b. Feb.
      28,1952, son of Harry & Dorothy Thompson.(1 child)
        a. Rebecca Dawn b. June 18,1976
   3. Tammy Elaine b. Nov. 13,1965

No. 5239

Vol. 10

Page 52/

The State  of Texas.

To all Regularly Licensed or Ordained Ministers of the Gospel, Judges of the District and County Courts, and all Justices of the Peace.

You are Hereby Authorized to solemnize the RITES OF MATRIMONY

Between .... N. H. Wiese .... and .... H. Neumann

and shall within sixty days thereafter make return of this License, with an endorsement thereon, showing your action in the premises, to me at my office in the City of Brenham, as the law directs.

In Testimony Whereof, I O. A. Seward Clerk of the County

Court of Washington County, hereunto subscribe my name and affix the seal of said Court, at my office in the City of Brenham, this .... 19th .... day of

.... October .... A. D. 1891

O. A. Seward
Clerk of the County Court of Washington County.

By R. V. Hoffmann Deputy.

THE STATE OF TEXAS,

THIS CERTIFIES that I joined in marriage as husband and wife

.... Mr. Fred Wiese ....

and .... Miss Hulda Neumann .... on the 22nd day of .... October .... A. D. 1891

Charles Montgomery Jr,
Minister of the Gospel

Fred

Hulda

Fred

Hulda

31-c

Hulda & Fritz Wiese

Friedricka Janka and Sigmond
Neuman, parents of Hulda

Fredrick Sigmond Wiese
and Lillie Edwards

Fred S. Wiese

.Fred and son,Joe

Lillie and Fred

Lillie,Fred, and Joe's
son, Bob

Joe,Ray and Roy
Helen,Lillie and Fred

Lillie and Gary,Fred and Larry,
Bob with Brenda and Vivian

Lillie and Fred Wiese

Ray and son, Sidney Wiese

Vivian and Gary

Neil and Ray

Megan

Colleen and Sidney

Ettie and Carl

Frieda and Henry

Walter and Malinda

Hulda and Fritz

John and Lydia Stuth

Henry and Lydia Wiese

Walter and Carleen

Walter and Emma

Birthday for Fritz

"...a few years later"

Fritz and Hulda

Sons

Daughters

"...more years later"

1976

Fritz and Hulda Wiese
Reunion, Cameron Park
Waco

Fritz and Hulda Reunion 1978, Riesel,Tx.

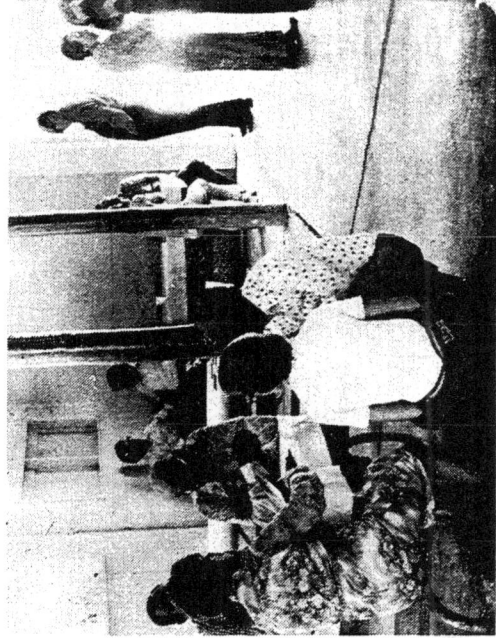

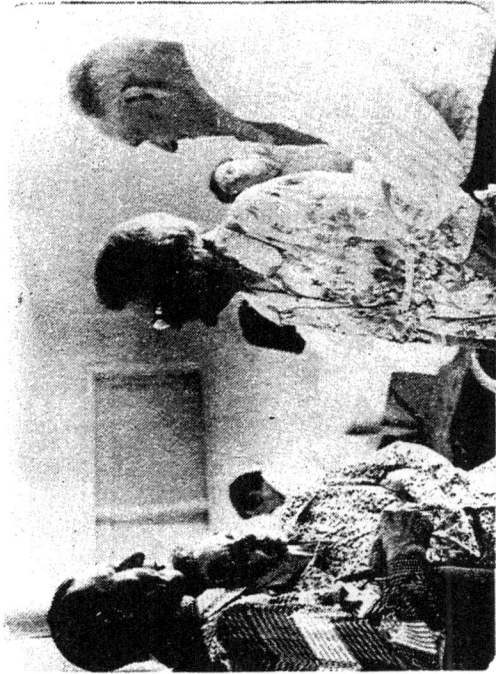

CHILD #2: <u>Otto Charles</u> b. Sept.14,1894 Washington Co. Tx.m. Jan.21
1920 McGregor to Ella Ernestine Albertine Christian Stuth b. Jan.4,
1902 Falls Co. Tx., dau. of Minnie and John Stuth (2 children)
  a. Esther Pauline b. Nov.26,1923 Bell Co.Tx. m. Nov.2,1945 Waco
    to Floyd C.Bagby b. June 19,1921, son of Charley and Mary
    Bagby (3 children)
      1. Shirley Sue b & d. Dec. 1946
      2. Carolyn Kay b. Apr.22,1948 McLennan Co. Tx. m. Westly
        Schmedthorst b. Aug.23,1945, son of Fritz Schmedthorst
        and Hattie Winkleman.Carolyn and Westly married Sept.
        11,1965 Riesel, Tx. (2 children)
          a.Bradley Craig b. Dec. 30,1968 Waco.
          b. Christi Lynn b. July 8,1972 McLennan Co.Tx.
      3. Dennis Wayne b. July 16,1958 McLennan Co. Tx.m.Aug.20,
        1977 to Janet Gail Bishnow b. Apr.7,1958, dau. of
        Bernie and Joyce Berndt Bishnow
  b. Edgar (Eddie) Otto b. Jan.11,1930 McLennan Co. Tx.m. Dec.31,
    1949 to Nelda Faye Paul b. Feb.4,1931, dau. of Elbert C. &
    Eva Paul(4 children)
      1. Regina Gail b. Aug.27,1951 McLennan Co.Tx. m. Aug.1,
        1970 to Alan Dale Patterson b. Jan.27,1949 son of Louis
        and Ethel Patterson.

      2. Shirley Jenise b. Oct. 8,1952 McLennon Co.Tx. m. Jan.
        28,1971 to John T. Coburn b. June 26,1946 , son of Gladys
        and Ewell Coburn(1 child)
          a. Justin Wayne b. Nov. 9,1973 Tarrant Co.Tx.
      3. Roger Paul b. Mar.29,1959 Dallas Co. Tx.
      4. Jennifer Lynn b. Oct.22,1970 Tarrant Co.

CHILD #3: <u>William Lewis</u> b. Jan.21,1895 d. Aug. 24,1973 Moody, Tex.
  m. Lydia Charolette Stuth b. Nov.26,1896 d. Sept.29,1970,dau. of
  Minnie and John Stuth (1 son)
    a. Ruben Will b. 1919 m. 1st. Mary Jo Sharp (2 children)
      1. Mary Ann b. Oct. 15,1947 m. Joe Mack Laird (3 children)
        a. Marion Elizabeth b. May 18,1964
        b. Joe Shack b. Oct.5,1968
        c. William Wiley b. May 18,1971
      2. Pamela Sue b. June 24,1950 m. Dennis Clay Wilson
        (2 children)
        a. Dennis Clay Jr. Oct.8,1973
        b. Denise Charolette b. Apr.3,1976
Ruben married 2nd to Betty Jo Brashear b. Nov.25,1927, dau of
Arthur Price and Lois Leona Ward Brashear. Ruben adopted Betty
Jo's three children.
      3. Deborah Lynn b. Oct.20,1955 m. James R. Hess (1 child)
        a. Shelley Bena b. May 2,1973
      4. Nan A. Lois b. July 29,1946 m. Tommie Haydon(2 children)
        a. Sterling Ruben b. Nov.4,1964
        b. Dana Louise b. Dec. 7,1965

33

                    5. Robert Elton b. Apr.3,1948 m. Linda Bates
                       (3 children)
                           a. Janel b. Jan.27,1971
                           b. Betty Lynn b. May 27,1972
                           c. Robert Elton b. Sept.13,1974
                    6. Gary Price b. Apr.15,1952 m. Cheryll Bochat.

CHILD #4: Henry b. Jan.2,1898 m. Oct.10,1926 Washington,Tx. to
    Frieda Krueger b. Oct.7,1898 Washington,Tx. d. Jan.25,1967 and is
    buried in Prairie Lea Cemetery, Brenham, Tx. Sister to Etta, wife
    of Carl, Henry's brother.(2 children)
        a. Joyce b. Jan.9,1929 Washington, Tx. m. Apr.23,1950 to Willie
           Kelling. b. Jan.31,1924, son of Willie F. Kelling and Nelda
           Blum Kelling.(1 child)
               1. Joylene b. Oct.11,1951 m. Richard Jolly b. Oct.18,1949.
                  m. Brenham July 21,1973 to Richard Jolly, son of Fred
                  and Florine Dehnel Jolly. (1 child)
                      a. Dirk Alan b. Dec.3,1977
        b. Janice b. Aug.20,1932 Washington, Tx. m. Sept.12,1955 to
           Jesse Menke b. Aug.24,1924, son of John H. and Annie Menke.
           (2 children)
               1. Alan Menke b. June 30,1957 Brenham
               2. Bonnie b. March 13,1961 Brenham

CHILD #5: Lydia Friedricka b. Oct.30,1899 between Gay Hill and
    Brenham, m. Oct.20,1920 to John Stuth b. Sept.13,1899, d. May 7,
    1967, son of John C. Stuth and Wilhelmine Whehrmann Stuth. John's
    sister's Ella and Lydia married Lydia's brothers Otto and
    William. (2 children)
        a. Elmer John b. Moody, Tx. b. Aug.21,1921 m. Sept.7,1946 to
           Mildred Lucille Weber b. Mar.21,1929, dau of William Henry
           Weber Jr. and Clara Fischgrabe Weber. (2 children)
               1. Jerry Wayne b. Nov.4,1947 Waco, m.Aug.1,1970 to Nadine
                  Ruth Rittimann of Houston b. Feb.20,1949 San Antonio
                  Tex. dau. of Roy Sidney Otto and Nellie Nadine Miles
                  Rittimann
               2. Judy Ann b. Sept.19,1953 Waco m. Feb. 13,1971 to Rickey
                  Glenn Wilkins b. March 29,1951 Waco,Tex. son of Louie
                  Alexander Wilkins and Thelma Moore Wilkins(1 child)
                      a. Brandon Scott b. Sept.7,1971 Tuscon, Arizona
        b. Edgar Arnold b. Feb.22,1925, died 5 weeks later in Moody, Tx.

CHILD # 6: Hulda b. May 11,1902 Austin Co. Kenny,Tx. m. Nov.25,1926
    McGregor Tx. to Fritz Carl Goessler b. May 18,1901 Washington Co.Tx.,
    son of William Goessler and Bertha Loesch.Fritz was the grandson of
    Louise, the sister of Henry, Hulda's grandfather.(2 children)
        a. Hilbert Fritz b. Jan.11,1931 Washington Co. m. Dec.2,1956
           Brenham, Tx. to Lena Mae Holtkamp b. Nov.24,1934 in Whitehall,
           Grimes Co.,dau. of Charlie & Lena Holtkamp. (3 children)
               1. Gary Lyn Goessler b. Apr.26,1959 Bryan,Tx.
               2. Kevin Lyn b. Oct.18,1962 Bryan,Tx.
               3. Karl Frederick b. Apr.16,1964 Bryan,Tx.

b. Ruby Marie b. Sept.14,1932 Washington, Co. m. Feb.20,1955
to Mace H. Meekins b. Nov.24,1932, son of Rufus and Pearl
Meekin (2 children)
   1. Cecil Elliott b. Aug.31,1956 Navasota,Grimes Co.
      m. Melissa Sanders on June 11,1977
   2. Danny Joe b. Aug.11,1964

CHILD #7: <u>Zelma</u> TWIN TO HULDA. Zelma died as an infant and is buried
in the Phillipsburg Cemetery, Austin,Co., along with her parents.

CHILD #8: <u>Carl H.</u> b. Feb.27,1905 Kemmey, Tx. m. Oct.24,1926 to Ettie
Krueger b. Aug. 18,1905 Washington, Tx. Carl and Ettie were married
in the Friedens Evangelical Church in Washington, Tex. Ettie is the
dau. of Albert and Johanna Schawe Krueger(2 children)
  a. Ruth Violet b. Apr.13,1929 Washington, Tx. m. Jan.9,1954
    St.Paul's Evangelical Luthern Church in Brenham, Tex. to
    Clyde W. Thomas b. Apr.30,1926 (1 child)
      1. David Charles Thomas b. Dec. 15,1954 Brenham, Tx.
  b. Nancy Claire b. Nov.24,1932 d. Jan.19,1933 buried in Frieden's
    Evangelical Church Cemetery, Washington, Tx.

CHILD #9: <u>Malinda Emma</u> b. Feb. 19,1908 Washington Co.Tx. m. Oct.25,1928
McGregor to Walter John VonRuff b. July 14,1904 (3 children)
  a. Edwin Walter b. Dec.15,1929 Moody, Tx. m. 1st to Alyce Glass
    (4 children)
      1. Eddie b. Jan.6,1955
      2. Mike b. Jan 27,1957
      3. Kirk b. Sept.29,1959
      4. David b. March 13,1961
    Edwin married 2nd to Sketter
  b. Mildred Louiese b. Apr.20,1931 Moody m. Oct.14,1950 to Albert
    Z. Foster b. Oct.22,1949, son of Thomas Z.Foster (2 children)
      1. David b. July 23,1951 m. Nov. 17,1973 to Juli Ann Curtis
        dau. of Jay Curtis (1 child)Juli b. Sept.7,1954
        a. Mellissa Michele b. Mar. 17,1976
      2. Wade b. Aug.31,1953 m. Aug.2,1974 to Patty Louise Poole
        b. Sept.10,1953, dau. of Bill Poole
  c. Alvin John b. Mar.4,1934 Moody, Tx. m.Lynn Litchy dau. of
    Tony Litchy(4 children)
      1. Timothy John b. Jan.29,1963
      2. Daniel John b. Mar.26
      3. Thomas John b. Jan. 18
      4. Alvin John b. Nov. 26,1956

CHILD # 10: Robert Fritz b. Aug.27,1910 Washington Co. Tx. m. Apr.27,
1929 to Nellie Cox b. Dec.25,1909 Coryell Co. Gatesville, Tx. dau.
of Richard and Hattie Humpries Cox (4 children)
  . Robert Charles b. Oct.25,1933 McGregor m. Aug.21,1954 to Wanda
    Mildred Beeman b. Jan.17,1937 Eula,Tx. dau. of Thomas Emmett
    Beeman and Jessie Goff Beeman (4 children)

   1. Dawn IdaNell b. Sept.2,1956 Hanford, Washington.
   2. Suzanne Carol b. May 9,1960 Waco
   3. Robert Charles Jr. b. Nov.28,1961 Waco
   4. Mark Alan b. Feb.22,1972 Waco

 b. Louise Nell b. Apr.3,1936 Waco m. Nov.27,1950 to Robert Lee
  Tate (2 children) divorced.
   1. Robert Lee Tate II b. Apr.12,1961 Waco.
   2. Cynthia Ann Holmes Tate b. Mar.5,1956 Waco.
    Natural father : James Holmes of Spar anberg,S.C.
    Adopted by Robert Lee Tate of Lorena,Tx. Cynthia
    m. Feb.12,1976 to Terry Joe Jeffery of Northridge,
    Calif., son of Robert Lee and Lois Elizabeth Jeffery
    (1 child)
     a. Jodie b. Aug.3,1976
 c. Billy Gene b. Aug.5,1939 Crawford Tx. m. Sept.3,1960 West,
  Tx, to Josephine Ann (Jo An) b. July 22,1939, dau. of
  Joseph Frank and Lillie Ann Trlica Matus. (3 children)
   1. Craig Alan b. Sep.11,1961 Bryan
   2. Paula Catherine b. Nov.16,1964 Waco
   3. Donna Elizabeth b. Oct.21,1965 Waco
 d. Edward Joe b. Aug.12,1945 m. June 12,1971 Hinesville Ga.
  Liberty Co. to Christine (Kit) Stanford, b.Sept.27,1949, dau.
  of Chris and Fleta Stanford of Hinesville, Georgia(2 children)
   1. Julia Errin b. Oct. 24,1975
   2. Joshua Kristof Nov. 1977

CHILD #11: Walter Henry b. Mar.20,1912 Washington,Co. m. 1st: Carleen
 Frances Adler b. Apr.11,1928 d. Oct. 13,1953 McGregor, Tex. Buried
 in the McGregor Cemetery, Bosque,Co.(3 children)
  a. Walter Jr. b. Feb. 10,1947 McLennon, Co.
  b. Linda Marie b. May 18,1948 McLennan Co. m. Nov.29,1975 to
   Gene Keadle b. Aug. 9,1929, son of Nora Mae Hesser and Wyle
   Eugene Keadle Sr.
  c. Shirley Jean b. Dec. 8,1950 McLennan Co.
Walter married 2nd: Emma Marie Goessler of Washington Co. Tx. on
Dec.11,1955. Emma b. July 24,1913, dau. of Wm & Bertha Loesch
Goessler. Emma is a sister to Fritz Goessler who is married to
Walter's sister Hulda.

CHILD #12; Lillie Emma b. Jan.18,1915 d. Aug.3,1974 m. Oct.18,1934
 Coryell City, Texas. to Gus Adler Jr. b. Nov. 15,1914 Coryell Co.
 d. Nov.3,1977, son of Gus Adler Sr. and Carolyn Rodebeck (1 child)
  a. Louise Marie b. Apr.9,1937 m.Apr.25,1953 to Horold Wayne Fair
   b. Feb.10,1934, son of Joe Charles and Lilly Fair. Louise
   and Wayne divorced. (2 children)
   1. Michael Wayne b. Feb.6,1954 McLennan Co. m. Marisa Jan
    Glasco Wolske b. Apr.9,1953 dau. of Maurice and Veronica
    Glasco.(2 children)
     a. Amy Nicole b. Feb.18,1973 adopted by Mike
     b. Chris Chad Wolske b. June 13,1975
   2. David Alan b. Aug.24,1960

CHILD #2: <u>Melinda</u> b. Sept.10,1869 d. Jan.5,1957 m. Louis Schmidt
  b. Nov.25,1864 d. April 13,1938(12 children lived,1 died)

    a. Louis b.June 20,1890 d.Nov.11,1965 m.Jan.1,1914 to Tonie
      Moellar b. Sept.25,1893 d.Feb.4,1965,dau. of W.E. and
      Hermina Moeller (3 children)
      1. Ruby b.Feb.13,1917
      2. Viola b.June 5,1923 m.March 1,1947 to Eugene Schorn
        b. Sept.18,1915,son of Theodore and Bertha Schorn
        (1 child)
        a. Dennis Eugene b. Sept.29,1948
      3. Freda Mae b. March 28,1931 m. Oct.12,1951 to Melvin
        Semff b.Jan.2,1931,son of Richard and Rosa Semff
        (1 child)
        a. Brenda Ann b. June 22,1957
    b. Hanna(Johanna) b. Sept.8,1891 m. Henry Beerwinkle Jr.
      b. May 29,1889 d. Feb.2,1965, son of Mr.& Mrs. Henry
      Beerwinkle Sr.(7 children)
      1. Ruben b. Oct.20,1912 m. Esther Haas in Temple,Tx.
        b.April 29,1918, dau. of Fritz and Emma Wiese Haas
        (Refer to chapter 7,August Wiese) (6 children)
        a. Kenneth b. Apr.4,1938 m. Dec.19,1964 to Jean
          Hildebrand b. Jan.28,1941,dau. of John and
          Lorene Neiman.(2 children)
          1. Tammy b. Feb.10,1966
          2. Kenneth Allen b. June 39,1970
        b. Donald b. Oct.7,1939 m. Patricia Nichols on
          July 10,1964 b. Jan.18,1945,dau. of Shirley
          and Bernice Traylor (3 children)
          1. Shelli b. Sept.5,1965
          2. Staci b. May 21,1973
          3. Si Donavan b. Dec.14,1976
        c. David b. Feb.9,1942 m. July 28,1968 to Sidney
          Kerr,b.Dec.26,1941, dau. of Warren Kerr and
          Merle Germany(2 children)
          1. Amy b. Feb.12,1974
          2. Rachel b. April 26,1977
        d. Linda b. Feb.18,1945 m. July 2,1966 to Tommy
          Birch b. May 4,1943,son of Oniel and Doris
          Whatley(2 children)
        e. Larry b. Apr.12,1949 m. July 28,1975 to Margaret
          McVey, dau. of Raystelle and Laverne McVey
          (1 child due in April,1978)
          1.
        f. Dale b. Nov.2,1953

    2. Esther b. Dec.31,1913 m. Dec.12,1934 Moody-Leon Church
to William(Bill)Haas b. Mar.11,1910, son of Emma Wiese
(Refer to chapter 7,August Wiese) and Fritz Haas.
(2 children)

        a. William E.Haas b. Feb.3,1938 m. Sept.27,1975
Temple.Tex. to Shirley Marie Tate(Lucky) b. Mar.
10,1946,dau. of Leroy Tate and Katherine Doughty
Tate(3 children)

            1. Steven Mathew Lucky b. March 3,1964
            2. Melissa Marie Lucky b. Feb.4,1967
            3. Kevin Eugene Haas b. Nov.12,1977

        b. Marjorie Ann Haas b. Nov.25,1945 m. Dec.18,1965
at 7th Street Methodist Church in Temple,Tx. to
David Vaughan Lewis b. Mar.18,1945, son of Carl
H.Lewis and Mattie A.Jane Ewing Lewis (2 children)

            1. David Todd Lewis b. Mar.20,1969 Kentucky.
            2. Paula Annette Lewis b. Feb.24,1976 Temple.

    3. Pearl b. Aug. 11,1936 m. Aug.11,1936 in Moody-Leon
Church to Arthur Haas b. Dec.22,1907 ,son of Emma Wiese
(Refer to chapter 7,August Wiese) and Fritz Haas
(2 children)

        a. Arthur Bruce Haas b. June 6,1942 m. Jan.12,1973
to Lanetta Holiman b. March 5,1946. Her father
died when she was an infant, and her mother remarried to Mr.Walker . Their home is in Payen,
Arkansas.

        b. Stanley Haas b. Nov.27,1950

    4. Marvin b. Feb.23,1919 d. Oct.20,1977
    5. Ewaldine b. Aug.29,1920 Lives with her Mother in Moody.
    6. Louise died at 2½ years of age.Buckhorn Cemetery
    7. Albert b. Oct.28,1928 m. Feb.1953 m. Martha Ann Wright
dau. of John D. and Minnie Wright. Albert was killed
in Veitnam. Martha's father,John D. died and Minnie
is now the wife of Henry Schmidt(#8 child)

c. Emanuel b. April 1893 m. Edna Weiting(3 children)
    1. Evelyn Fay b. 1925 m. Ben Shull (4 children)
        a. Timothy
        b. David
        c. Rachel
        d. Sarah
    2. Harvey b. 1928
    3. Homer b. 1930 m. Diann   (3 children)
        a. Peter
        b. Paul
        c. Amy

d. Paul August b. Nov.2,1894 d. June 27,1971 m. Aug.12,1920
to Clara Schuette b. Apr.26,1901,dau. of Wm Henry Schuette
and Emma Dorothy Kuhlmann.TWIN TO NETTIE

e. Nettie b. Nov.2,1894 d. July 14,1975 m.Jan.9,1915 in the
   home of her parents to W.H.Moeller b. Jan.19,1890(3 children)
   1. Grace b. Aug.12,1922 m.Dec.24,1950 to Vaughn Renfro
      b.June 15,1924,son of Omega Cronkrite and Luther
      Burleson Renfro(1 child)
      a. Grace Marie b. May 14,1952
   2. Wallace b. Dec.10,1915 m.Feb.21,1937 to Ila Mae
      Meals b. Dec.27,1915,dau. of Leta Ila Reeves and Oscar
      Meals(3 children)
      a. Virginia Kathryn b. Oct.2,1941
      b. Keith Edwin b. Oct.3,1947
      c. Margaret Ann b. June 26,1945 d.Jan.10,1946
   3. Elva Moeller b. Oct.1,1918 d. March 26,1927
   4. Eva Mae b. July 30,1929 m.Dec.31,1948 to L.J.Miller
      b. Dec.20,1924,son of Cornelia Miller and Willis
      Burgess Miller (1 child)
      a. David Glenn b. Sept.30,1960

f. Ella b. July 15,1897 m.July 28,1920 to Otto Winkler b. Sept.
   16,1889 d. Apr.30,1962,son of Chas A.and Katherine Winkler
   (6 children)
   1. Milton b.July 6,1921 m.Carolyn Schmidt June 4,1946,
      b. May 15,1924,dau. of Gustave and Bertha Schmidt
      (3 children)
      a. Daphne Lynn b. Sept.10,1949
      b. Timothy Craig b.Dec.11,1953
      c.Mark Milton b.July 15,1957
   2. Weldon Homer b.Jan.11,1924,d. June 14,1926
   3. Bernie b.Dec.5,1925 m.Oct.10,1959 to Carlyn Hansman
      b.Jan.8,1938,dau. of Wilbert and Hermina Hansman
      (5 children)
      a. Brian W.b.Nov.19,1960
      b. Beverly Ann b.Aug.9,1962
      c. Carrie Lynn b. Sept.27,1963
      d. Chris Allen b.Mar.10,1965
      e. Donna Kay b.Jan.20,1967
   4. James Carl b.July 21,1927 m.Nov.1951 to Rebecca
      Simmons b.Dec.3,1934 dau. of Mr.and Mrs. Daniel
      Simmons(2 children)
      a. James Daniel b.Aug.16,1953
      b. Rebecca Lynne b. Nov.13,1954
   5. Lawrence Edward b. May 26,1933 m.Sept.18,1956 to
      Geraldine Lora Barrett b.Nov.11,1935, dau. of Ernest
      and Lora Barrett (2 children)
   6. Gerald Sidney b.Jan.18,1937 d. June 5,1949

g. Willie b. May 20,1900 m. March 14,1923 to Alma Weber b. July
11,1903 d. Aug.6,1978 buried in Moody-Leon Cemetery
dau. of Will Weber and Lydia Spross from Moody(2 children)
   1. Vernon b. Sept.22,1924 m. 1948 to Amy Lou Vowell b.Mar.
     14,1923,dau. of Roy Vowell and Hester Vowell
   2. Arvell b. Aug.26,1928 m. 1950 to Nelda McDonald b.Oct.
     25,1929,dau. of Roger & Zona McDonald (4 children)
       a. Lana Sue b. Mar.25,1952 m. Chris Frantz (1 child)
         1. Amanda b. Feb.24,1976
       b. Gary b. Sept.16,1956 m. Sherry Seawright b. Feb.
         3,1956,dau. of Jack and Betty Seawright.
       c. David Ray b. Feb.24,1961
       d. Lou Ann b. May 31,1963

h. Henry b. Dec.7,1902 m. 1st: Daisy Lydia Urbankt b. June 19,
1912,d. Sept.1965,dau. of Mr.& Mrs. Willie Urbankt(5 children)
   1. Carolyn Sue died at 2 years of age.
   2. Daisy Nell b. March 31,1942 m. Gene Huntsinger (2 children)
       a. Randel Cory b. Aug.4,1976
       b. Bryan Chris b. July 12,1974
       c. Carol Sue b. Oct.9,1946 TWIN TO LINDA LOU
       d. Linda Lou b. Oct.9,1946
       e. Henry Narvell b & d 1944
Henry married 2nd to Minnie Wright b, July 10,1908,dau. of
Francis Collin Green and Laura Clara Rebecca Jane Aldrich.
i. Charles Arthur b. Dec.22,1905 Bell Co.Tx. m. April 4,1931
at Collinsville, Ill. to Virginia Ruth Ficke b. Jan.11,1909,
dau. of James Alfred Ficke & Talitha Virginia Wiseman Ficke
(4 children) Charles is a Physician in Gerald,Mo.
   1. Charles Robert b. March 3,1935 St.Louis,Mo. m.1st: Dec.
     18,1956(4 children)to Janet Nidy.
       a. Steven Allen b. Jan.14,1957 Washington,Mo.
       b. Andrew Robert (Chuck) b. July 6,1958 Memphis,Tenn.
       c.Charles Robert 2nd b. Feb.5,1960 Memphis,Tenn.
       d. Catherine Talitha(Kathy) b. Jan.1,1962 Wichita,
       Kansas.
   Charles m.2nd Oct.14,1977 St.Louis,Mo.Valeria Tonies.
   2. Virginia Ann b. April 6,1938 m. 1955 to Wm.A.Pogue,
     son of Harold and Audrey Pogue(5 children)
       a. Virginia Lynn b. Mar.12,1957 Columbia,Mo.
       b. Bryan Charles b. July 31,1959 Columbia,Mo.
       c. Wiliam Lisle b. Nov.30,1960 Columbia,Mo.
       d. Christian(Chris) Horold b.Sept.27,1962 Columbia
       e. David Allan b. Aug.29,1963
   3. Audrey Leah b. Jan.17,1941 m. Ray E.Busch in 1962,
     son of Von & Grace Brown Busch.(3 children)
       a. Amanda Louise b. Mar.15,1965 Wyandotte,Mich.
       b. Talitha Ann b. Sept.25,1967 Wyandotte,Mich.
       c. George Douglas b. Apr.21,1969 Washington,N.J.

Malinda Wiese & Louis Schmidt

Hannah & Henry Beerwinkle

Nettie & W.H.Moeller

Ella & Otto Winkler

Charley, Walter & Ed.

The Schmidt Home

Nettie & Ella Schmidt

Louis & Antonio

Walter & Lucille

Paul & Clara

(Refer to pg 50, #c)
Raymond Eakin and
Emma Wiese

(Refer to pg 50, #b)
Ervin Wiese and Irene
Kamman

Henry Schmidt & Daisy Urbankt

Ed Schmidt & Edna Haas

Emmanuel Schmidt & Edna Weiting

Charles & Ruth

Charles, Ruth & Children

Ella Schmidt and Otto Winkler

39-f

Arvel, Vernan, Alma and Willie

Willie Schmidt and Alma Weber

Paul Schmidt

1931
Louis, Erna, Walter, Willie, Henry, Paul, Nettie, Ed
Emanuel, Hannah, Malinda, Louis Sr., Ella & Charley

Whitehall,1960
Emanuel,Louis,Henry,Willie,Ed, Walter
Hannah,Nettie,Ella,Erna,Charles, and Paul

4. Julia Mae b. May 19,1944 m. June 17,1972 to Rev.
Andrey G.Kunz II,son of Andrew G.& wife,Lee.

j. Walter: TWIN TO CHARLES b. Dec.22,1904 m. Nov.22,1934 in
Moody-Leon Church to Lucille Klingleman b. Mar.16,1907
dau. of Monroe Klingemann and Hilda Trapp(1 son)
   1. Weldon Floyd b. Oct.18,1938 m. Dec.16,1961 to Mary
      Ellen Erxleben b. Dec.22,dau. of Helmuth Erxleben
      (3 children)
         a. Mark Anthony b. Oct.15,1962
         b. Trisha Deene b. July 15,1964
         c. Michael Allen b. March 7,1971

k. Edwin Joe b. April 13,1907 d. Feb.1,1977 m. Dec.28,1932
to Edna Haas b. Oct.26,1912, dau. of Fritz Haas and Emma
Wiese(Refer to chapter 7,August Wiese) (2 children)
   1. Edward b. Nov.25,1933 m. Roberta Kramer b. Jan.19,
      1937,dau. of Stella & Robert Kramer (3 children)
         a. Sharon b.Nov.20,1957 m. June 10,1977 to Rick
            Lynch.
         b. Steven b. Dec.18,1959
         c. Susan b. Aug.25,1965
   2. Doyle b. Sept.13,1940 m.1st to Rita Meador
      (2 children)
         a. Scott b. April 5,1967
         b. Michael Lynn b. Oct.11,1970
      Doyle married 2nd to Mary Ann McElwreath(2 children)
         c. Debbie Ann m. Randy Threadgill
         d. Donna
l. Erna b. May 10,1909 m.Dec.22,1926 to Fred Beerwinkle b.
Nov.27,1896,son of Fritz Beerwinkle and Sophie Muegge
Beerwinkle(3 children)
   1. Florine b. Jan.18,1928 m. May 8,1947 to George Beimer,
      son of Leolo H. Beimer and Martha Locka(2 children)
         a. Carolyn b. Nov.3,1949 m. Aug.10,1968 to Mark
            Hafley(2 children)
            1. Brian b.Dec.9,1969
            2. Malinda b. Sept.30,1975
         b. Sharon b. Feb.23,1954
   2. Joyce b. Sept.16,1930 m. Nov.25,1948 to Herbert
      Kattner b. July 24,1922,son of Robert L.Kattner and
      Juania Fudge (4 children)
         a. Glen b.Nov.8,1951m.Sherry Johnson Dec.2,1977
         b. Vivian b.Feb.19,1954 m.July 29,1977 David
            Blankemeier
         c. Rickie b.Jan.12,1957
         d. Gordon b.Nov.15,1959
   3. Shirley b. Jan.16,1943 m.Nov.23,1961 to Billy Mac
      McCutchen b.July 13,1939,son of Eric McCutchen and
      Lois Brazzil(1 child)
         a. Billy Fred b.Jan.16,1965

Wilhimena(Minna) Wiese b. July 27,1871 d. March 4,1953. Married
Jan.21,1892 to Henry Brockermeyer by Pastor Oscar Samuel in the
Evangelical Luthern Church in Brenham,Texas. Henry was born around
1869 in Germany and was brought to the United States by his father
in 1872. Henry's mother had died during childbirth and both he and
his father came into Texas from old Me ico and evidently resided
near the Houston area for awhile. His father died when Henry was
7 or 8 years of age and nothing is known concerning who reared
Henry. However, he became a citizen of the United States in Brenham
on Sept.21,1906. His grandson, Kae L.Brockermeyer of Ft.Worth has
his naturalization papers.

After Henry and Minna married, they moved to McGregor where they
lived for many years and reared nine children to adulthood.Three
children died young.

Henry and Minna Brockermeyer Bible is in the possession of their
son R.W.Brockermeyer, 712 So.Main Street,McGregor,Tx.76657.

The Bible measures 6'x9" and is printed in German. The cover sheet
is of Dr. Martin Luther . Printed in 1904 by the Wartburg Publish-
House, Chicago,Ill.It lists parents,children;Sophie,Henry,Robert,
Carl,Willie,Rosa,Lillie,Ben,Rienhard,Albert,and Fred.There are also
listed confirmations and deaths.

Henry and Agnes Wiese, Emma Wiese, and the Brockermeyer Family in
front of Henry and Sophie's home

Child #3: <u>Willimena (Minna)</u> b. July 27,1871 d. Mar.4,1953 m. Jan.21,
1892 in Evangelical Luthern Church by Oscar Samuel: Pastor. Witness:
her brother, Carl, and Anna Brockermeier.(Vol 2,p.56 Brenham,Tx.)
Married Henry Broekermeier (Brockermeyer) b.Dec.1869   d. Aug.15,
1940. (12 children) (1900census: Immigrated 1872 -Henry)
  a. Sophie b. 1892 d. Dec. 23,1977 m. Herman Mutscher (3 children)
      1. Marvin Paul m. Louise
      2. Esther Clara
      3. Clarence Gustav b. Dec. 17,1926 Lee Co., Giddings,Tx.
         m. Feb.16,1947 Lincoln Co. , Sylvan Grove, Kansas in the
         Bethlehem Luthern Church. to Doris Heine(3 children)
           a. Glenn Allen b. May 27,1948 b. Houston m. Patricia
              Grossman in Gidding,Tx. in the Immanuel Luthern
              Church June 1, 1969(2 children)
                1. Keith Allen b. Oct,28,1970 Austin Tx.
                2. Randy Wayne b. Sept.25,1974 Austin Tx.
           b. Ralph Dennis b. Dec.2,1949 Houston m. Linda Mitschke
              in Giddings in the Martin Luthern Church on April
              10,1971(2 children)
                1. Jeffrey Dean b. Nov.18,1971 Austin,Tx.
                2. Travis James b. June 10,1975 Brenham,Tx.
           c. Shirley Mae b. Nov.20,1950 Houston,Tx. Harris Co.
  b. Henry b. Feb. 19,1894 Brenham, Tx. m. Lillie Mae Amanson and
     is buried inEl Campo, Tx. Died Jan.5,1960(7 children)
      1. Evelyn Nesbit b. Oct.21,1916 Brenham,Tx.m. Jan.15,1944
         in Houston(1 child)Married J.C. Hemphill
           a. Baby Hemphill b. Aug.4,1944 d. Aug.4,1944 Houston
         Evelyn and J.C. would later rear her sister's son,Jerald.
      2. Nola Marie b. March 26,1919 Chappell Hill, Tx. Washington,
         Co.m. to James Homer Cummins on Feb. 27,1937 in Navasota,
         Tx.(2 children)
           a. Ruth Marie b. Mar.2,1938 WmPemm,Tx. m. Emil Charles
              Pulido on Nov.27,1957 in Houston(3 children)
                1. Lesha Lynette b. Apr.27,1960 Houston
                2. March Charles b. April 10,1961 Houston
                3. Gregory Anthony b. May 8,1964 Houston
           b. Billy Marius b. May 24,1939 Navasota,Tx. m. to Linda
              Lee Dawson on Aug.5,1961 in Houston.(2 children)
                1. Keith b. Dec.13,1966 Houston
                2. Kari Marie b. Sept.29,1969 Houston
      3. James Floyd
      4. Girl (name unknown)
      5. Wilhelmina Juanita b. Jan.22,1927 Wm.Penn,Tx.m. Olson
         She divorced Olson after having a son,Jerald Wayne.
         Jerald lived for many years with Evelyn and J.C. Hemphill
         until Juanita took him back and gave him the name of Olson.
         Jerald later returned to his uncle and aunt and makes his
         home with them today.
         Jerald Wayne Hemphill Olson b. Nov.25,1946 Houston,Tx.

         Juanita married James Kirchner July 2,1977 in Liberty,Tx.

6. Dora Adell b. March 11, 1928 Washington Co.m.Oct.24, 1947 to Archie J.Wade in Harris Co. Houston,. Archie b.Jan.27,1926 Travis,Co.Austin,Tx.(3 children)
    a. Patricia Ann b. Oct.13,1948 Houston m. March 24, 1967 to Rondle Lee Hartley b. May 3,1943 Freestone Co.,Teague,Tx(4 children)
        1. Rondle Lee Hartly III b. Nov.4,1969 Houston
        2. Crispin Patrice b. April 8,1973 Houston
        3. Amanda Denise b. May 17,1975 Houston
        4. James Wade b. Feb.7,1978 Houston
    b. Joyce Marie b. Sept.19,1951 Houston . m. Sept.17 1971 Houston to Richard Lee Henderson b. June 20, 1949 Tarrant Co.Ft.Worth (1 child)
        1. Amy Marie Henderson b. May 30,1975 Orange Co. Nederland,Tx.
    c. Ronnie Fred Wade b. Jan.27,1953 Houston, m. Debbie Jo Samuels b. Dec.17,1956 Pushmataha Co. Clayton Oklahoma. Married April 6,1978 Houston. (1 child)
        1. Meysa Diane Samuels b. May 27,1975 Nacog- doches Co. Nacogdoches,Tx.(Debbie's dau.)

Dorothy Louise

Aunt Agnes Wiese,92 yrs. and James Wade 3 mo.
"She has not lost her touch"

#5426   Vol.11

43-a

To all Regular Licensed or Ordained Ministers of the Gospel Jewish Rabbis

Judges of the District and County Courts and all Justices of the Peace, Greeting

YOU ARE HEREBY AUTHORIZED TO SOLEMNIZE THE

RITES OF MATRIMONY

Between Mr. *Henry Broeckermeyer*

and Miss *Minna Wiese*

and make due return to the Clerk of the County Court of said County within Sixty days thereafter, certifying your action under this License.

WITNESS my official signature and seal of office at office in Brenham this *16th* day of *January* AD 1892

R. V. Hoffmann
Deputy.

O. A. Seward
Clerk County Court, Washington County.

I *Oscar Samuel* Hereby Certify that on the *twenty first* day of *January* A.D. 1892 I united in Marriage *Henry Broeckermeyer* and *Minna Wiese* the parties above named

WITNESS my hand this *21* day of *Jan.* AD 1892

Oscar Samuel
Pastor of Evgl. Luth. Church

25th anniversary of Sophie and Herman Mutscher

Wilhelmina and children
and grandchildren

Wilhelmina Wiese Brockermeyer

c. Robert b. Oct.6,1896 d. Aug. 13,1942
d. Carl b. Aug.22,1898 d. June 14,1943 m. June 24,1926 Brenham,
   Tx. to Ella Schwartz. Carl buried Wm.Penn, Washington Co.Tx.
   (6 children)
  1. Walter b. Jan.23,1927 Wm.Penn. m. Dec. 7,1947 Washington
   Co. to Sadie Tappe (3 children) Sadie b. Aug.5,1927
    a. Sharon Sue b. Dec.14,1948 Navasota,Tx. m. June 5,
     1970 Houston, Tx. to Don S.Lindahl (2 children)
      1. Steven Jay b. Jan.15,1971 Houston
      2. Jayson Jay b. Sept.9,1975 Gouston
    b. Nancy b. Aug.23,1952 Navasota m. June 19,1970
     Houston to David Bishop. Divorced. Jan.3,1973
     (1 child)
      1. Cinnamon Kay Bishop b. Feb. 15,1973 Houston
    c. Janie TWIN TO NANCY b. Aug. 23,1952 Navasota, Ts.
     m. April 1,1974 Houston to Alton Jones.
  2. Ora Dell b. June 15,1928 Wm Penn, m. Dec.29,1962 Houston
   to Tommy Hagan b. Jan.6,1926 (1 child)
    a. Sherry Renee b. Nov.7,1963
  3. Floyd Carl b. Jan.3,1930 Washington Co.Brenham, Tx. m.
   June 18,1950 Prairie Hill, Washington,Co.Tx. To Earline
   Schulze b. Nov.30,1931, dau. of Reinhard and Velma
   Ceissmer Schulze (4 children)
    a. Daniel Ray Sr. b. June 10,1951 Harris Co. Houston
     Tx. m. Deana Deutscher Jan.24,1970 Houston. Divorced
     Sept.18,1972 (1 child)
      1. Daniel Ray Jr. b. Aug.29,1970 Houston
    b. Linda Lee b. and d. Dec.8,1952 Harris Co. Houston
     buried in Wm. Penn, Tx.
    c. Allen Wayne b. Mar.27,1954 Houston m. Feb.17,1973
     Houston to Kathleen Thompson.
    d. Karen Lynn b. Dec.10,1955 Houston,Tx.
  4. Gladiola b. Nov.18,1931 Wm.Penn m. Oct.5,1973 Houston
   to James Oscar Lampley b. May 20,1928.
  5. Fred Henry b. Mar.26,1938 Wm.Penn Washington, Co.Tx.
  6. Ruth Marie b. April 1,1942 Wm.Penn. m. Sept.1,1961 Houston
   to Max Moretz Hengst (3 children)
    a. Debra Lynn b. Nov.9,1962 Houston
    b. Kimberly Kay b. Jan.15,1965 Houston
    c. Max Kevin b. Dec.29,1972 Lubbuck,Tx.
e. Willie b. Dec.16,1900 d. Aug.17,1901
f. Rosa Lina b. Aug.25,1901 d. Oct.3,1918 Sandy Hill, Washington,
   Tex.
g. Lillie b. Oct. 24,1903 d. Aug.21,1970
   Beloved by many people.
h. Ben b. Oct.24,1905 McGregor d. Apr.12,1927 Killed in Houston
i. Rienhard (Putsun) b. 1908 Lives in McGregor. Without his help
   this chapter could not have been complied.
j. Albert b. May 31,1911 WmPenn, Tx. m. Dec.15,1935 in McGregor,Tx.

45

to Mabel Reed. Lives in Ft. Worth (2 children)
    1. Ben Abbie b. Aug.10,1937 Waco,Tx.m. March 11,1957
      Ft. Worth, Tarrant Co. to Francis Eppers (2 children)
        a. Tamera Kay b. April 10,1959
        b. Tanya Kim b. June 30,1961
    2. Kae Louis b. Oct.7,1939 McGregor,Tx. m. April 1, 1967
      Tyler,Tx. to Kay Bridewell (2 children)
        a. William Brent b. Sept.1,1970
        b. Blake Weeks b. April 11,1973
k. Fred b. Feb. 4,1913 d. June 2,1973 Houston
l. Child unnamed.

HENRY HOLLE
and his
DESCENDENTS

HENRY HOLLE immigrated to Washington County, Texas from Hanover Germany. He was born Feb.16,1820 and died Aug.27,1890. He had two children from his first marriage; Sophie, born Dec.11,1845 and William, born Sept.12,1847. It is not known at this time just when Henry came to the United States, however, William arrived in 1851 and Sophie in 1855.

Henry married the second time to a Winkleman, some think her name was Caroline or Heneritta and it is thought that she is buried in St. John's cemetery at Prairie Hill but no record can be found to confirm this fact. Four children were born from this union, Charles in 1862, Friedrick in 1865, Adolph in 1867 and Frieda on Aug.7, 1869.

Child #1. Sophie b. Dec. 1845 d. June 23,1932(87 years). Buried in Phillipsburg Cemetery between Brenham and Kenny,Tex. on Hwy #36. Sophie married Henry Wiese on Jan.12,1867 (M.B.2,p. 396). They lived for years in Prairie Hill , a community near Brenham,Tex.Later they moved to Kenny in the Phillipsburg community in Austin County. 13 children were born to this couple, and 11 lived to become adults. (See Henry Wiese,chapter 3).

Child #2. William b. Sept.12,1847 d. May 6,1932 and is buried in Prairie Lea Cemetery, Brenham,Tex. He married Willimenna Elnora Brant, b March 1,1844, d. Dec.22,1 23, on Jan.21,1869 (M.B.2,p.158, Brenham). In 1900, nine children had been born but only eight were living.

1. William Jr. b. 1873 m. 1894 to Louise Sternberg(V.12,p. 245) In 1900, 3 children had been born,Lille b. 1896,Emma b. 1898, and Alma b. Oct.1899.
2. Henry b. Oct.5,1876 m. Mary Caroline Luckmeyer (V10,p.386) on Dec.5,1890.Henry died April 25,1959.
3. Fritz b. June 1882
4. Charley b. Dec. 1879 never married.
5. Albert b. March 1885
6. Minnie married Mr. Eickhorst
7. Emma married A.H. Shitzer (V13,p.8) and moved to Clifton,Tx.
8. Louise married Mr. Jaster and moved to Clifton Tx.

Child #3. Charles b. Nov. 15,1862 d. June 21,1941. Married three times.
    1st marriage to _____Schulte (4 children)
1. Charlie(C.H.) Holle b. Nov.26,1908 (V16,p.136) m. Caroline Bohne b. Mar.29,1887. (3 children)
    a. William C. b. Dec.1,1909 m. Olga Jensen (For additional information, see page 72)

b. Charles F. b. Jan.4,1911 m. Nelda Krueger (3 children- for additional information refer to page 72)

c. Caroline Holle Peterson

Child #4. Fredrick W. b. March 19,1865 d. Aug.21,1900 and is buried in the Salem Cemetery. m. Dec.31,1885 (V9,p.14) to Louise Muller who immigrated in 1869 from Germany.(3 children). Louise later married, had another child by her second husband. then she died. The child was reared by the husband's family. Name unknown.

1. Fred. b. Nov.1886 born in Texas d. 1964 and is buried in Otto Cemetery,Otto,Tx. married Rose Stchanke who died on Nov.13,1954. (5 children)

   a. Alma m. Lennie Krumnow and lives in Mart,Tx.
   b. Lonnie (Otto) m. Ida Diekker.
   c. Fred Jr. m. Catherine Berry from Gatesville. Fred is a barber in Riesel,Tx.
   d. Charles W. (C.W.) b. 1917. married 1937 to Alice Pankonien b. Apr.23,1920.They live in Mart,Tx.(2 children)
      1. Charlene Olga b. June 20,1938 m. Dale Smith(1st) 1 child
         a. Charles Dale,B.Dec.13,1955
         m. 2nd, to Ralph Bailey (1 child) They live in Austin,Tx.
         b. Jackie b. Sept.1954 m. John Bailey b. 1955

      2. Darlene Hazel b. Nov.23,1939 m. Kenneth Chaney (4 children)
         a. Vicci Lyn b. Mar.10,1957
         b. Debra Kay b. Mar.1959
         c. Tina Marie b. Apr.20,1962
         d. Kimberly Ann b. Nov.18,1963 They live in Austin,Tx.

   e. Bennie died at 18 or 19 years of age.
2. Annie b. Oct.1,1887 m. 1st Albert C. Wist who died in 1910. m.2nd. Albert Hueske who died in 1953 (5 children)
   a. Albert F. b. Oct.23,1912
   b. Milton R. b. Sept.27,1915
   c. Louise b. Feb.14,1918
   d. Annie Mae b. Aug.11,1921
   e. Ruth Marie b. July 28,1928 lives in Brenham,Tx.

3. William b. Sept.1899 d. July 5,1971 m. Ella Grebe in 1925 (1 child)

   a. Josephine Holle b. Sept.26,1929 m. Clarence Folterman in 1950. (2 children)
      1. Douglas Keith b. Feb.4,1955
      2. Jan Renee b. 1962

Child # 5. Adolph b. Feb. 1867 , married 1st to Melinda Lehrman on Oct. 26,1887 (V9,p.379) Lidia b. Apr.1867. In 1900 they had been married for 12 years. Adolph later married her sister,Louise Lehrman.(8 children by Melinda and 1 by Louise)
   1. Louis b. May 1889 m. Rosena Lueck. (4 children)
      a. Melvin m. Elfrieda (3 sons)
         1. Melvin Jr. 2. son   , 3.   son
      b. Walter m. Neta Bethke (2 children)
         1. Sam m. Adaline and 2. Julie
      c. Erwin Henry m. Adaline Dietrich on June 29,1946. Erwin b. Mar.10,
         1919 and Adaline b. Oct.15,1925.(3 children)
         1. Ralph Brian b. Sept.19,1951
         2. Sharon Kay b. Jan.8,1957 m. May 20,1978 to Larry Smith,son of
            J.B. and Doris Smith.
         3. Joan Kathleen b. Dec.7,1965
      d. Louis m. Esther Albrecht. (3 boys)

2. Bertha b. Sept.22,1890 m. Roudolph Jahnke
      a. Erwin Jahnke
      b. Dorothy Mae Jahnke
3. Frieda b. Mar.1,1892 m. Henry Haferkamp. (7 children)
      a. Alberta m. Bill Wolske. They live in Gatesville,Tx.(2 children)
      b. Esther m. Ben Wolske(5 children)
      c. Linda m. Arthur Fenske (1 child) Lives in Houston
      d. Vernon m. _____Kettler . Lives in Clifton
      e. Almo m. Georgia Sykora (2 children)
      f. Wilma B. (Pudden) married Hellen. Lives in Hewitt. (3 children)
      g. Pee Wee m. Mary, Lives in Gatesville (4 or 5 children)

4. Clara b. Dec.20,1894 m. William (Bill) Koester.Lives in Riesel(8 children)
      a. Wilburn (Scotter) married Lena LaCater. Lives in Waco.(1 child)
         1. Kenneth Janks m. Penny Robertson and lives in Houston
      b. Albert m. Dorothy (2 children)
         1. Curtis
         2. Caroline
      c. Alvin m. Gracie Dietrich from Riesel (1 child)
         1. Bobbie Sue m. Bob. Glazeman
      d. Milton m. Josephine (Jo). Riesel(3 children)
         1. Keith,2. Karol, 3. Kavin
      e. Bruce m. Dorothy Fleishour   Mart.(3 children)
         1. Connie, 2. Cynthia, 3. Stanley
      f. Lucille m. Ervin Denke   Mart. (4 children)
         1. Dwayne,2.Paul,3.Doloras,4. Marylyn
      g. Bernice m. Walter Kuehl   Mart (2 children)
         1. Walter Jr. 2.Janice.

5. Adolph Jr. Feb.13,1897 m. Eddie Bettis . Adolph d. 1974(6 children)
      a. Billie Lee m. Hilda Marks (1 child)
         1. Margaret m. John Kelley (1 child- Heather)

   b. Donald m. Alice Hood Salt Lake City (3 children)
    1. Garth, 2. Gayle, 3. Greg
   c. Adolph W.(A.W.) m. Zella Kaster Austin (4 children)
    1. Dan, 2. Eric, 3. Gill, 4. Scott
   d. Betty Joyce m. Don Beachamp Ft.Smith Ark.(5 children)
    1. Michael Jack, 2.Vita, 3. Judy, 4. Donna 5.Tammie
   e. Ira Jean m. Thomas Cobbs Waco (4 children)
    1. Steve, 2.Tonie, 3. Jim, 4. Ed
  f. Bobbie Sue m. Keith Saltzman Los Angles(2 children)

6. Malinda(Linda) b. Mar.30,1899 m. Nathan Pate. Lives in Robinson,Tx.

7. Hedwig(Hattie) b. Dec.20,1902 m. Henry C. Wegner.Lives in Waco,Tx.
   a. Bonnie Jean m. Calvin Finstad.Bonnie b.Dec.19,1931 and
    Calvin b. Sept.16,1924 (2 children)
     1. Richard Allen b. Aug.23,1955
     2. David b. March 9,1957

   b. Charles W.Wagner b. Oct.22,1940 Lives in Houston

8. Berthold(Bernard)m. Meddie Steinke (3 children)
   a. Billie
   b. Linda Lou
   c. Gloria

9. Alvin,Half brother, married Alvena Steinke

Child #6: Frieda Holle b. Aug.7,1869 married Henrich Kokemor on
Sept.15,1887. Frieda died Oct.5,1962 and Henry b.Feb.22,1865
died Sept.17,1946. Both buried in St.John's Cemetery in Prairie Hill
Texas. (4 children)
   a. Louis m. Emma Reue
    1. Arthur m. Rosalee Brauner
   b. Hennie m. Bill Schlotman
    1. Bill
    2. Otto
    3. Lonnie
    4. Lidia
   c. Edwin m. Annie Lehman
    1. Ervin
    2. Roy
   d. Selma m. Henry Luech
    1. Lonnie
    2. Henry Jr.

Child #4: <u>Unnamed child</u>

Child #5: <u>Charles</u> b. Jan.1,1896 TWIN TO BETTY d. March 7,1956. m. Nov.16,
    1905 to Lena Wellman b. Aug.28,1886 (6 children)
        a. Walter (Spitz) Henry William b. Sept.17,1906 Kenney, Tex.
        married Oct.9,1929 Moody, Tx. to Nancy Jane Comer b. Oct.10,
        1908 and d. Apr.19,1959 Moody. Buried in the Moody Cemetery,
        dau. of John Edgar and Tina Adelene Comer (1 child)
            1. Frances Loraine b. Feb.19,1934 Moody, Tex. m. Oct.15,
              1960 Moody to Dr. Jack Lewis Akins, b. June 27,1928,
              Haskell, Tx., son of Odus Otto and Sarah Jane Wilson
              Akins (1 child)
                a. Jane Ann Akins b. June 26,1970
        b. Ervin Fritz b. May 26,1908 Kenney, Tex. m. Oct.4,1930 Moody,
        Tex. to Artle Irene Kamman b. May 30,1908, dau. of Theodore
        and Artle Kamman (3 children)
            1. Doris Irene b. Sept.30,1931 d. Feb.8,1932. Buried in
              Moody-Leon Cemetery, Moody, Tex.
            2. Iris Marie b. Apr.7,1934 d. July 2,1934. Buried in
              Moody-Leon Cemetery, Moody, Tex.
            3. Debora Ervin b. June 11, 1945 d. Aug.5,1945. Buried
              in Moody-Leon Cemetery.
        c. Emma Sophie Wilhelmine b. Jan.12,1914. m. Oct.19,1933 Moody,
        to Thomas Raymond Eakin b. Jan.24,1909, son of Thomas Duncan
        and Ella Carberry Eakin of Moody. Thomas b. Aug.8,1888 and
        d. Jan.8,1977. Ella b.Sept.21,1892 and d. Jan.8,1972. Both
        are buried in the Buckhorn Cemetery, near Moody, Tex.
        (2 children)
            1. Dolores Faye b. May 10,1937 m. June 30,1967 to Billy
              Russell Choat b. June 14,1934, son of Herman and Margie
              Choat of Temple, Tx. (1 child)
                a. Melissa Michelle b. Feb.15,1969 Austin,Tx.
            2. Jeffery Don (adopted) b. Sept.10,1965
        d. Gilbert b. Sept.14,1919 Moody m. Sept.28,1939 to Juanita
        Marie Whittemore b. Aug.31,1920 Moody, Tx. dau. of Lillie
        and M.H. Whittemore of Moody (3 children)
            1. Donnie Milton b. Jan.10,1941 Moody,Tx. m. Dec.19,1959
              to Elizabeth Ann Pryor b. Apr.14,1942 Waco,Tx. dau.
              of Claude and Ann Elder Pryor of Waco. Claude was a
              barber.(2 children)
                a. Lori Beth b. Aug.1,1963 Lubbock,Tx.
                b. Kelli Dawn b. Nov.19,1966 Lubbock, Tx.
            2. Gary Layne b. Dec.24,1944 Moody,Tx. m. July 28,1975
              to Debra Sue Qualls , b. Nov.19,1953, dau. of Alfred
              Perry Qualls and Billie Jo Qualls of Ft.Worth.
            3. Mark Dwain b. May 11,1954 Temple,Tx. m. Aug.1,1974 to
              Sharla Ann Forrest b. Mar.20,1956,dau. of Charles Iqvin
              Forrest and Ethel Ann Forrest Legan, Temple,Tx.

51

e. Myrtle Lena b. Apr.13,1924 Moody,Tx. m. June 3,1943 to
   Preston Lee Nelson b. Apr.24,1924 Moody., son of Hershel Lee
   and Dolly Russel Nelson (2 children)
   1. Michael Ray b. Nov.23,1956 Eddy,Tx. m. June 21,1975
      Waco,Tx. to Robin Lynn Elmore b. Jan.15,1954, dau of
      Wm.C. and Jackie Elmore.
   2. Pamela Kay b. Jan.26,1960 Eddy,Tx.

f. Eldon Charles b. Jan.7,1930 Moody,Tx. m. March 3,1956 Houston
   to Mary Frances Stevens b. Aug.17,1934 La Porte,Tx. dau. of
   Morris and Hazel Stevens (2 children)
   1. Carolita Denise b. Nov.30,1956 Dallas,Tx.m.Dec.28,
      1974 Dallas, to Carroll Ray Lumpkin. b. Oct.2,1950
      Waco, son of Laura and Calvin Lumpkin Sr.(2 children)
      a. Benjamin Ray b. Nov.4,1975
      b. Cary Charles b. Oct.6,1977
   2. Kim Lisa b. Mar.20,1959

Ervin Wiese and Irene Kamman   Raymond Eakin and Emma Wiese

To any regularly Licensed or Ordained Minister of the Gospel, Jewish Rabbi, Judge of the District or County Court, or any Justice of the Peace, Greeting:

You are Hereby Authorized to Solemnize the

RITES OF MATRIMONY

Between Mr. _Chas Wiese_

and _Lina Willmann_

and make due return to the Clerk of the County Court of said County within sixty days thereafter, certifying your action under this License

Witness my official signature and seal of office at office in Brenham, the _9_ day of _Nov_ 190_5_

J. A. Seward

Clerk County Court Washington County, Texas.

By _____ Deputy

I _Wm Harroski_ hereby certify that on the _6_ day of _Nov._ 190_5_, I united in marriage _Chas Wiese_

and _Lina Willmann_ the parties above named.

Witness my hand this _7_ day of _November_ 190_5_

Rev. _Wm Halowski_

Pastor of the German M.E. Church

Returned filed and recorded in Book No. _15_ _Page_ _151_ _of Marriage Record the_ _16_ _day of_ _Nov_ 190_5_

By _R. Hoffmann_ Deputy

O. A. Seward

Clerk County Court Washington County, Texas.

Charles and Lena

Charles Wiese

Gilbert,Walter,Emma,Lena and Charley,Ervin
Eldon and Myrtle
1931

Walter and Ervin

Walter and Nancy Jane

Gilbert and Emma

Lena,Frances,Charley,& Dolores

1st Wiese Reunion,1950
Donnie,Gary,Lena,Charlie,2nd: Preston & Myrtle,Frances,
Delores,3rd: Ervin & Irene,Walter & Jamie,Emma & Raymond,
Juanita,& Gilbert and Eldon

Charley and Lena
50th Anniversary

Walter,Ervin,Gilbert,Myrtle,Emma
and Eldon

Nov.13,1955

Charley and Lena
Delores,Frances,Gary and Donnie

Donnie,Gary,Mike,Pam
Mark,Delores,Kim,Frances and Carlotta
Reunion 1977

Reunion 1977
Walter,Ervin,Myrtle,Gilbert,Emma and Eldon

Great, grandchildren
Kelli,Lori,Jeffery,Melissa, Jane Ann and Benjamir

Child # 6. Bertha (Betty) b. Jan.1,1876 d. June 7,1954 m. April 4,1896
Brenham,Tx. by L.C. Zettner, Pastor(Vol.2,p.313. to Fritz W.Korth
b.Apr.23,1876 d.Sept.29, (7 children) 1958
    a. Minnie b. Aug.29,1896 Brenham. m. Fred Rosentreter on Dec.26,
       1920 in Berlin Eben-Ezer Luthern Church. Fred son of Gottlieb
       and Louise Schwarze Rosentreter.
    b. Henry b. Sept.1898 Brenham, Rte 4, m. Helen Sternberg b. Aug.
       23,1900 on Nov.16,1921 Berlin Luthern Church. , dau. of Louis
       and Ida Windt Sternberg.
    c. Lillie b. Nov.22,1903 Brenham, Rte 4, m. March 16,1924 to
       O.A. Weidner at the family residence near Brenham. O.A. born
       Aug.24,1900 , son of Herman and Annie Appel Weidner. He died
       April 19,1973 (1 child)
           1. Lillie Belle b. Nov.17,1928 m. W.A.Bass, son of Sam
             and Lula Jenkins Bass at St. Pauls Luthern Church in
             Brenham.(3 children)
               a. Patricia Ann b. Feb.3,1951 Freeport,Tx.married
               1st: Rusty Ward(1 child)
                  1. Shannon b. Jan.20,1972
               2nd: Ray Januzewski Feb. 14,1976 (1 child)
                  2. Brandy b. Jan.25,1977
               b. Robert Douglas Bass b. Dec.3,1953 Freeport,Tx.
                 m. Nov.26,1976 to Amanda Fitts in Clute Tx.
               c. Brian Howard b. Nov.19,1954 Giddings,Tx.
    d. Walter Korth b. April 17,1906 Rt.4,Brenham. m. Sept.1927
    in Berlin Church to Cora Stegman b. Oct.14,1908, dau. of Henry
    and Betty Sandhoff Stegman(4 children)
           1. Ruth Lois b. May 14,1929 Rt.4,Brenham. married 1st:
           H.C.Rodden (2 children)
               a. Linda Ruth Rodden b. Sept.16,1951 m. Howard Ray
                 b. April 9,1947 (3 children)
                  1. Carey Lee b. Aug.2,1971
                  2. Corey Allen b. Jan.11,1973
                  3. Cristina Ann b. Jan.17,1977
               b. Janet Ann Rodden b. Sept.4,1953 m. 1st: to Mr. King.
               (2 children)
                  1. Jenny Lynn b. Sept.22,1969
                  2. Renee Michelle b. Dec.15,1972
             married 2nd: John Victor Mikolajewski Jr. b. Sept.
             8, 1951 (2 children)
                  3. Randy Gene b. May 25,1976
                  4. Ruth Catherine b. Nov.14,1977
        Ruth married 2nd: Hubert Adams b. Apr.26,1921 in Houston
           2. Walter Korth Jr. b. April 7,1931 Rt.4,Brenham. m.
           Carolyn Williams b. Aug.19,1935(2 children)
               a. David Wayne b. Aug.11,1957 m. Donna Haas Aug.13,
                 1977
               b. James Allen b. May 25,1960
           3. Cora Lee Korth b. Apr.10,1933 Rt.4,Brenham. m. J.F.
           Naumann b. Oct.16,1925 , son of Mr & Mrs. Ed Naumann
           (1 child)
               a. Ray Allen b. Nov.21,1955 Houston,Tx.

        4. Howard Korth b. Jan.1,1936 Rt.4,Brenham.m. Judy
           Franke b. Sept.30,1943, dau. of Ervin and Velma
           Krause Franke (3 children)
             a. Michael b. Nov.24,1961
             b. Keith Allen b. Apr.17,1967
             c. Kimberly Kay b. Dec.23,1975
  e. Edwin Korth b. July 5,1910 Rt.4,Brenham m. Dec.6,1936 Salem
    Lutheran Church near Brenham to Annie Rodenbeck b. Feb.19,
    1914 Pleasant Hill Community near Brenham, Rt.1,dau. of Otto
    and Annie Jahnke Rodenbeck(2 children)
        1. Joy Ann b. Jan.15,1941 near Brenham, Rt.1,m. Aug.9,
           1959 at Salem Lutheran Church to Raymond Dickshat
           born Jan.5,1934, son of Fred and Frieda Mohr Dickschat
           (3 children)
             a. Brian Keith b. May 19,1960 Brenham, Tx.
             b. Rodney Allen b. Aug.4,1962 Brenham,Tx.
             c. Mark Wayne b. Aug.28,1969 Washington,Tx.Rt.1
        2. Gloria Jean b. June 29,1943 Brenham Rt.1,m.Dec.19,
           1964 at Salem Luthern Church to John A.Sommer b. Aug.
           23,1942, son of John and Malinda Krueger Sommer(2 children
             a. John Ashley b. Oct.28,1966 Houston,Tx.
             b. Richard Dean b. July 14,1970 Houston,Tx.
  f. Eleanor Korth b. March 30,1913 Brenham Rt.4,m. July 14,1951
    in Houston to Tom Cecil b. Feb. 1904, d. Nov.24,1963.,son of
    Mr.and Mrs. Bill Cecil (1 child)
        1. Mary Beth b. July 10,1952 Houston m. Berlin Eben -Ezer
           Luthern Church near Brenham to Donald Wayne Holle
           born Nov. 1946, son of Willie and Amanda Boenker Holle
           (2 children)
             a. Angela Beth b. Dec.20,1971 near Brenham
             b. Christel Wynn b. Sept.23,1975 near Brenham
g. Herbert died as an infant:TWIN TO ELEANOR

#7043

53-a
Vol.11, p.313

To any Regularly Licensed or Ordained Minister of the Gospel, Jewish Rabbi, Judge, District or County Court, or any Justice Peace, Greeting:

You are hereby Authorized to Solemnize the

RITES OF MATRIMONY

Between Mr. F. W. Korth and M. Bertha Wiese

and make due return to the Clerk of the County Court of said county within sixty days thereafter, certifying your action under this License.

Witness my official signature and seal of office, at office in Brenham, the 4 day of April 1896

O. H. Seward
CLERK COUNTY COURT WASHINGTON COUNTY
By R. V. Hoffmann Deputy

I, S. C. Tetters hereby certify that on the 4 day of April 1896 I united in Marriage F. W. Korth

and Bertha Wiese the parties above named.

Witness my hand this 4 day of April 1896

S. C. Tetters
Luth. Min.

Returned and filed for record the 26 day of Feby 189_7 and recorded the ___ day of ___ 189_

Deputy

O. H. Seward
CLERK COUNTY COURT WASHINGTON COUNTY

A 109 CLASS 4.

Clarke & Courts, Stationers, Printers & Lithographers, Galveston.

Betty Wiese and Fritz Korth

Edwin,Minnie,and Lillie
Eleana,Betty,Fritz, Walter and Henry

53-c

"Mother"

Lillie and Otto

Minnie and Fred

Helen and Henry

Korth Family
Henry,Lillie,Betty,Fritz,Walter,Edwin,& Minnie

Korth Home

Child #7: <u>Lidia</u>: b. Feb.1877. She was 2 years old in the 1880 Census, and it is thought that she died soon afterwards. TWIN TO CHRISTOPH

Child #8: <u>Christoph</u> (Christe) b. Feb. 1877. married in Gay Hill on Nov.3,1898 to Augusta Wenzel b. Jan.21,1879. (M.B. Vol 13,p.172, #7961 Brenham,Tx.) Chris d. May 25,1964 and Augusta died July 10,1949. Both are buried in the Phillipsburg Cemetery. (9 children)

Their wedding is vividly remembered by Chris's first cousin,Ben Wiese of McGregor,Texas. Ben's father Carl , an accomplished musician, was asked to play for the wedding ceremony. For some reason of his own, Carl refused . However, the couple in their wedding dress, came and asked him to play--and he agreed to do so.

   a. John Henry (Johnny) b. June 8,1899 d. Dec.22,1954. married
      Hazel Brandes b. Dec.2,1904. (2 children)
       1. Eugene Everett b. Oct.12,1923 m. Erlene Copeland
         (4 children)
           a. Candice Lorraine b. July 15,1951
           b. Eugene Everett Jr. b. Jan.2,1955
           c. John Henry II b. Jan.2,1955 TWIN TO EUGENE JR.
           d. Jerry Alexander b. April 7,1963
       2. Fern Lorraine b. Oct.11,1927 m. Herbert Oliver Quebe
         b. Sept.24,1924

   b. Henry Chris b. Dec.18,1900 d. Aug.16,1966 Eagle Lake Tex.
      Buried in Gidding,Lee Co.Tx. m. to Elsie Alice Meier b. Jan.9,
      1901 Calvert, Robertson Co.Tx.,dau. of Carl Meier b. Oct.18,
      1953 Germany and Augusta Kasky (Koukosky) b. Sept. 6,1863
      Germany. Both are buried in Calvert, Tx.(2 children)
       1. Estelle
       2. Leroy Henry b. Oct.4,1929 Brenham, Washington Co.Tx.
         m. Aransas Pass,Tx. Aug.16,19 56 to Patricia Hall
         b. Corpus Christi, Tx. Jan.16,1935, dau. of Ollie
         Volman b. Nacogdoches Co. Tex, March 4,1901,d.June 15,
         1967 and Cora Lee Chapman b. Oct.1,1906,Dallas,Tx. Both
         are buried in Denton,Tx.(2 children)
           a. Karla Ann b. Feb.26,1958 Aransas Pass,Tx.
           b. Kris Deane b. Mar.18,1959 McAllen,Tx.
   c. Leona Amelia b. Sept.13,1902 m. Raymond Luhn b. April 6,1901.
      on Nov.8,1922. Raymond son of Robert Luhn and Caroline
      Klopstad Luhn (1 child)
       1. Florine Elsie b. Oct.23,1926 m. Melvin Pomikal b. Nov.8,
         1922, on Nov.1946. Melvin,son of Willie and Minnie Pomikal
         (2 children)
           a. Wayne Melvin b. July 13,1947 m. Nov.17,1970 to
             Kay Smidt b. Apr.19,1947 (1 child)
               1. Stacey b. Oct.17,1972
           b. Melba Joe b. Nov.10,1950

d. Arthur Edward Fredrick b. Feb.14,1907 m. Dec.24,1941 Hunts-
   ville,Tx. to Lola Irene Clevenger,dau. of Arthur M.and Esta
   Miller Clevenger (2 children) Arthur is known as "Tex" Wiese.
     1. Arthur Edward Fredrick Jr.b.May 13,1946 m.Sept.2,1967,
       Huntsville to Nanetee Susan Arnold b. March 16,1947,dau.
       of Betty Underwood Arnold and Mr.Arnold(1 child)
         a. Kimberly Susan b. Feb.27,1971 Austin,Tex.

     2. Larry Clevenger b. May 30,1949 m. Aug.12,1972 in Cross
       Plains,Tex. to Patricia Petty Barr b. June 17,1951,dau.
       of Clara Nell McCermett Barr and R.H.Barr.

e. Regina Martha b. May 29,1909 d. March 25,1978 m. August Hold
   Jr.on Nov.27,1930.August b. Jan.24,1907(2 children)
     1. Janet Elaine b. Mar.12,1932 m. Oct.2,1950 to Harry G.
       Namken b.Feb.22,1927(2 children)
         a. Donna Gail b. Oct.20,1953 m. Mar.9,1974 to Thomas
           Swonke b. Feb.2,1951
         b. Kathie Elaine b. Dec.22,1955 m.Aug.17,1975 to Garry
           Nitsche.
     2. Winston Curtis b. Aug.12,1942 m. June 6,1965 to Darlene
       Dana Teichelman(1 child)
         a. Allen Wayne b. Oct.12,1968

f. Raymond Henry b. Jan.10,1911 m. Nov.28,1936 at St.Paul Lutheran
   Church in Phillipsburg,near Brenham,Texas to Anne Frances Miller
   b. May 21,1916,dau. of Theresa Schmitt and Joe Miller.Raymond
   and Annie live at Chappell Hill,Tx.

g. Lillie Augusta b. Aug.13,1913 d. 1967 m. 1st to John L.Lindsey
   (1 child)
     1. Ronnie Lindsey Lemm b. Mar.5,1946. He is married and has
       two children.
   Lillie married 2nd. to Charles Lemm.(1 child) Charles adopted
   Ronnie.
     2. Millie Augusta b. Nov.10,1953.She is married and has one
       child.

h. Oscar Herman b. April 7,1916 m. Elsie Tillie Goeke b. Jan.8,
   1918

i. Ruth Agnes (Toodie) b. Oct.12,1920 m. Ervin Charles Henske
   b. May 4,1916 (3 children)
     1. Terry Ervin b. July 19,1946 m. April 6,1974 to Janice
       Carlson b. Jan.14,1952
     2. Nancy Ruth b. Oct.14,1947 m.Dec.9,1967 to A.V.Hartman,Jr.
       b. Aug.15,1946(3 children)
         a. Melanie Kris b. Oct.18,1970
         b. Tina Renee b. Aug.20,1976
         c. Dana Michelle b. Aug.20,1976 TWIN TO TINA RENEE
     3. Billy Chris b. Mar.19,1950 m. June 18,1977 to Rebecca
       Kraemer

COUNTY OF WASHINGTON,

Vol. 13, p.172

To any Regularly Licensed or Ordained Minister of the Gospel, Jewish Rabbi, Judge of the District or County Court, or any Justice of the Peace, Greeting:

You are Hereby Authorized to Solemnize the
RITES OF MATRIMONY

Between Mr. *Christoph Wiese* and Miss *Augusta Wenzel* and make due return to the Clerk of the County Court of said County within sixty days thereafter, certifying your action under this License.

Witness my official signature and seal of office, at office in Brenham, the 31st day of *October* 1898

O. H. Seward
Clerk County Court Washington County.

By — Deputy.

I. *W. Vollbrecht* hereby certify that on the 3rd day of *Nov* 1898 I united in Marriage *Christoph Wiese* and *Augusta Wenzel* the parties above named.

Witness my hand, this 4th day of *November* 1898.

W. Vollbrecht.
Pastor at Gay Hill, Tex.

Returned, filed and recorded in book No. *13* Page *172* of Marriage record the *19* day of *July* 1899

By Deputy.

O. H. Seward
Clerk County Court Washington County.

Chris & Augusta

Annie & Leona

Lydia and Otto Koeppen
(twin to ~~Chris~~) *William*
(p. 58)

Chris Wiese

Chris,Augusta and Family

Child #9: <u>Henry Wiese Jr.</u> b. June 3,1880 m. Agnes Glaser Dec.20,1906
born Feb.24,1882. They were married at Chappell Hill, near Brenham,
Tx. by Pastor Alefelbach (M.B.15,p.366)dau.of Louise Dahse & Fritz
Glazer
Henry died June 3,1970 on his 90th birthday. Agnes lives in Ganado
where she celebrated her 92nd birthday on Feb. 1978. At the"Henry
Wiese" reunion in Brenham held every two years, she has been the
the oldest member attending, for many years.(6 children)
- a. Irene b. July 24,1909 d. Nov.5,1910

- b. Ewin Henry b. Sept.22,1907m. June 23,1921 Kenney,Tx. to Neddie
  Richter b. Dec.15,1909, dau. of Fritz Richter and Louise
  Schroeder Richter (3 children)
    1. Milton b. July 19,1927 m. Aug.10,1954 to Mildred Rush.
       Divorced. July 1972.(4 children)
        a. Frankie Clarence West b. Jan.1952 (adopted)
        b. Becky June b. Oct 11,1955 m. Oct.23,1976 to Mike
           Foly
        c. Douglas b. Nov.29,1961
        d. Theresa b. Dec. 10,1962

    2. Harold b. May 18,1928 m. Oct.4,1953 to Lucy Mercer in
       Ganado,Tx. Lucy b. Mar.27,1955,dau. of Henry E.Mercer
       and Alma L.Franklin Mercer (2 children)
        a. Brenda Marie b. Dec.1,1955 m. May 21,1977 to
           Michael Lloyd Chandler, son of Lloyd and Opal
           Chandler
        b. Karen Sue b. Aug.28,1959
    3. Elroy b. Aug.30,1931 m. May 9,1953 Ganado,Tx. to Louise
       Selma Webel b. Mar.5,1934,dau. of Fritz Webel and Lydia
       Tegeler Webel (3 children)
        a. Michael Ray b. Dec.31,1953 d. Feb.6,1954
        b. Sandra Kay b. Oct.22,1955 m. May 24,1975 to Charles
           (Chuck) Hasdorff b. Aug.16,1955, son of Fred
           Hasdorff and Mary Gabrysch.

- c. Della b. Dec.6,1911 m. Jan.18,1951 to Raymond Hultquist
  in the St.James Luthern Church Ganado,Tex.,son of Albert
  Hultquist and Lydia Oaks Hultquist.

- d. Gerald b. Nov.19,1913 m. June 13,1946 to Blake Freeman Patton
  b. July 12,1923,dau. of Dee Patton and Vonie Shaw Freeman. Dee
  d. May 6,1972 and Vonie d. Oct.1956 (5 children, 2 of Blakes)
    1. Imogene deceased.
    2. Bobby Alton Patton b. May 17,1938 m. Linda(2 children)
        a. Shanon b. 1972
        b. Kimberly April b. May 1977
    3. Robert Gerald Wiese b. Apr.6,1947 m. May 22,1976 to
       Allison Jeanne Smith b. Oct.2,1958 dau. of Mr. and Mrs.
       Claude Smith
    4. Eddie Doyle b. Feb.10,1951 m. June 15,1973 to Wol Mae Yum
       b. Feb.10,1947 Korea
    5. Bradford Wiese b. June 11,1959

e. Mildred b. Sept.30,1915 m. Jan.5,1937 Ganado,Tx. to Bernard
   Kuretsch b. Mar.15,1914, son of Louis Kuretsch and Lena
   Buddenburg Kuretsch (2 children)
     1. Weldon b. Feb.6,1940
     2. Marjorie Ann b. Dec.26,1942 m. Aug.27,1961 to Milton
       Bain Ganado,Tx. Milton b. Dec.12,1938, son of R.T.
       and Helen Tucker Bain (2 children)
         a. Dennis Alan b. July 26,1962
         b. Shari Renee b. Feb.8,1966

f. Viola L. Wiese b. June 18,1921 m. Dec.4,1947 Ganado,Tx. to
   Billie Robert MClanahan b. Oct.21,1925, son of Collier Joseph
   and Fannie Pearce McClanahan (2 children)
     1. Diana Marie b. Mar.24,1949 m. June 2,1973 Austin,Tx. to
       Edward Anthony DeFrancesco b. Dec.17,1949, son of Pasquale
       DeFrancesco and Levia Dippolito De Francesco(1 child)
         a. John Edward b. July 25,1977
     2. Billy Lynn b. Sept.22,1950 m. Sept.7,1974 Corpus Christi,
       Tx. to Carolyn Joan Zdansky b. May 10,1955,dau. of Julius
       Joseph Zdansky and Eleanora Ann Malik Zdansky.

Viola,Mildred,Gerald,Della,and Ervin
Agnes and Henry

Vol. 15, p. 366

To any regularly Licensed or Ordained Minister of the Gospel, Jewish Rabbi,

Judge of the District or County Court, or any Justice of the Peace, Greeting:

You are Hereby Authorized to Solemnize the

RITES OF MATRIMONY

Between Mr. *Henry Wiese Jr.*

and *Agnes Glaser*

and make due return to the Clerk of the County Court of said County within sixty days thereafter, certifying your action under this License.

Witness my official signature and seal of office at office in Brenham, the *19* day of *December* 190*6*

O. H. Seward

Clerk County Court Washington County, Texas.

By *R V Hoffmann* Deputy.

I *O. Appelbach* hereby certify that on the *2d* day of *December* 1906, I united in marriage *Henry Wiese, Jr.*

and *Agnes Glaser* the parties above named.

Witness my hand this *18* day of *March* 190*7*

O. Appelbach Pastor

K. E. Chapel Hill, R. J. Tex.

Returned, filed and recorded in Book No. *15* Page *366* of Marriage

Record the *19* day of *March* 190*7*

By *R Hoffmann* Deputy.

O. H. Seward

Clerk County Court Washington County, Texas.

Agnes & Henry

Agnes 1978

1978
5 generations: Milton,Edwin,
Becky June with Sherira & Agnes

Henry and Agnes 1966

1976 Wiese Reunion
Della, Mildred,Agnes and Viola

Wiese Reunion 1978: Della and Agnes (92 yrs.)

Kuretsch Family
Bernard,Mildred,Marjorie,Milton Bain,Dennis,Shari & Weldon

92nd birthday,Feb.24,1978
Shari,and Marjorie Bain,Mildred and Agnes: Four generations

CHILD #10: William H. b. Oct.5,1882 TWIN TO LYDIA d. Dec.8,1958
Buried in the Oak Knoll Cemetery in Bellville Tex.
William lived on the "homeplace"

CHILD #11: Lydia b. Oct.5,1882 TWIN TO WILLIAM d. April 24,1901,
married to Otto Koeppen. She was carring her first
child when she was accidently shot.Buried in the Phillipsburg Cemetery.

CHILD #12: Emma b. Feb.18,1885 d. May 9,1973. M.Herman Pfeffer b. July
24,1886 d. Jan.15,1971. Both are buried in the Oak Knoll
Cemetery in Bellville Tex. with their son Rolf.(1 child)
    a. Rolf H. b. June 26,1917,killed by a train on Nov.8,
        1942. Buried by his parents.

Emma Wiese and Herman Pfeffer
1886

Child #13: <u>Sophie</u> b. Feb.13,1887 d. Jan.31,1974. M. Nov.9,1905 in
Brenham, Phillipsburg Community, Texas. MB 15,p.151, #10174. to
Paul Glaser b. April 28,1884 d. Jan.15,1960, son of Fritz
and Louise Glaser. Both buried in the Ganada City Cemetery,
Ganada, Tx. (2 children)
  a. Ervin Henry Fritz. b. April 5,1906, christened April 5,1906
     died July 31,1977. Married June 1,1952 to Marie Katherine
     Haegelin, dau. of Mr.and Mrs. Louie Haegelin of Banders, Tx.
     Marie Katherine died Jan. 1963. Both buried in Ganado.
     (2 children)
       1. Katie Mae, b. Feb.1946
       2. Vernan Paul b. Apr.25,1954 m. Feb.19,1975 to Suzanne
          Dieterich b. Jan.19,1957, dau of Carl Dieterich and
          Eula Mae (Jean, Swanner Dieterich of Waco. (1 child)
            a. Robert Paul b. Jan.4,1975

  b. Ronald b. 1900, lives in Ganada,Texas

Paul Glaser Home: Sophie Wiese, Ervin,Ronald and Paul

Vol. 15, p. 151 #10175

59-a

To any regularly Licensed or Ordained Minister of the Gospel, Jewish Rabbi, Judge of the District or County Court, or any Justice of the Peace, Greeting:

You are Hereby Authorised to Solemnize the

RITES OF MATRIMONY

Between Mr. *Paul Glaser*

and *Sophie Wiese*

and make due return to the Clerk of the County Court of said County within sixty days thereafter, certifying your action under this License

Witness my official signature and seal of office at office in Brenham, the *9* day of *November* 190*5*

O. H. Seward
Clerk County Court Washington County, Texas.

By *R V Hoffmann* Deputy.

I *F. Uffelshaffen* hereby certify that on the *11* day of *Nort.* 190*5*, I united in marriage *Paul Glaser* and *Sophie Wiese* the parties above named.

Witness my hand this *11* day of *November* 190*5*

F. Uffelshaffen Luth. Pastor
Philippsburg, Tex.

Returned, filed and recorded in Book No. *15* Page *151* of Marriage Record the *18* day of *Dec* 190*5*

By *R V Hoffmann* Deputy.

O. H. Seward
Clerk County Court Washington County, Texas.

Sophie and Paul

Sophie and Paul

Ronald,Ervin,Sophie and Paul

Paul and Sophie

Sophie Wiese

Ronald and Ervin Glaser

PARENTS: A.F. CARL WIESE AND CHARLOTTE WILHELMINE D. MEYER

CHILD # 4: <u>Marie Wilhelmine Henriette</u>,b.Jan.3,1847, Baptized Jan.
     10,d. Feb.13,Register No.1,Wehden,Germany.

CHILD #5: <u>Carl Hermann Wilhelm</u>, b. Nov.16,1848 Baptized: Nov.26,
     <u>1848</u>,Register No.118,Wehden,Germany. d.Feb.8,1868.

Hermann arrived in the United States on Sept.30,1866,
at the port of Galveston,Tx.(Roll 3,18 0-1873,#149 Micro-
film list H.Wiese from Westphalan,Prussia, 17 years of
age and a farmer).

He went to work for a Mr. Bohne and at the age of 20, he
was killed one night as Mr.Bohne was robbed. Herman
Hermann climbed out an upstairs window and chased the
robber over a fence. The man turned and shot Hermann.

Hermann is buried in the Salem Cemetery on the Winkle-
mann Place 2½ miles southwest of Brenham,Tx.Washington
County.

CHILD #6: Henriette Louise Caroline b. Feb.10,1851 Baptized: Feb.
16,Register No.23,Wehdem,Germany. d. Dec.2,1884. Buried Eicholt
Cemetery in the Cedarhill Community. Family cemetery enclosed
with an iron fence. Married twice.1st to Herman Loesch on Jan.5,
1871,MB.Vol.4,p.68,Brenham,Tx. 3 children were born: Bertha,
reared by Louise's sister Caroline Bohne, Annie and Charlie were
reared by her brother Fritz and his wife Caroline. Louise's
husband died and she married the 2nd time on Jan.6,1880 to Herman
Grube, MB,Vol. 6,p.467. Again, Louise had 3 children but died in
childbirth when Minna was born. Her oldest child from this
marriage, Fritz Grube was reared by her sister,Minna Wehmeyer.
Another brother, August and his wife Louise, took the baby Minna,
and Carl. Both later died of diptheria while young children.

Herman Grube later returned to Osmbruck,Germany and died in 1910.
It is believed that he never remarried.

No photographs available.

   Child #a. Bertha b. Dec.18,1874 d. March 2,1955. m.Jan.4,1894
      to Wm.Goessler b. Oct.18,1871 d. June 22,1945.Both buried
      in Washington Quadrangle,Freiden Cemetery,Washington Co. Tx
      For many years they lived in the "Goessler House"a beauti-
      ful two-story house 1 mile from Old Washington,Texas.
      (7 children)

   They married in the Ev.Luth.St.Johannas Church in Washington
   County and celebrated their Golden Anniversary on Jan.4,1945.

      1. William b. Dec.31,1894 Prairie Hill on their Uncle
         August's place. m.Washington,Tx.Dec.4,1919 to Clara
         Krueger,dau. of Albert and Johanna Schawe Krueger.
         Clara b. Aug.22,19 d. Mar.18,1962.Buried in the
         Oaklawn Memorial Cemetery,El Campo,Tx.(2 children)
            1. Edna b. June 9,19 m. Werner Wendt(2 children)
               a. David m.Glenda
               b. Charles m. Kathy (2 children)
                  1. Charles
                  2. Kathy
            2. William A. b.March 1,1925

      2. Hanna b. Sept.25,1896 Prairie Hill on her Uncle
         August's place.d.Feb.4,1965.

      3. Fritz Carl b. May 18,1901 Washington Co.Tx. m. Hulda
         Wiese b. May 11,1902, dau. of Henry Friedrick(Fritz)
         Wiese and Hulda Neumann. Henry was the son of Henry
         and Sophie Holle Wiese. Henry Sr. was the brother of
         Fritz Goessler's grandmother,Louise.

         Fritz and Hulda celebrated their Golden Anniversary on
         Nov.25,1976 (2 children)

The State of Texas---County of Washington.

To any Regular Ordained Minister of the Gospel,
Judge of the District Court, or Justice of the Peace:

I hereby authorize any one of you to celebrate the **Rite of Matrimony** between

Hartman Lösch and Louisa Friede Wiese

and due return of your proceedings hereon to me, at my office, make, within sixty days, as the law directs.

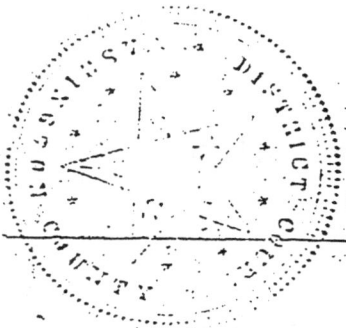

In Witness Whereof, I, J.J. Stockbridge

Clerk of the District Court of Washington County, hereto subscribe

my name and affix the seal of said Court, this 4th

day of January A. D. 1871.

J.J. Stockbridge
Clerk D. C. W. C.

By A.M. Hughes
Deputy.

RETURN.

The Rite of Matrimony between the above named parties was duly celebrated by the

undersigned P. G. Fiek, Minister Gospel on the fifth day of

January A. D. 1872. P G Fiek, M.G.

Left to right: Mother,Bertha
with baby Bertha,Willie,
Hannah,Fritz and William

50th Anniversary,1944
Grandchildren with
Bertha and William

The Goessler Home in Washington,Tx.

Hulda and Fritz
1978

1922: 25-30 gallons

Hulda and Fritz

WARRANTEED

COMB HONEY

Net Weight _____

Packed and Guaranteed By

F. C. GOESSLER

WASHINGTON, TEX.

Clara and Willie

Emma and Walter Wiese

Walter and Emma,1978

a. Hilbert Fritz b. Jan.11,1931 Washington Co.m.Dec.2,
1956 Brenham,Tx. to Lena Mae Holtkamp b.Nov.24,
1934 Whitehall,Grimes Co.,dau. of Charlie and Lena
Holtkamp.(3 children)
    1. Gary Lyn Goessler b. Apr.26,1959 Bryan,Tx.
    2. Kevin Lyn b. Oct.18,1862 Bryan,Tx.
    3. Karl Frederick b. Apr.16,1964 Bryan,Tx.
b. Ruby Marie b. Sept.14,1932 Washington,Co.m.Feb.20,
1955 to Mace H.Meekins b. Nov.24,1932,son of Rufus
and Pearl Meekins(2 children)
    1. Cecil Elliott b. Aug.31,1956 Navasota,Grimes
       Co. m. Melissa Sanders on June 11,1977.
    2. Danny Joe b. Aug.11,1964

4. Bertha Minnie Emma b. Aug.27,1904 Washington,Tx.m.in the
Friedens Ev. Church by Rev.Alvina Blume on Aug.27 to
Herman Jaster b.March 3,1906 Brenham,Tx.(1 child)
    a. Betty Lou b. April 3,1944 m.College Station in Our
       Saviour's Lutheran Church by Pastor Carl Ruk on June
       6,1965 to Garland Leneal Sparks b.Apr.22,1943.,son
       of Emmett Elwood Sparks b.Apr.12,1895 and Jamie
       Estella Garrison b. Nov.6,1902(1 child)
          1. Jeffery Scott b.Aug.22,1968 in Fayetville,N.C.

5. Henry b. Aug.2,1907 d.June 2,1908

6. Charlie Henry b.Sept.11,1909 m.Prairie Hill on Oct.2,
1930 to Emma Schmidt dau. of Heneritta Schmidt and Richard
Schmidt(1 child)
    a. Herbert Goessler b.Feb.28,1931 m.Jan.21,1956 to
       Norma Jean Kneschke,dau. of Alive Dubbe and Ferdinand
       Kneschke(2 children)
          1. Mark Anthony b.May 14,1958
          2. Paul Fredrick b.July 31,1963

7. Emma Marie b.Washington Co.b.July 24,1913 married on Dec.11
1955 to Walter Henry Wiese b. Mar.20,1912,son of Fritz Wiese
and Hulda Neumann. Fritz was the oldest child of Henry and
Sophie Holle Wiese. Henry was the brother of Emma's grandmother,Louise. Walter is also the brother of Hulda Wiese,
wife of Fritz Goessler,Emma's brother(child #3)

Emma became the "mother" of Walter's three children by his
first marriage to Carleen Adler who had died at the age of
25 years,leaving 3 small children. Emma is beloved by all
who know her.

    a. Walter Jr.b.Feb.10,1947 McLennan Co.
    b. Linda Marie b.May 18,1948 McLennan Co.m.Nov.29,
       1975 to Gene Keadle b.Aug.9,1929,son of Nora Mae
       Hesser and Wyle Eugene Keadle Sr.
    c. Shirley Jean b. Dec.8,1950 McLennan Co.

CHILD #2: <u>Annie</u> b. Dec.4,1876 d. May 16,1952 m. Herman C.Burmeister
d. 1948. Lived in Temple,Texas. (5 children)

    a. Bertha Loesch b. Aug.22,1891 Wiedeville Community, Brenham,
       Tx. Married Sept.26,1912 Wiedeville to Oscar Fuelberg, b.April
       7,1887, Kuykendall Community, Brenham, Washington Co.Texas.
       Son of Ludwig Fuelberg and Marie Welticke Fuelberg. Oscar
       died July 25,1959 and is buried in the Chappell Hill Quadrangle,
       Wiedeville Cemetery, Wiedeville Community (10 children)
          1. Otto b. June 21,1913 Wiedeville Community, d. Dec.3,1913
            Buried in the Wiedeville Cemetery.
          2. Hilda b. Sept.1,1915 m. Immanuel Lutheran Church
            in Wiedeville on Jan.16,1936 to Herbert Wellmann.
            (5 children)Hilda d.Nov.22,1976 buried Wiedeville Ceme.
               a. Vernon Herbert b. Aug.9,1938 m. Eben Nezer Lutheran
                 Church (Berlin) on Nov.20,1960,to Kathyrn Ullrich
                 b. Dec.12,1939, dau. of Jacob Ullrich,Sr. and Tonie
                 Spies Ullrich.(3 children)
                    1. Wayne Allen b. Sept.29,1961 Brenham
                    2. Kathy Renee b. Oct.8,1963 Brenham
                    3. Becky Lynn b. Oct.29,1968 Brenham
               b. Ralph Reinhard b. Oct.21,1942 m. at St.Rose of Lima
                 Catholic Church in Schulenberg,Tx. on Sept.5,1966
                 to Patricia Elizabeth Dittrich b. Dec.7,1946, dau.
                 of Henry Joseph Dittrich,Sr. and Elizabeth Christ
                 Dittrich. (2 children)
                    1. Brian Scott b. Oct.31,1967 Brenham
                    2. Rodney Alan b. Jan.21,1970 Brenham
               c. Merle Helen b. Aug.27,1946 , m.Immanuel Lutheran
                 Church on April 25,1969 to James Ronald Kyzar b.
                 Jan.21,1946, son of Elmo Ben Kyzar and Dorothy
                 Sanberg Kyzar.
               d. Pauline Sue b. Sept.12,1952,m. in Bryan,Tx. on Jan.
                 23,1978 to Mickel Norman Hodges b. Mar.24,1950,son
                 of Norman Hodges and Willie Maude Jetter Hodges.
                 Pauline has 2 children by 2 previous marriages.
                    1. Stephen Chad Roliard b. Feb.11,1971
                    2. Janie Marie Salazar b. Jan.20,1976
               e. Tommie Lee b. Aug.6,1954 m. Immanuel Lutheran Church
                 in Wiedeville to Carolyn Foster b. July 22,1953.Dau.
                 of Nathan Gordon Foster and Esther Corene Grant of
                 Tahlequah.Oklahoma. Carolyn was born July 22,1953
                 at Richmond,Contra Costa Co.,California(3 children)
                    1. Toby Eugene Rogers b. Nov.30,1969 Vallejo,
                      Solano Co.California. Father: Harmon Eugene
                      Rogers, Carolyn's 1st marriage.
                    2. Kristy Renee' Rogers b. Oct.20,1971 same as
                      above.
                    3. Nathan Herbert Wellmann b. April 4,1975 at
                      Okland,Contra Costa Co,California.

3. Arthur Carl b. Feb.4,1917 Wiedeville Community,Brenham
   Washington Co. Tx. m. Lydia Helen Muehlbrad b. Feb.15,
   1908, on June 24,1939 in Brenham, dau.of Emil Muehlbrad
   and Wilhelmine(Minnie) Krause Burton of Washington Co.
   (1 child)

       a. Gene Arthur b. Dec.17,1946 Brenham,m. Nancy Elsie
          Rauch of Carmine,Tx. b. Feb.22,1947, on June 24,
          1967.Nancy born Burton,Tx.,dau. of W.Otis Rauch
          and Ida Belle Light of Carmine,Tx.,Fayette Co.
          (1 child)
             1. Kristine Kay b. June1,1968 Houston ,Tx.

4. Reinhard b. Feb.28,1919 Wiedeville Community,Brenham.
   m. Dec.23,1945 to Mabel Caroline Haarmeyer b. Jan.29,
   1923,dau.of Otto Haarmeyer and Bertha Becker of Brenham,
   Tex.(1 child)

       a. Betty Lynn b. April 27,1954 Brenham,Tx. m.Oct.16,
          1976 to Kenneth Lee Beckman b. Sept.28,1951 at
          Bellville,Austin Co.Tx.Married in Bellville,dau.
          of Wilbert Gus Beckman and Hazel Mewia Beckmann
          Prause. Step-father: Harvey Prause of Bellville.

5. Dora b. Dec.24,1921 Wiedeville m. Oct.30,1949 to Charles
   Wesley Steele b. Nov.16,1924 in Midway Community, Winkler
   Navarro Co.Tx.,son of Edward Elijah Steele and Mary
   Naoma Richmond of Fairfield,Tx.

6. Oscar Jr. b. Sept.14,1924 Wiedeville Community, Brenham.
   Lives with his mother on the homeplace.

7. Edward b. June 26,1926 Wiedeville Community,Brenham.
   m. March 18,1978 to Carol Moore b. June 19,1929 Denver,
       Colorado.Married at Wiedeville. Dau. of Charles Richard
       Cooper and Miriam Black of Waco,McLennan Co.Tx.
       (Carol's two children)

       a. Joyce Moore b. Nov.28,1966 Houston,Harris Co.Tx.
          Father: Buell Moore
       b. Dale Moore b. May 10,1968 Houston,Harris Co.Tx.
          Father: Buell Moore, son of Obe Ebeneezer and
          Adele Moore of Yoakum,Lavaca Co.Tx.

8. Bertha b. Feb.21,1929 Wiedeville.m. Sept. ,1950 to Elmo
   Emshoff b. July 22,1930,Kenny ,Austin Co.Tx.,son of Otto
   Emshoff and Laura Glaser of Brenham.(2 children)

       a. Tina Marie Emshoff b. July 17,1956 Austin,Travis Co.
       b. David Alan b.Oct.10,1960 Austin,Travis Co. Tx.

9. Robert b. March 23,1931 Wiedeville m. Oct.22,1955 to
   Mary Nell Finley Foster b. Oct.30,1926 at DeKalb,Bowie Co.
   Tx. Robert and Mary Nell married in DeKalb.,dau.of Chester
   Finley and Donnie Oliver of DeKalb.(2 children)

       a. Marsha Lenell b. June 10,1948 Texarkana,Ark.Father:
          Houston Foster
       b. Mary Dale Fuelberg b. Nov.12,1957 Angleton, Brazoria
          Co.Tx.

10. Annie Marie b. April 10,1935 Wiedeville.m. April 10,1955
    to Joel Ernest Lovell b. June 31,1932 at Bryan,Brazos Co.,
    son of Ernest Lovell and Alene Davis of Kurten,Tx.

CHILD #2: <u>Annie</u> cont.

    b. Annie b. Mar.31,1903 d. Mar.1944 m. Fritz Beltz.,son of John
       and Helena Heide Belz of Sands,Ala(4 sons)
         1. John lives in Victoria
         2. Rev.Fredrick Wm.Beltz lives in Ft.Worth
         3. Franklin D.Belz lives in Brownwood
         4. Charles Herman Belz lives in Austin
    c. Martha Lorina Wilhimina Burmeister b. March 9,1898 Weideville
       Community,Washington Co.Tx.near Brenham,Tx.Lives in Temple.
    d. Lillie b.June 28,1907 m.Ben Kosel b.Feb.22,19
    e. Herman b. 1910 d.1973,buried in Temple,Tx.m.Naomi J.Embree
       of Glenrose on Oct.1947.

CHILD #3: <u>Charlie</u> H.Loesch b. Sept.29,1881 d. June 20,1959 m.Dec.
22,1899,MB.Vol.13,p.232 #8081,to Lorina
Wiese b.Apr.5,1881 d.Feb.14,1969,dau of
Alonzo(Lonnie) Wiese born Morgan,and Rene
Charlotte(Lottie)(Refer to Fritz Wiese,
Chapter 1)
Charles and Lorina were married in the German
Ev.Lutheran Church in Wiedeville by Pastor
P.Dyck(6 children)
a. Johnnie Mae b. Feb.22,1900
b.Roy b.March 27,1903 d.Apr.25,1976 m.
August 14,1929 to Gracie Simank b.Jan.4
1902,dau. of Charles and Sullie Simank.
c. John b.Nov.4,1904 m.Nov.29,1934 to
Louise Kochwelp b.Jan.9,1912 dau.of Ernest
and Louise Kochwelp.
d. Louise Belle b.May 2,1917
e. Melvin b.Aug.14,1907 d.Dec.20,1953
f. Mary b.Feb.7,1910 d.Mar.20,1954 m.Erich
William Tappe Nov.26,1928 b.Oct.15,1906,son of E.W.Henry Jr.b.Oct.
25,1862 d. Oct.13,1938, and Henriette Tappe b. April 5,1863 d.Nov.
7,1944 (7 children)
    1. Dorothy Mae b. March 13,1929 d.March 19,1929
    2. Mary b.May 24,1947 m.1st Wilbert Schroeder b.Sept.11
      1920(3 children)
        a. Bobby Ray b.Sept.12,1948 m.Mary Jo Hustfield on
          June 28,1969.Mary born Sept.26,1953(1 child)
           1. Len Anthony b. Sept.23,1971d. Mar.3,1974
        b. Ronald E.Schroeder b.Nov.23,1951 m.Sept.2,1978
          Patti Ann Shelton b.March 11,1955
        c. Michael Glenn Schroeder b.Sept.3,1954 m.June 2,
          1973 to Billie Kay Pessarra b.May 30,1954
        (2 children)
          1. Kelley Marie b.Nov.19,1973
          2. Jared Dakota b.Oct.2,1976
Mary married 2nd to Charles R.Doiron Jan.29,1972 b.
Oct.24,1929.

COUNTY OF WASHINGTON,

To any Regularly Licensed or Ordained Minister of the Gospel, Jewish Rabbi, Judge of the District or County Court, or any Justice of the Peace, Greeting:

You are Hereby Authorized to Solemnize the

RITES OF MATRIMONY

Between Mr. _Charley H. Loesch_ and Miss _Lorina Wiese_

and make due return to the Clerk of the County Court of said County within sixty days thereafter, certifying your action under this License.

Witness my official signature and seal of office, at office in Brenham, the _24_ day of _December_ 1898

O. A. Seward
Clerk County Court Washington County.

By _R. W. Hoffmann_ Deputy.

I, _P. Lyck_, hereby certify that on the _22_ day of _Dec_ 1898 I united in Marriage Mr. _Charles H. Loesch_ and Miss _Lorina Wiese_ the parties above named.

Witness my hand, this _22_ day of _Dec._ 1898

P. Lyck
Pastor Germ. Ev. Luth. Church
Wiedeville, Tx

Returned, filed and recorded in book No. _13_ Page _232_ of Marriage record the _24_ day of _July_ 1899 _O A Seward_

By _____ Deputy. Clerk County Court Washington County.

Annie and Herman Burmeister

Lillie and Herman

Bertha and Oscar Fuelberg

Lonnie Wiese

Lora and Charles Loesch

Lora

Charlie Loesch

3. Lucille b. Feb.7,1932 m. Nov.26,1953 to Gene Meyer
   b. Dec.13,1930 (6 children)
   a. Debora b. July 3,1954 m. 1970 to Larry Lewis
      (2 children)
      1. Biran b. Sept.1971
      2. Melissa b. Aug.1976
   b. Darrel b. Aug.1956
   c. Beverly b. May 1958 m. 1977 to Kenneth Hickness
   d. Mary b. Dec.1960
   e. Linda b. Dec.1961
   f. Diana b. Nov.1965

4. Charles Hy b.April 22,1936 m. June 6,1959 to Gerldine
   Hester.b.April 11,1936 (1 son)
   a. Charles Hy Jr. August 26,1960

5. Geneva b. March 16,1940 m.1st Jimmie Means Bowden on
   Nov.30,1957 b. Feb.28,1935 (3 sons)
   a. Jimmie Means Jr.b. Sept.14,1958
   b. Terry Lynn b. April 6,1960
   c. John Bowden b. Jan.14,1962 (John Abney)
Geneva married 2nc to Douglas Cructhers May 29,1971,
b. May 29,1938
6. Darla Neikamp b. Feb.1,1942 m. April 18,1959 to Edmund
   B.Neikamp Jr. b. Jan.12,1940 (3 children)
   a. James b. June 12,1960
   b. Sidonia Charisse b. June 19,1963
   c. David b. April 8,1965 (David Randall)
7. Carol Lois Carlile b. May 29,1946 m. March 6,1964 to
   Joseph Nelson b. May 29,1963 (3 children-1 due Jan.1979)
   a. Joesph Nelson Jr. b. Aug.9,1964 d. Aug.12,1964
   b. Kimberly Jo b. Sept.21,1965
   c. Anthony Joesph b. Dec.2,1969
   d.

CHILD #4: <u>Frederick (Fritz R.) Grube</u> was born in Washington Co. near Brenham on Nov.20,1 81. He was baptized and confirmed in the Lutheran Church. He accompanied his parents to Maxwell, Tx. as an infant and later moved to Port Lavaca. After his mother died in childbirth, he was reared by his Aunt Minna Wehmeyer, his mother's sister. His father Herman Grube returned to Germany where he died on Jan.10,1910.

He again moved to Maxwell and there he met and married Miss Selma Schawe. This union was blessed with eight children. Norman, as an infant, preceded his father in death and the oldest son Hilbert also died before his father. He was killed in an automobile accident. They were both buried in the Lutheran Cemetery in Maxwell,Tx.

Fritz and Selma then moved to Reedville where he purchased and operated both a general store and a farm. In 1924 he sold his business and moved to Hondo and again purchased a farm. Here he and his family joined St.Paul Lutheran Church. He was survived by his wife and six children at the time of his death, Nov.1,1956. He was buried in the Oakwood Cemetery, Hondo,Texas.

Selma and Fritz Grube

Fritz Grube family

No. 181

STATE OF TEXAS.

Page. 467

Vol 6, P. 467

To All who Shall See these Presents:

Know Ye, That any person legally authorized to celebrate the rites of matrimony is hereby licensed to Join in Marriage, as husband and wife, _Florentine Stieby_ and _Mathildene Finck_ and for so doing this shall be your authority, and you will make your return of this License to me, at my office in the City of Brenham, in sixty days, as the law directs.

IN TESTIMONY WHEREOF, I, _Will Beers_ Clerk of the County Court of Washington County, hereunto subscribe my name and affix the seal of said Court, at my office in the City of Brenham, this _6th_ day of _January_ A. D. 1880.

W. Beers
Clerk of the County Court of Washington County.

THE STATE OF TEXAS.

This Certifies that I joined in marriage as husband and wife _Florentine Grube_ and _Miss Mathildene Finck_ on the _7_ day of _January_ A. D. 1880.

_Rev. G. F. _____._

<u>Fritz Grube</u> b. Nov.20,1881 d. Nov.1,1956 m.Nov.17,1904
to Selma Schawe b. May 23,1884 d. Sept.26,1978. Both
are buried in the Oakwood Cemetery in Hondo. Selma,dau.
of Dora and W.F. Schawe.(8 children)
- a. Hilbert b. Sept.3,1905 d, June 14,1925 (Maxwell Ceme)
- b. Otto b. Sept.22,1906 d. June 1,1977 (Oakwood Ceme)
- c. Elma b. Dec. 4,1907 m. in Hondo at Saint Paul Lutheran
  Church on Aug.21,1928 to Alfred Breiten b. Jan.22,1901
  son of John N. and Emma Loesberg.(4 children)
    1. Evelyn Joyce b. Aug.25,1930 m. Hondo,Tx. Dec.16,
    1951 at St.Paul Lutheran Church to George Dawson
    Jr. b. May 14,1926, son of George and Vera
    Dawson (5 children)
        - a. Gary George Dawson b. Nov.10,1955
        - b. Bruce Ray Dawson b. April 26,1958
        - c. Robin Gayle Dawson b. April 2,1959
        - d. Sandra Joyce Dawson b. April 15,1961
        - e. Thad Alfred Dawson b. April 16,1971

    2. Wilma Alene b. Aug.14,1931 m. Hondo,Texas on
    Oct.15,1950 at St.Paul Lutheran Church to Harold
    Bohlen b. Feb.3,1924, son of John and Emma
    Breiten (3 children)
        - a. Harold James Bohlen b. Nov.6,1951
        - b. Sharon Elaine Bohlen b. Sept.11,1953
        married St.Paul Lutheran Church in Hondo
        Jan.14,1978.
        - c. Robert Allen Bohlin b. April 3,1955

    3. John Allen b. Feb.17,1938 m. Augsburg Germany
    April 13,1963 to Susan Ruth Adams b. Nov.8,1938
    dau. of Mr. Adams and Susan Ruth Walker (2 child-
    ren)
        - a. Sarah Ann Breiten b. Dec.6,1965
        - b. John David Breiten b. May 16,1967

    4. Alfred Ray B.July 7,1942 m. Castroville Tx. on
    June 20,1970 at St.Louis Catholic Church to
    Mildred Jean Werzbach (Urerzbach) b. Mar.8,19??
    dau. of August.(2 children)
        - a. Sean Ray Breiten b. May 23,1971
        - b. Bret Allen Breiten b. Sept.7,1973

- d. Melanie b. Feb.28,1909 m. St.Paul Lutheran Church in
  Hondo, on March 12,1929 to Robert Graff b. April 17,
  1900,son of Louis and Elizabeth Leinweber Graff.
  (5 children)
    1. Frances Bernice b. March 30,1930 m. Hondo,Tx in
    her home on Aug.20,1950 to Wilford L.Richter
    b. Sept.22,1929, son of A.J. and Florence
    Richter. (3 children)

       a. Kim Richter b. June 4,1957
       b. Kirk Richter b. Aug.2,1960
       c. Kris Richter b. Oct.17,1962

  2. Robert J. b. Oct.4,1932 m. St.John Catholic
     Church on July 20,1952,Hondo,Tx. to Patsy Zeir
     b. Sept.27,1932,dau. of Arnold and Luciene Finger
     Zeir (3 children)
       a. Susan b. Sept.20,1953 m.May 30,1976 to James
         Weimers
       b. Joey Stephen b. Feb.5,1955
       c. Tommie Allan b. Dec.24,1961

  3. Barbara Annette b. July 7,1935 m. St.Paul Lutheran
     Church,Hondo,Tx. on Aug.21,1954 to Arthur H.
     Schroder b. June 1,1928,son of Arthur H and Thelma
     Schroder.(3 children)
       a. Stephen b. Oct.18,1956
       b. Bryan b. March 18,1957
       c. Karen b. Sept.15,1961

  4. Fred Louis B.Oct.28,1942 m. Hondo,Tx. at home to
     Dianne Tondre b. April 13,1944 dau. of Charles
     and Ginger Fussleman Tondre.(3 children)
       a. Robert Charles b. July 15,1966
       b. Tina Rene b. June 22,1968
       c. Fred Louis Jr. b. June 2,1973

  5. Kathy Marie b. May 11,1952 m. Hondo, Tx. on Aug.
     19, 1972 in the St.Paul Lutheran Church to Stephen
     Frank Billiot b. Dec.17,1951, son of Frank and
     Katherine Billiot (1 child)
       a. Nathan Christfer b. Jan.5,1973

f. Louis b. Oct.25,1910 d. June 6,1962 (Oakwood Cemetery)

g. Dorothy b. June 19,1912 m. Hondo,Tex. at St.Paul
  Lutheran Parsonage on June 31,1934 to Clarence Neuman
  b. Aug.25,1910,son of Louis and Martha Bohmfalk Neuman
  (5 children)
  1. Fanelle Dorothy b. Sept.11,1935 m. Hondo,Tx.on
     Jan.17,1954 at St.Paul Lutheran Church to Douglas
     Bohnfalk b. April 26,1934,son of Erwin and Alleen
     Weimers Bohmfalk (3 children)
       a. Gordon Douglas Bohmfalk b. July 24,1956
       b. Larry Wayne Bohmfalk b. May 10,1961
       c. Kathy Fay b. May 10,1968

  2. Betty Louise b. July 21,1937 m. Ft.Sam Chapel,
     San Antonio ,Tx. on Feb.20,1960 to Jack La Spina
     Jr. b. Sept.5,1937,son of Jack and Louise
     La Spina(2 children)
       a. Lisa Michelle b. Jan.19,1961
       b. Mark Scott b. Oct.28,1965

3. Charles Larry Neuman, b. July 29, 1944 m. Hondo, Tx. on June 25, 1965 at St. Paul Lutheran Church to Bobbie Gail Melton b. June 21, 1946, dau. of Ray and Burle Melton (3 children)
    a. Charles Larry Jr. b. Dec. 26, 1965
    b. Michael Ray b. June 15, 1968
    c. Daniel Louis b. Jan. 26, 1972

4. Lynn Ray b. Sept. 3, 1948 m. Weslaco, Tx. on Aug. 12, 1972 at United Method st Church to Janet Hansen b. Dec. 1, 1948, dau. of Harold and Polly Hansen

5. Dennis James b. April 3, 1953 m. in Castroville, Tx. on March 20, 1976 at St. Louis Catholic Church to Marva Louise Hutzler b. Feb. 22, 1954, dau. of Wilford and Martha Tschirhart Hutzler

CHILD #5: CARL DIED OF DIPTHERIA

CHILD #6: MINNA, DIED OF DIPTHERIA Both children were with their Uncle August and Aunt Louise Wiese after their mother died. When the family returned home from burying Carl, they found Minna ill.

CHILD # 7: HENRIETTE WILHELMINE CHARLOTTE, b. May 26, 1854, bapt. June 5, Died, Aug. 11, 1855 Register No. 65. Wehdem, Germany

CHILD # 8: <u>Henriette Luise Caroline</u> b. Oct.19,1856 Baptized: Nov.2,
Register No.23,Wehdem,Germany d. Jan.22,1941 m. Christ.W.Bohne
b. Jan.6,1855 d. April 4,1945.Both buried Freiden Cemetery near
Frieden Church on FM Road #1155 near Old Washington,Tx. (11 children) They also reared Caroline's sister Louises' child of her first
marriage, Bertha who would later marry Wm.Goessler.

   a. Minnie
   b. Emma   Both died as infanta(2½ years) and are buried in St.
      John's Cemetery at Prairie Hill under the lone tree in the
      Cemetery. No other information known.
   c. Karl Fredrich Wilhelm b. Oct.29,1877 d. Feb.25,1895
   d. Fritz b. Aug.22,1880 d. Jan.25,1964 m. Johanna Roesler Dec.
      7,1908 (MB Vol.15,p.25 Brenham Tx.) b. June 15,1885 d. Jan.
      21,1975 (2 children)
       1. Fritz Jr. b. Aug.23,1910 m. Lillie Kupott b. Nov.5,
         1908 (3 children)
         a. Fritz III b. Oct.24,1940 m. Wanda Wiatt b. June
           27,1939 (3 children)
            1. Ronda b. May 21,1964
            2. Kimberly b. May 14,1960
            3. Fritz David b. May 30,1967
       2. Marie Jane b. De.9,1946 m. Victor Shaper b. Aug.27,
         1946 (1 child)
         a. Christopher b. June 6,1975
   e. Minnie b. Feb.19,1882 Prairie Hill d. Dec.17,1963 m. Fritz
      Vahrenkamp Dec.8,1904 (MB Vol.15,p.25 Brenham) Fritz b.
      Dec.16,1882 at Wiederville Tx. d. Dec.22,1966,son of
      Heneritta Spreen.Both buried in Frieden Cemetery, Old
      Washington,Tx.(9 children)
       1. Willie C. Fahrenkamp b. July 28,1906 at Old Washing-
         ton ,Tx.
       2. Emma b. Jan.26,1908,Old Washington m. Roland Roese
         Nov.17,1927.Roland b. Dec.7,1904,son of Wm.Roese
         and Minetta Wehmeyer (5 children)
         a. Robert
         b. Wilbert
         c. Christine b. Feb.13,1931 d. Nov.23,1941
         d. Larry Gene b. Jan.12,1935 d. Nov.6,1935
         e. Milton
       3. Annie b. Aug.23,1909 m. Willie Fleischlauer March 5,
         1935 (2 children)
         a. Herbert
         b. Raymond and wife have 2 girls
       4. Elsie b. Jan.24,1911 m. Nelson Clyde Smith Jr. on
         March 1,1947,son of Nelson Clyde Smith Sr. and Opal
         Junice Clary(1 child)
         a. Kitty Ann b. Aug.16,1949 m. Nov.4,1967 to Colin
           Clyde Miller,son of Athol and Joan Miller of
           Madison,West Virginia (1 child)
            1. Stephen Lee b. July 11,1969

Carolina

Carolina Wiese and Chris Bohne

Minnie and Lena

5. Minnie b. Sept.17,1912 m. March 9,1944 to Herbert
   Roese, son of Willie Roese and Bertha Lohmeyer
   (3 children)
      a. Carol
      b. Judy
      c. John Robert
6. Rosa Fahrenkamp b. Dec.12,1914
7. Fritz Fahrenkamp b. Sept.27,1916 m. to Edie Mae
   Heckman (1 child)
      a. Linda Kay
8. Ida b. June 25,1918 m. Leo Schmalriede d. Oct.1955
   Later married Albert Alaminski
9. Clara b. March 3,1920 m.Fritz Benker Jr.,son of
   Fritz Benker Sr. and Pauline Renn (3 children)
      a. Valgene
      b. Larry
      c. La Nelle
f. Henry Bohne b. Feb.16,1884 d. June 5,1969 m. Elsie Krueger
   b. Aug.27,1894 d. Dec.12,1968
g. Caroline Lena b. March 29,1887 d. Dec.28,1913 m. Charley H.
   Holle Nov.26,1908 in the Evangelical Church of Peace by
   Rev.Fr. Lueckhoff (MB Vol.16,p.136 Brenham) C.H ,son of
   Charles Holle and _____ Schulte Holle.(3 children)
      1. William C.Holle b. Dec.1,1909 m. Olga Jensen on
         June 30,1938 (4 children)
            a. Rebecca Holle b. Aug.5,1941 m. Aug.5,1962 to
               T.C. Kolhhorst (2 children)
                  1. Christina Lynn b. Aug.30,1971
                  2. Todd Christopher b. April 17,1975
            b. Ralph W. b.Mar 26,1943 m. Donna (2 children)
                  1. William Geoffrey b. Oct.39,1970
                  2. David Garick b. Nov.21,1975
            c. Thomas N. b. June 28,1947 m. Lois Goessler
               Sept.25,1971 (1 child)
            d. Ronald C.b.May 10,1949 m. Dorothy Wellman
               Aug.23,1971 (2 children)
                  1. Stacy Renee b. Sept.20,1972
                  2. Kyle Bradley b. Feb.28,1977
      2. Charles F. b. Jan.4,1911 m. Nelda Krueger (3 children)
            a. Frances Anderson b. Feb.24,1935 (2 children)
                  1. Dean Alan Anderson
                  2. Doyle Anderson
            b. Dennis Holle b. Feb.23,1937 m.Nancy Rogers
                  1. Charles Holle
                  2. Chris Holle
            c. Bobby Jean Holle Hobbs m. Billy Joe Hobbs
               (2 children)
                  1. Roddy Joe b. March 28,1960
                  2. Brenda b. March 26,1962

3. Caroline Holle Peterson
   a. Judy
   b. Charles Wayne
   c. Susan,deceased
h. Emma b. May 30,1889 d. April 5,1969 m. Frank C.Dickschat
(Vol.16,Nov.28,1910) b. Feb.8,1884 d. Feb.11,1950
(5 children)
   1. Edwin Christoph b. Oct.24,1912 d. Mar.31,1973
      m. Hildegarde Borgsted b. April 6,1918 (3 children)
      a. Nina b. May 28,1943 m. James T.Hall b. May ,
         1939
      b. Reba b. Nov.28,1945
      c. Carol b. July 14,1954
   2. Otto Fritz b. Dec.5,1913 d. Feb.1978 m. Annie Mae
      Bohot b. Mar.3,1916 (6 children)
      a. Dorothy Ann b. Dec.22,1939 m Herbert William
         Stolz Jr. b. Feb.8,1941 (1 child)
         1. Kelli b. Jan.11,1969
      b. Betty Jane b. Oct.15,1942 m. Raymond Wilson
         Varner b. Nov.29,1943 (2 children)
         1. Shannon Rhea b. Jan.22,1967
         2. Shelli Kae b. Oct.18,1971
      c. Peggy Elaine b. Jan.14,1947 m. Gene Smith
         b. Sept.2,1946 (2 children)
         1. Robin b. June 22,1970
         2. Kimberly b. Sept.4,1974
      d. Joyce Lynn b. Oct.14,1948 m. James Allen
         Pelkemeyer b. Sept.14,1947 (1 child)
         1. Jennifer Leigh b. Mar.30,1974
      e. Linda Kay b. Dec.13,1955 m. Pat Lynn Jolly
         (1 child)
         1. Aimee Lynn b. July 30,1974
   3. Rosa Karoline b. Oct.20,1915 m. James Ennis Lambert
      b. Sept.1,1902 d. Nov.22,1965(1 child)
      a. Renee b. Mar.5,1957
   4. William Henry b. Feb.18,1918 d. Dec.11,1977 m.Doris
      Schwartz b. Sept.2,(1 child)
      a. Danny b. Dec.21,1949
   5. Frank William b. Nov.26,1922 m. Edith Roese b. May
      25,(1 child)
      a. Alton Carl b. July 17,1957 d. May 25,1977
i. Bertha b. Feb.17,1891 d.Oct.18,1977.Never married.She was
   dared for in her last days by her niece Elsie Smith.
j. Annie b. Mar.25,1893 d. Oct.19,1960 buried in the Brenham
   Quadrangle,Prairie Lea Cemetery.
k. Willie C.b. Sept.16,1897 d. Feb.11,1975 m. Lydia Schamberg
   in 1963

CHILD #9:CHRISTOPH HEINRICH WILHELM.b. Mar.30,1859 1:AM Germany,
  died July 16,1878 buried Prairie Hill.Nothing known about death.
CHILD #10: TWIN TO CHRIS: CARL FRIEDRICH WILHELM.b&d.Germany

CHILD # 11: Heinrich Friedrich <u>Carl</u> b. Feb. 1861,Baptized, May 5,
Register No.48,Wehdem,Germany. d. March 15,1940, McGregor.Tx.
m. Nov.19,1885 Prairie Hill, Washington,Co.Tex. by Pastor O.
Samuel to Louise Wehmeyer, b. July 11,1865 d. Jan.15,1951, dau. of
John Friedrich Wehmeyer and Marie Henriette born in Hambury,Whedem,
Germany. Louise was christened on July 23,1865 and confirmed on Palm
Sunday,1879.(5 children)

    a. Carl Fredrick Wilhelm (Wm.) b. Oct.22,1886 Prairie Hill,
       Christened. Godparents: Wiese,Wehmeyer,Aunt Charlotte Weiss,
       Confirmed June 27,1902 by P.O.Bracher in Mosheim. William
       married Alda Barber and lived in Triboli,Refugio Co.
       (2 children)
         1. Elaine(Elana)
         2. Bill married Louise and died in 1942

    b. Friedrich (Fred) b. Feb.24,1888 at Prairie Hill. Christened
       April 1,1888. Godparents: Frau Wiese, Wilhelm Weymeyer, Sophie
       Wiese. Confirmed June 27,1902. Married Dec.11,1910 at Coryell
       to Nora Hering b. Dec.29,1893 at Welcome Tex. Presently lives
       in McGregor. (2 children)
         1. Charlsey Louise b. Mar.15,1912 m.Nov.20,1929 to Robert
           Edwin Duncan b. July 28,1907, d. Dec.20,1963,son of
           Robert Ewell Duncan and Mary Lee Brunson. (1 child)
             a. Mary Lee b. Sept.16,1930 m. Dec.3,1951 to Ruben
               Etzel b. Roundtop,Tx. Feb.28,1912,son of Louis
               and Minnie Quade Etzel. (1 child)
                 1. Richard Duncan b. Apr.21,1953 m. Aug.14,1977
                    Greenville,Tx.Methodist Church to Ann Weis
                    b. Jan.10,1954
         2. Freddie (Carl) b. Oct.13,1916 m. Oct.12,1939 in Rev.R.S.
           Morgan's home in Pendleton,Tx.,near Temple to Eva Nell
           Connally b. McClennan Co.,April 8,1916,dau. of Lonie
           Wade Connally and Tennie Heffington Connally of Travis
           Co.Tx.(1 child)
             a. Alan Wayne b. March 27,1946

    c. Minna b. June 15,1891 Prairie Hill, Christened.Godparents
       Herman Weymeyer,Wilhelmine Wiese, Henriette Weymeyer. Confirmed
       Palm Sunday,1905 at Coryell. m.Nov.19,1911 to Ed Weiss(2 child-
       ren)
         1. Harold b. Aug.25,1912 m. Oct.7,1939 in McGregor to Mary
           Ruth Sharp b. Aug.7,1917 ,dau. of Sidney Thomas Sharp
           and Eliza Bell Clemmer Sharp of McGregor (2 children)
            a. Horold Charles b. Jan.3,1942 m. Ann Roussear
              b. Jan.20,1942 (2 children)
               1. Christopher Charles b. Dec.11,1966
               2. Robin Beth b. March 3,1971
            b. Mary Carol b. Aug.2,1949 m. Christopher Michael
              Foster (2 children)
               1. Gretal b. Dec.6,1974
               2. Gillian Elizabeth b. April 24,1978

2. Carlos b. Jan.8,1915 m. Juanita Hunter Thompson
   (3 children)
   a. Anita Frances Thompson
   b. Martha Louis Weiss m. Fritz Herman Becker
      (2 children)
      1. Infant died
      2. Traci b. Aug.1969
   c. Thomas Edward m. Janice

d. Anna Caroline b. Sept.6,1892 Washington Co. d. Aug.20,1966
   Buried by her parents in the McGregor Cemetery,Godparents:
   Caroline Bohne, Wilhelmine Wehmeyer and Fritz Rosenbaum.
   Confirmed April 12,1908 Coryell (Pastor Ermisch)

e. Ben(Bernard) Friedrick,b. Aug.29,1894 at Prairie Hill
   Christened Oct.28,1894.Godparents: Mutter (Taunge) Fritz
   Wehmeyer, Henriette Wiese. Confirmed April 12,1908 at Coryell.
   Married March 31,1920 at McGregor by Pastor James Schwarz to
   Hulds Bishoff b. June 23,1893,dau. of Caroline Schlechte and
   William Bishoff. Married in her parents home.(1 child)
   1. Esther b. Sept.9,1925 m. June 3,19 0 to William Thomas
      MacNutt,b. Sept.24,1922,son of Dorothy Weaver and Wm.
      MacNutt of Detroit,Mich. (4 children)
      a. Robert Carl b. Sept.11,1956
      b. Wm.Phillip b. May 27,1959
      c. Thomas Lansing b.Aug.21,1963
      d. Mark Benjamin b. Oct.27,1967

Ben died September 18,1978

Ben and Hulda 1978

Louise Wehmeyer

Carl Wiese

Son, William

Carl Wiese

Carl and Louise Wiese

Nora and Fred Wiese

Minnie Wiese and Ed Weiss

Hulda and Ben,"Newlyweds"

Mary Lee,Fred,Will,Ben,Esther,Carl, and Tom, the cat
with Buster, the English Bulldog

Reading the material from Wehdem, Germany

Ben and Hulda's 50th anniversary

Ben Wiese 1918

MacNutt Family
Phillip, Robert,Bill,Mark,Tom,and Esther

CHILD #12: AUGUST WIESE b. June 1862 d. Nov.1936. Born in Germany and
was seven years old when he arrived with his family in 1869.TWIN
TO WILHELMINA. August married Nov.3,1885 in Brenham,Texas by Oscar
Samuel,Minister of the Lutheran Church at Prairie Hill,Texas, a
community six miles northeast of Brenham.Louise immigrated to
Texas when she was 14 years old.She was born in Germany on Sept.
25,1866 and died in Jan.1961.

August and Louise lived in the Prairie Hill community until after
his parents died in 1903. From there they moved to Prairie Dell
near Salado until 1915 when they made their home in the Whitehall
community a few miles from Moody,Texas. Both are buried in the
Buckhorn Community Cemetery,Bell County,Texas.
(9 children born to August and Louise)

1. Elizabeth Louise m. Rev.Henry Houy

2. Carl   died

3. Emma m.Fritz Haas

4. Ernest m. 1st: Ida Bischoff
             2nd: Toni Karnowski

5. August Jr.m. Esther Nichols

6. Ida m. Anton Haas

7. Minnie m. Otto Beerwinkle

8. Heneritta m. August Houy

9. Lydia   died

CHILD #1: <u>Elizabeth Louise</u> b. Sept.8,1886 d. Aug.22,1928.b.Liberty
Hill,Texas,married and moved to Fredericksburg,Texas.M.to Rev
Henry Houy b. May 14,1865 d. June 7,1935 (7 children)
- a. Henry H. b. June 5,1904 Fredricksburg,d.Nov.15,1964
  married Dec.27,1926 to Anida Durst b. Feb.8,1908 Fredricksburg.
- b. Eward Wesley b. Apr.18,1907 d. Sept.11,1965 m. Oct.16,1929
  to Alice Koening b. May 20,1908 Divorced (1child)
  - 1.Edward W.b.Oct.3,1931 m. Oct.12,1957 to Anna Pace
    Gastle b. May 27,1927 Munich,Germany,m.at Ausberg,
    Germany.
- c. Ernest William b. Aug.6,1914 Fredericksburg,m.Ruth Wyle
  b. May 14,1919 at Bohoshe,Okla.m.Carlsbad,New Mexico (2child-
  ren) TWIN TO CARL
  - 1. Barbara Jo b. Oct.25,1945 at Carlsbad,N.M. m. Aug.10,
    1968 in Artesia,N.M. to Richard Wyckoff b. Sept.26,
    1945 at Quakerstown Pa.(1 child)
    - a Carter Wyckoff b. July 5,1976 Quakerstown,Pa.
  - 2. Cheryl Ann b. Nov.28,1955 Carlsbad,N.M.m.Bradford
    Milner b. July 19,1955.m.June 17,1978.
- d. Carl Arthur b. Aug.6,1914 Fredericksburg TWIN TO ERNEST
  m. Aug.7,1940 Rockville Center,N.Y.to Anne Hershey b.June
  18,1917 New York(4 children)
  - 1. Charles Arthur b. Feb.4,1945 Ellinwood,Kansas m.Aug.
    29,1967 Littleton,Colo.to Margaret Lowe b.May 9.
  - 2. Mary Anne b. Aug.13,1946 Dallas,Tex.
  - 3. John David b. May 21,1951 Dallas,Tex.
  - 4. Stephen William b. Aug.5,1952 Dallas,Tex.
- e. Esther C.Houy b. Nov.17,1911 b. Fredericksburg,Tx.m.Oct.23,
  1939 to Richard Clay Locke b. July 18,1896 Zanesville,Ohio
  (1 child)
  - 1. Rose Louise b. April 15,1943 San Antonio.
- f. Dorothy Louise b. Aug.30,1924 Fredericksburg,Tex.m.June 8,
  1947 to James Ewald Eckert b. Aug.30,1923 Stonewall,Tex.
  (3 children)
  - 1. Patricia Elaine b. July 18,1948 Fredericksburg m. Dec.
    29,1967 to Jesse Patrick Slovacek b. Oct.13,1947
    Austin,Tex.(1 child)
    - a. James Daniel b. March 4,1972
  - 2. Rodney Wheeler b. March 15,1952 Fredericksburg m.Feb.
    5,1972 to Peggy Ann Schuch b. Oct.17,1951 Fredericks-
    burg (1 child)
    - a. Jary Lyn Eckert b. Nov.7,1976
  - 3. James Ewald Eckert,Jr.b. Oct.5,1955 Fredericksburg
- g. Verdie Helen b.Nov.23,1925 Fredericksburg,m.Jan.20,1944 to
  Wilburn Lee Hahn b. Feb.18,1923 Fredericksburg m.Yuma,
  Arizona (3 children)
  - 1. Helen Ann Hahn b.Jan.17,1946 m.Stephen Sembritzy
    Divorced (3 children)

No. 1906

Page 359

THE STATE OF TEXAS,

To all Regularly Licensed or Ordained Ministers of the Gospel, Judges of the District and County Courts, and all Justices of the Peace:

You are hereby authorized to solemnize the **RITES OF MATRIMONY**

Between _August Will_ and _Louisa Schulenberg_ and shall within sixty days thereafter make return of this License, with an endorsement thereon, showing your action in the premises, to me at my Office in the City of Brenham, as the law directs,

H. M. Lewis Clerk of the County

In Testimony Whereof, I, _H. M. Lewis_ Clerk of the County

Court of Washington County, hereunto subscribe my name and affix the seal of said Court, at my

Office in the City of Brenham, this _3rd_ day of _Nov_ A. D. 188__

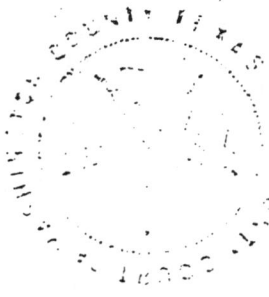

H. M. Lewis
Clerk of the County Court of Washington County.

By _A. Wehring_ Deputy.

THE STATE OF TEXAS:

This Certifies that I joined in marriage as husband and wife

August Will

and _Louisa Schulenberg_ on the _____ day of _November_ A. D. 1887

Oscar Samuel
Luth Pastor

August Wiese Family

Ernest,Louise,Emma,Louise,
Heneretta,August,Ida & August Jr.

Four generations: Louise,Emma,Fritz,Albert,
and son

August Wiese's Homeplace

August Jr.,Louise,Emma,Minnie,Louise,August & Ernest

Emma and Fritz Haas

Louise and Rev. Henry Houy

Ida and Ernest Wiese

Minna and Otto Beerwinkle

        a. Sherry Ann b. Feb.13,1965 Memphis,Tenn.
        b. Coreen Colleen b.Oct.22,1966,Oak Ridge,Wash.
        c. Steve Lee b.June 22,1969,Fredericksburg,Tx.
    2. Carol Lynn Hahn b. Dec.26,1947 Fredericksburg,Tx.
      m.Nov.29,1969 to Dennis Meglow b.Feb.26,1945 Wenat-
      chee,Wash.m.Fredericksburg.Divorced.(2 children)
        a. Moncia Lynn Menglos b.Feb.9,1971 Austin,Tx.
        b. John Andrea Menglos b.Apr.5,1943 Wenatchee,Wash.
      Married 2nd:to Tom Green b.Aug.1943,m.May27,1978.
    3. Kathy Lee Hahn b.July 6,1956 Fredericksburg,m.Aug.24,
      1974 to Ronald Keith Klier b.June 27,1952 Fredericks-
      burg,Tx.(1 child)
        a. Jessica Klier b. July 5,1977 Austin,Tx.

CHILD #2: _Carl_ died of diptheria as an infant.No other infomation
  is known.

CHILD #3: _Emma_ b.Nov.8,1889 d.June 20,1967 married Oct.1904 (MB Vol.
  14,p.625,Brenham,Tx.) to Fritz Haas b. April 6,1876 d. March 6,
  1962.Both buried in the Moody-Leon Cemetery,Buckhorn Community,
  Bell Co.Tx.

Emma and Fritz lived for many years in Bartlett,Texas where all
nine children were born and reared.(9 children)

    a. Ervin b. Aug.9,1905 m.July 10,1933 at Moody to Nannie Haar-
      meyer b. July 10,1908 dau.of Fred and Emma Haarmeyer.
      (2 children)
        1. Wayne b. Jan.24,1937 m.June 2,1957 Rosebud Tx. to
          Irene Fisk (Fick)dau.of Carl Fisk(Fick) and Alma
          Schroeder (3 children)
            a. Larry b. Aug.6,1958
            b. John b. May 14,1962
            c. Kevin b. Nov.101964
        2. Shirley Ann b. Feb.18,1945 m. Walter F.Winkler in
          the Moody-Leon Methodist Church on July 4,1965.
          Walter is the son of Joseph J.Winkler and Louisa
          Wallart Winkler.
    b. Arthur b.Dec.22,1906 m.Pearl Beerwinkle Aug.11,1936 at
      Moody-Leon Church. Pearl b. Oct.25,1916,dau. of Henry Beer-
      winkle and Hanna Schmidt Beerwinkle(Ref.3rd son;Henry Wiese-
      Hanna was the dau. of Melinda Wiese and Louis Schmidt)
      (2 children)
        1. Arthur Bruce Haas b.June 6,1942 m.Jan.12,1973 to
          Lanetta Holiman b. March 5,1946. Her father died
          when she was an infant, and her mother married
          Mr.Walker.Home in Payen,Arkansas.
        2. Stanley Haas b. Nov.27,1950

c. Albert b.June 19,1908 m.Dec.20,1933 to Hella Karnowski
   b.March 23,1915 in her parents home,Rte.2,Moody.dau.of
   Henry Karnowski and Minnie Beerwinkle Karnowski(2 children)
     1. Charles Ray Haas b. April 5,1938 m.Nov.21,1964 in
       Seaton Brethren Church,Seaton,Tx. to Nancy Jane Andel
       b.May 28,1947 ,dau. of Willie Andel and Della Bravenec.
       (2 children)
         a. Kimberly Renee b. May 25,1966 Temple,Tx.
         b. Kasi Rachelle b. Oct.14,1968 Temple,Tx.
     2. James Henry Haas b. March 1,1943 m. Hov.8,1963 in
       the First Assembly of God Church of Moody,Texas to
       Carol Ann Patrick b.Mar.30,1945, day. of R.H.Patrick
       and Athlene Robinson Patrick.(3 children)
         a. Bradley Jay b. Aug.15,1964 Waco.
         b. James Paul b. May 5,1967 Waco.d.May7,1967
         c. Stacey Dianne b. Apr.26,1968 Waco.
d. William b. March 11,1911 m. Dec.12,1934 at Moody-Leon Church
   to Esther Beerwinkle b.Dec.31,1913 dau. of Henry F.Beerwinkle
   and Hanna Schmidt Beerwinkle (Ref to 3rd son;Henry Wiese--
   Hanna was the dau. of Melinda Wiese and Louis Schmidt)
   (2 children)
     1. William E.Haas b. Feb.3,1938 m. Sept.27,1975 Temple,
       Tex. to Shirley Marie Tate (Lucky) b. Mar.10,1946
       dau,of Leroy Tate and Katherine Doughty Tate.
       (3 children)
         a. Steven Mathew Lucky b. March 3,1964
         b. Melissa Marie Lucky b. Feb.4,1967
         c. Kevin Eugene Haas b. Nov.12,1977
     2. Marjorie Ann Haas,b. Nov.25,1945 m. Dec.18,1965 at
       7th St.Methodist Church in Temple,Tx. to David Vaughan
       Lewis b. Mar.18,1945,son of Carl H.Lewis and Mattie A.
       Jane Ewing Lewis.(2 children)
         a. David Todd Lewis b. Mar.20,1969 Kentucky.
         b. Paula Annette Lewis b. Feb.24,1976 Temple,Tx.
e. Edna Haas b. Oct.26,1912 m. Dec.28,1932 to Edwin Joe Schmidt,
   son of Melinda Wiese,daughter of Henry,and Louis Schmidt,(See
   Ref,Child: Henry F.Wiese #3.) (2 children)
     1. Edward b. Nov.25,1933 m.Roberta Kramer b. Jan.19,
       1937 dau. of Stella and Robert Kramer(3 children)
         a. Sharon b. Nov.20,1957 m. June 10,1977 to Rick
           Lynch
         b. Steven b. Dec.18,1959
         c. Susan b. Aug.25,1965
     2. Doyle b. Sept.13,1940 m. 1st to Rita Meador(2 child-
       ren)
         a. Scott b. Dec.18,1959
         b. Michael Lynn b. Oct.11,1970
       Married 2nd to Mary Ann McElwreath (2 children)
         c. Debbie Ann   m. Randy Threadgill
         d. Donna

f. Ben.b. May 30,1914 m. Nov.16,1938 at St.John Lutheran Church
   Bartlett,Tex.to Cora Gebert b. Oct.11,1916 dau. of Rudolph
   Gebert and Alma Andrens(3 children)
   1. Ben Haas Jr. b. May 22,1943
   2. Mike b. Dec.4,1947 m. Nov.1,1974 at Seventh Street
      United Methodist Church in Temple,Tx. to Shelia
      Graham b. Nov.1,1951 dau. of Curtis and Pauline
      Maxwell Graham (1 child)
         a. Chad Michael b. Oct.20,1977
   3. Jacque b. April 25,1959
g. Lorena (Tommie) b. Feb.18,1916 d. April 28,1977 m.Dec.2,
   1940 at Moody-Leon Methodist Church to Paul Karnowski
   b. Jan.5,1918 d. April 21,1978.
h. Esther b. April 29,1918 m. Dec.2,1936 Temple Tex. to Ruben
   Beerwinkle b. Oct.20,1912,son of Henry Fred and Hanna S.
   Schmidt Beerwinkle.(See ref. to 3rd son:Henry F.Wiese--
   Hanna was the dau. of Melinda Wiese and Louis Schmidt)
   (6 children)
   1. Kenneth b. Apr.4,1938 m. Dec.19,1964 to Jean Hildebrand
      b. Jan.28,1941 at College Station,Tx.dau. of John and
      Lorene Neiman(2 children)
         a. Tammy b. Feb.10,1966
         b. Kenneth Allen b. June 30,1970
Kenneth graduated from Texas A&M 1960.Served three years
in the Air Force, received M.S.degree from Texas A&M in 1965
P.H.D. Tex.A&M 1978 with the Toxocology Lab .
   2. Donald b. Oct.7,1939 m. Pampa,Tx. to Patricia Nichols
      July 10,1964.Patricia b.Jan.18,1945,dau. of Shirley &
      Bernice Traylor (3 children)
         a. Shelli b. Sept.5,1965
         b. Staci b. May 21,1973
         c. Si Donavan b. Dec.14,1976
Donald received B.S.from Tex.A&M 1962 M.S.from New Mexico
State 1964,P.H.D. Ohio State 1974.Prof.of Genetics at West
State Un. Canyon,Tx.
   3. David b. Feb.9,1942 m. July 28,1968 Antonita,Colo.
      to Sidney Kerr b.Dec.26,1941,dau. of Warren Kerr and
      Merle Germany Kerr.(2 children)
         a. Amy b. Feb.12,1974
         b. Rachel b. Apr.26,1977
David received B.S. from Texas A&M in 1964. He manages a
Feed yard in Pecos,Tx.
   4. Linda b. Feb.18,1945 m. July 2,1966 Temple,Tx. to
      Tommy Birch b. May 4,1943,son of Oniel and Doris
      Whatley (2 children)
         a. Christi b. Oct.18,1967
         b. Casey b. Sept.20,1973
Linda received B.A.West Texas State Un. in Canyon,Tx.1969.
She lives at Borger,Tex.

5. Larry b. April 12,1949 m. Madisonville,Tx.July 28,
   1975 to Margaret McVey,dau. of Raystelle and Laverne
   McVey.(1 child)
       a. Baby   April 1978
   Larry holds a B.S. from Tex.A&M 1971.Assistant Adm.
   of a Federal Meat Research Center in Clay Center,Neb.
6. Dale b. Nov.2,1953 received his B.S. from Tex. A&M in
   1976 and his M.S. from Un. of Arizona in May 1978 at

i. Infant died

CHILD #4: Ernest b. Jan.19,1889 d. Jan.30,1962. Married 1st
Dec.1911 Prairie Dell, Texas to Ida Bischoff b. Aug.23,1888.
d.Nov.16,1918. Ernest later moved to McGregor, then to Moody,Tx.
(3 children)
   a. Irene Carolyn Louise b. Oct.4,1912 Prairie Dell,Texas.
      m. Dec.17,1930 in Moody to T.G.Beerwinkel who died in Nov.
      1938.
      Irene married 2nd on Nov.1940 in Temple to R.H.Presley
      (1 child)
          1.Carolyn Sue b. July 7,1940 Temple m. June 1966 Temple
            to David Garcia .Living in Virginia.
   b. Lillie died at age 1½ years.
   c. Alice Agnes b. Mar.7,1917 McGregor m. Jan.24,1940 Temple
      to Herbert Fehler b. Aug.24,1911 McGregor,son of Henry
      Fehler and Emma Meiske (1 son)
          1. Edward Dwayne b. Aug.2,1945 Waco.m.July 27,1968 to
             Diane Mayfield b. March 10,1947, dau. of Jewel and
             Bill Mayfield of Lorena,Tx. (2 children)
                 a. Kimberly Diane b. June 21,1971
                 b. Stephen Edward b. April 24,1974
Ernest married 2nd on Oct.21,1920 Moody, Tx. to Antonia(Toni)
Karnowski b. Apr.24,1891,dau. of Louise and Albert Karnowski.
(2 children)
   d. Unnamed girl child b. 1921
   e. Ernestine Louise b. Aug.28,1930 Moody,m.May 31,1953 Odessa,
      Tx. to James Neal London b. Aug. 19,1929,son of Merle and
      Clarence London (3 children)
          1. Dennis Neal b. June 16,1954 Odessa,Tx. m.Marion
             Roberson Feb.8,1975 (1 child)
                 a. Leah Anne b. Feb.22,1976
          2. Ernest Ray b. July 17,1957
          3. Albert b. March 5,1961

CHILD #5: August Jr. b. Aug.7,1890 d. July 10,1973 m. Oct.1,1911,
in Jarrell Tex. to Esther Nichols b. Jan.13,1894 dau. of Jeff
Davis Nichols and Sidney Russell.They livedin Odessa,(1 child)
where Esther still lives alone.
   a. James Aubrey b. Sept.3,1918 in Jarrell,Tex, m. Dec.21,1941
      in San Antonio,Tex. to Florence (Flo) E.Rentz b. Oct.5,
      1923,Lake Providence,La.dau. of Lucien D.Rentz and Belle
      Brownley. (6 children)

1. James Michael Wiese b. Dec.12,1943,Stamford,Tx. m.
   Jan Barnett (1 child)
      a. Amy b. 1977
2. Suzanne Wiese (Culbertson) b. 1948,Lamesa,Tx.
3. Mary Jane Wiese (Ritz) b. 1952,Odessa,Tx.
4. Lisa Marie Wiese (Mangus) b. 1955, Odessa,Tx.
5. Debra Shannon Wiese b. 1959,Odessa,Tx.
6. Caroline Wiese b. 1963,Odessa,Tx.

August had moved to Odessa in order to be near their son and his family. August had moved from Roswell, New Mexico several years before he retired because of illness. He was called "Fritz" by his family and he was a registered pharmacist having drug stores in several Texas towns before he moved to Roswell and bought a prescription pharmacy that he ran until he retired at age of 70. He is buried in Odessa.

CHILD # 6: Ida b. Feb.6,1892 d. Aug.6,1953 m.Sept.1906 at Prairie Dell,Tx. to Anton Haas b. Sept.11,1883 d. Aug.25,1965. Buried Buckhorn Cemetery. Anton was the son of Robert Haas and Elizabeth Shabey(3 children)
   a. Raymond b. Nov.10,1910
   b. Leroy b. Sept.2,1913 m. Oct.14,1939 at Bartlett,Tx. to Estelle Geber b. Oct.3,1914 d.July 21,1950 buried at St. John's Lutheran Church Cemetery in Bartlett. Estelle was the dau. of Roudolph Gerbert and Alma Andrus (2 children)
      1. Robert b. Feb.20,1943 at Moody,Tx. m. Nov.26,1971 in Killeen,Tx. to Alice Douglas b. Jan.13,1948,dau. of Elmer Douglas and Agnes Isbell.

      2. Kathleen b. Aug.24,1944 Moody,Tx.
   c. Walter Henry b. Oct.23,1915 Bell Co.Tx. m. Jan.14,1945 in the Moody-Leon Methodist Church to Florence Emma Sophie Frase b. Aug.31,1923 in Moody,Bell Co.Tx.,dau. of Roy B. Frase and Melissa Beerwinkle. Both are buried in the Buckhorn Cemetery, Buckhorn Community,Bell Co.Tx.(2 children)
      a. Barbara Ann b. Feb.18,1946 Temple,Tx.m.Sept.10,1966 in Moody Methodist Church to Wm.Theodore Fredrich b. Jan.21,1962.

      b. Wm Walter b. Sept.22,1960 in Temple

CHILD #7: Minnie b. May 26,1893 d. Nov. 18,1961 married Otto Beerwinkel b. Dec.8,1892 d. June 25,1958 Moody,Texas. Both buried in the Moody-Leon Cemetery, Buckhorn Community,Bell Co. Texas.(5 children)
   a. Lorine Louise b. Nov.18,1916 ,m.June 20,1959 at Moody in her parents home to Horace Douglas Brown b. Dec.8,1920,son of Steve N.Brown and Elsie Adams.Lives in Rocksprings,Tx.

b. Wesley Henry Beerwinkle b. Aug.8,1919 m. Alice Gebert in 1943.KILLED IN WWII and buried in Hamm, Luxenburg,Germany on Feb.22,1945 in the Military Cemetery. Alice was from Bartlett,Tx. and her parents : Mr. and Mrs. Rudolf Gebert, Mother's maiden name: Andres.(1 son,Dwight)

Alice married 2nd to Roland Roselius. Dwight's name was changed to Roselius.
    1. John Dwight b. Aug.3,1945 after his father had died.
      m. Janice, Lives in Pomona,Calif.(1 child)
        a. Erica

c. Leona b. Oct.18,1920 m. Dec.31,1944 Moody,Tx. to John Henry Myrick b. July 12,1921,son of Ernest Myrick and Gladys Fondren Myrick.(2 children)
    1. Deana b. Jan.22,1950 m. June 1,1974 in Dallas,Tx.to David Murphy b. July 22,1949,son of Marion K.Murphy and Mignon Turner Murphy.(2 children)
        a. Michael Patrick b. Jan.2,1976
        b. Alicia Catherine b. June 18,1977
    2. Sandra Jean b. May 14,1953 m. Jan.8,1972 in Dallas,Tx. to Charles R. Thompson Jr. b. Dec.17,1952,son of Charles R. Thompson Sr. and Nita Jean McNeis Thompson (2 children)
        a. Robyn Elise b. August 23,1974
        b. Amy Christine b. July 6,1976

d. Milton August b. Oct.23,1922 m. Wanda Sue Smith b. Feb. 27, 1926, dau. Of Robert and Lois Moore Smith. Lives in Dallas. (3 children)
    1. Marshall b. Mar.14,1950 m. Kathy McQueen b. Aug.1952
    2. Patricia Louise b. Mar.3,1954
    3. Lynn Lorine b. Aug.9,1959

e. Elmer Otto Beerwinkle b. Oct.12,1928 m. Jan.19,1952 Moody, to Lula Jo (Lu) Hatter b. Jan.7,1932,dau. of Logan Thomas of Moody and Eunice Josephine Harvey .(2 children)
    1. Ronald Bruce b. Dec.12,1955
    2. Brenda Lou b. Feb.17,1959
    Lives in Moody on the "homeplace"

CHILD #8 : Heneretta b. Feb.1896 d.   m. August Houy and lived at Prairie Dell, Texas. Died in childbirth. Buried in Bartlett,Tx.

CHILD #9: LYDIA (LILLIE) b. Sept.1901 died a few short hours later.

Uncle August and Aunt Louise were at the home of Charles Wiese,(son of August's brother William) when Charley's wife Mitilda gave birth to their 3rd child,a girl. Uncle August asked permission to name this child afterhtheir little girl that had died. Therefore, the baby was named Lydia Louise and August and Louise were to become very close to this child and have her visit them many times.They called her their "little girl". Lydia was to marry Herman B.Hodel and live at Coryell City,Tex. Herman died as a young man and Lydia moved to Waco and became a nurse. She worked for many years on the OB Ward in the Hillcrest Hospital taking care of the newborn babies.

She was to be the instrument by which this book was written, for without her help and assistance, it would have been impossible to pull this clan together.

CHILD # 13 : WILHELMINE (Minnie) b. June   1862 in Germany.TWIN
    TO AUGUST.d. Jan.13,1925 married Jan.19,1883 (MB Vol.6,p.21) to
    Fritz Wehmeyer b. Dec.17,1861 d. March 12,1930 . Both buried at
    Westhoff Cemetery, Westhoff,Tex. Son of Frederick Wehmeyer and
    Henrietta Weiss from Hamburg,Germany(10 children and also reared
    Minnie's sister Louise's son Fritz Grube by her second marriage
    to Herman Grube.Louise had died in childbirth).
    a. Carl Frederick b. Nov.8,1883 Brenham,d.as an infant a few
       days after birth.
    b. Charlie William b. Brenham,date unknown,died as infant.
    c. Charlie b. 1886 Brenham. No married. Lived a bachelor
       with his mother and father. died 1938 buried San Jose
       Cemetery, San Antonio.
    d. Emma b. 1888 Brenham died 1913 of Typhoid.buried Pleasant
       Valley Cemetery,Pandora,Tx.
    e. August b. 1890 Port Lavaca d. Aug.28,1973 buried Mission
       Burial Park,San Antonio,Texas.married Sophie Kemper 1908.
       (7 children)
           1. Clara Wehmeyer b. Sept.5,1908 m.Paul Koehler b. Dec.
              13,1903 d. Nov.6,1966(2 children)
                  a. Irene b. Nov.8,1931
                  b. Paul b. July 27,1930
           2. Otto b. Nov.26,1909 d. Feb.20,1910
           3. Martha b. May 17,1911 married Roy Stahl(1 child)
                  a. JoAnn
           4. Helen b. July 2,1913 m. Connie Fletcher (1 child)
                  a. Harry
           5. Walter b. Feb.22,1915 married Duran Evans (1 child)
                  a. Linda Joy
           6. Lillie Wehmeyer b. July 25,1917 m. Gene Camp
              (2 children)
                  a. Bob
                  b. Geraldine
           7. Melvin b.June 23,1919 m. Faye Lois McCall (2 children)
                  a. Jim
                  b. Gary
    f. Willie b. Port Lavaca 1892 d. 1913 of Typhoid,buried in
       Pleasant Valley Cemetery ,Pandora,Texas
    g. Herbert b. 1894 d. 1913 Typhoid,buried in Pleasant Valley
       Cemetery,Pandora,Tx.
    h. Fred Henry b. 1896 Port Lavaca d. 1976 in San Antonio,buried
       Stockdale Cemetery.m.Cordie Collins in 1919 at Pandora,Tx.
       (1 child)
           1. Collins Fred b. Nov.1920 in Ganado,Tx.d.1938 in Ecleto
              Tx. buried in Stockdale Cemetery.Died in a car accident
    i. Bernie b. 1898 Port Lavaca d. 1934 buried in San Jose
       Cemetery,San Antonio
    j. Erna b. 1903 Port Lavaca married 1921 Westhoff,Tx. to Paul
       Christiansen,son of John and Lena Stienman Christiansen.
       Paul d. 1926 buried National Cemetery.Erna remarried 1930

to John Lee Price b. 1900 in San Antonio,son of Josephine
Atkin. Lee Price was widower with a small son,Lee Roy Price
b. 1924.His mother died at birth. Erna adopted the child as
her own. There were no other children during their married
life. John Lee Price died April 5,1964 and is buried in the
Mission Burial Park in San Antonio. Their son Lee Roy, married
Ruth Marsh in 1944,dau. of Cave and Dell Marsh. Lee Roy
died Aug.9,1968 at the age of 44 years.Buried in Mission
Burial Park. Lee Roy and Ruth had three boys.
  1. Roy Lee b. Nov.30,1947 m.1967 San Antonio to Carol
     Gunnufson b. 1946 St.Louis,Mo. (1 child) They live
     in St.Louis.
       a. Brent Lee b. 1968 in Illinois
  2. Still born son b. 1948
  3. Richard Mark b. June 19,1952 m. July 22,1978 in
     St.Louis to Pat Lenning b. 1951 St.Louis,dau of
     Irvin and Glendora Lenning.

Minna & Fritz Wehmeyer

Wilhelmina & Heneritta

87

"I do not have the exact date of our move from Port Lavaca to Pandora.Maybe you already have it. We left Port Lavaca early one clear morning in a covered wagon and a surry with the fringe on top. The boys in the wagon and Fred Wehmeyer from Brenham came with us (rode in the wagon with all my brothers) also, Henry Kemper from Port Lavaca, a friend,came with us to help build our house and barn etc. There was no house on the land and we had to haul water and lived as all pioneers did. Papa hired many people to help build and clear the land. Mama and Charlie, having asthma so badly,prompted the move. The furniture and cattle were shipped via freight cars.

Papa also had the well drilled as quickly as possible, and soon all was finished, wind mill pumping water, barns and sheds for cattle all completed.

We had one Negro working--hauling wood, digging post holes, fixing fences--he drove two oxen before a two wheel cart. His name I shall not forget was Grant. He was a very nice man,good worker,and Papa kept him on,even after the typhoid epidemic.

I believe we were five days arriving in Pandora. In the surry rode Mama,Emma,Papa,Henry Kemper and I. It was fun for Ben and I and we would walk sometimes. At night we stayed in a pasture near a home in the countryside and bought milk and eggs,milk in a bucket for 5¢ and eggs 10¢ a dozen. Of course, my Papa always got permission from the home owners when we stopped for the night. I can't imagine the hard work it must have been for my mother an sister to prepare meals for eleven people for days on an open fire until our home was built(9 of us and 2 carpenters). Papa hired many carpenters, so it wasn't too long before everything was up and ready for us.

The first year the cotton crop was great--50 bales of cotton,which was a great help toward finances and also harvested plenty of feed for the cattle.

I believe in about 1919 or 1920 we sold our place and moved to Westhoff,Texas . This time by car and furniture and cattle in freight cars. My parents lived there until their death. Fred and I were married and moved away. Fred worked in Ecleto, Texas, was a Postmaster, had a grocery store, and leased a ranch with cattle. When it came retirement time he sold his cattle and was Deputy Sheriff in Ecleto for the time he lived. He never tired of working.

I lived in San Antonio and worked as a secretary and later worked eighteen years for Civil Service at Kelley Field for which I am glad.Now I draw Social Security and Civil Service retirement checks.I retired 30,June, just before being 70 years old on Aug.5. I will soon be 75 in a day or so--"Erna Wehmeyer Price (1978)

Vol 8, p. 21

No. 1037

Page 21

Vol 8, p. 21

THE STATE OF TEXAS,

To all Regularly Licensed or Ordained Ministers of the Gospel, Judges of the District and County Courts, and all Justices of the Peace:

You are hereby authorized to solemnize the RITES OF MATRIMONY

Vol 8, p. 21

Between _Friedrich Wehmeyer_ and _Miss Maria Miese_ and shall within sixty days thereafter make return of this License, with an endorsement thereon, showing your action in the premises, to me at my Office in the City of Brenham, as the law directs.

In Testimony Whereof, I, _Chris Roeve_ Clerk of the County Court of Washington County, hereunto subscribe my name and affix the seal of said Court, at my Office in the City of Brenham, this _____ day of _____ A. D. 188_5_

W. H. _____

Clerk of the County Court of Washington County.

By _____, Deputy.

THE STATE OF TEXAS:

This Certifies that I joined in marriage as husband and wife _Friedrich Wehmeyer_

and _Maria Miese_ on the _____ day of _January_ A. D. 188_3_

Carl Gerhard

Pastor

Vol 8, p. 21

Husband and son

Erna and Mother

Erna Wehmeyer Price

August Wehmeyer Family

Erna with grandson & great,grandson

Fred Wehmeyer

Left to right, Herbert, Emma, Charlie, Mother, Dad, Willie is
outside the fence, Bennie, Erna and Fred. The dog was Fred's
hunting dog.

"The picture you have of our home and family was taken just before
the house was painted and some of the rooms not completed. There
were four bedrooms and porch upstairs and one bedroom, a parlor,
kitchen and dining room down stairs. This was a large house for a
large family.

All too soon --came the terrible fever.(typhoid) An epidemic swept
through the entire country and small town of Pandora, Texas causing
the death of two brothers and my only sister;plus my mother and
two brothers lay near death for days. Those were bad days for my
father and brother, Fred. I was sent to Port Lavaca to live with
my brother August and family until my mother recovered completely.
It left mother broken hearted when she got well enough to realize
our loss of family.

Herbert took sick first--died within two weeks, then Emma, and next
Willie."

Erna Wehmeyer Price (1978)

Willie Kluck, "Uncle Wehmeyer wrote to my mother, Heneretta(Setta)
of an epidemic of Typhoid fever. He was very depressed as he was
losing his loved one one after another."(1977)

CHILD # 14: <u>Henriette Luise Caroline (Setta)</u> b. April 22,1864
Baptized: May 5,Register No.48,Wehdem,Germany.Died July 8,
1946,at the age of 82 years. She lived with her son Charlie
in her last years. Married Jan.13,1887 (Vol.9,p.262 Brenham
Tx.by Pastor Oscar Samuel) to Emile Kluck b. Oct.26,1865
d. Mar.24,1923,son of Gottlib Kluck.Both Setta and Emile are
buried in the Perry Cemetery,Perry,Tx.

Emile, along with his brothers Gus,August,William and sister
Marrida immigrated from Germany.

When Emile died, Heneretta bought an eight grave plot in
the Perry Methodist Cemetery. Neither of the daughters
married and both were R.N.'s.The Kluck family has lived in
Perry since 1902 and Willie E.Kluck is the only living
child of this union.(6 children)

    a.Wilhelmina A.Christine (Minnie) b. Jan.20,1888,Bapt.
      Feb.26,1888.d. Jan.15,1964.Buried in Travis Park
      Cemetery,Austin,Tx. in the single grave section.
    b.Charley(C.W) Wesley b. Sept.12,1889 d. Oct.14,1966 Prairie
      Hill,Tx. m.Marie Wolf b. Aug.19,1894 d. Oct.14,1966.Both
      died in a tragic automobile accident.(4 children)
        1. Carl Wesley b. Nov.28,1923 m. Aug.25,1947 Ft.Worth
          to Margie Ruth Sandridge b. Mar.14,1927 (2 child-
          ren) Baptist Minister.
            a. Sharon Dianne b. Mar.15,1950 m. July 11,1976
              to Jawn Townsend.
            b. Carl Wesley Jr. b.Jan.25,1955
        2. Ruth Evelyn b. Mar.9,1922 m. Nov.10,1945 Marlin,Tx.
          to Lester Lee Ledbetter b. May 15,1909 (3 children)
            a. Debra Sue b. Mar.14,1949 m. Dec.10,1966 to
              Domingo Peralias Castro b. Sept.3(1 child)
                1. Edmond Lee b. March 30,1968
            b. Doloras Ann b. Mar.24,1951 m. July 7,1967
              to John Wayne Region b. March 17,1949
              (6 children)
                1. John Houston b. July 26,1968
                2. King Wayne b. May 20,1970
                3. Tammie Sue b. Dec.20,1972
                4. Lynelle b.July 28,1975
                5. Tonya Gay b. Nov.2,1974
                6. Michael DeWayne b. April 5,1977
            c. Karen Gay Jones b. Nov.2,1956
        3. Homer Roy b. June 16,1928,chr'nd Sept.4,1928 m.1st:
          Le Ruth Bentley b. Aug.21,1932 King's Daughter
          Hospital,Temple,Tx. d. Feb.12,1958(1 child)
            a. Marguerite Marie (Margi) b. July 31,1957
              Scott and White Hospital,Temple,Tx.
          Married 2nd Feb.23,1962 Trinity Methodist Church
          Waco,Tx. to Virginia Ann Hailey,b.Oct.9,1937
          Lampasas,Texas. Homer is a Methodist Minister.

4. Lois Marie b. April 21,1931 m. Jan.1951 Houston to
   Kelley Walter Coker b. Sept.13,1924 (4 sons)
       a. Kelly Russell b. Nov.12,1951 m. Waco,Tx. to
          Ellen Kay Swearengen b. Jan.16,1952 in La.
          (2 children)
              1. Kristhopher Kelley b. Sept.24,1976 in
                 Wichita,Kansas.
              2.
       b. Curtis Charles b. Dec.8,1952
       c. Burl Dean b. Sept.13,1955

       d. Bradley Thell b. April 5,1960

c. Heneritta (Hennie) died
d. Emile F. b. July 1,1891 d. June 24,1952 TWIN TO HENERITTA
   m. Willie Castleberry b. 1890 d. May 7,1977. Methodist
   Minister.
e. Wm.Emanuel (Willie) b. Dec.16,1892 at Cottonwood or
   (Maxwell,Tx),m. Oct.18,1924 by Rev.Theo Hanekost to Laura
   Neumann b. Nov.8,1898 d. Aug.15,1976 .Lives in Perry,Tx.
f. Rosalie(Rosie) b. Aug.20,1896 d. June 9,1940. Kendleton,Tx.

CHILD # 15: Marie Wilhelmine Charlotte,B.Oct.11,1865 Baptized:
   Oct.22,1865 Register No.124. Died Jan.1,1867,Register No.5
   Wehdem,Germany.

No. 3518

Page 262

THE STATE OF TEXAS,

Vol 9, P. 262

To all Regularly Licensed or Ordained Ministers of the Gospel, Judges of the District and County Courts, and all Justices of the Peace:

You are hereby authorized to solemnize the **RITES OF MATRIMONY**

Between _Emil Klink_ and _Henrietta Wiese_

and shall within sixty days thereafter make return of this License, with an endorsement thereon, showing your action in the premises, to me at my office in the City of Brenham, as the law directs.

In Testimony Whereof, I, _J. M. Rew_ Clerk of the County Court of Washington County, hereunto subscribe my name and affix the seal of said Court, at my office in the City of Brenham, this _11_ day of _Jany_ A. D. 1887

A. Wehring, Deputy.

Clerk of the County Court of Washington County.

By _____

THE STATE OF TEXAS,

This Certifies that I joined in marriage as husband and wife _Emil Klink_

and _Henrietta Wiese_ on the _12_ day of _January_ A. D. 1887

Carl Learner, Pastor

Vol. 19 P. 262

v.19.

Heneretta(Setta) Wiese

Setta and Emile Kluck
with Minnie and Charley(C.W.)

Emile Kluck Jr.

C.W. Kluck

Emile,Minnie,Charlie and Willie

Emile,Aunt Willie,Ruth Ledbetter,Zess Ledbetter,C.W.,Homer,
Minnie,Laura,Carl and Willie Kluck

Emile Kluck

Setta Wiese Kluck

William Kluck 1978

William Kluck 1918

ADDITIONAL INFORMATION

p. 15: Paulita,child #3. Husband,Leo Robins died Sept.9,1978

p. 61: Child #1 of Bertha and Wm. Goessler. William and Clara
    Krueger's children:
    1. Edna b. June 9,1921 m. Oct.21,1945 to Werner Wendt
        b. July 23,1921(2 children)
            a. Werner David b.Feb.23,1947 m. Glenda Sample
            b.Dec.14,1944,Glenda's child by her first
            husband who is deseased:
                1. Cheryl Lanzer b. ug.27,1970
            b. Charles Allen b. Dec.8,1949 m.Dec.23,1971
            to Brownie Katherine Neason b.May 7,1948
            (2 children)
                1. William Charles Wendt b.Mar.31,1976
                2. Edna Katherine(Katie) b.Aug.8,1977
    2. William A.Goessler b.March 1,1924

p. 25: Liane Marie Worley b.July 2,1977 born to Charles and Martha
    Worley.

p.77: Jimmy Eckert married Sept.23,1977 to Cathy Bierschevale,
    b.Sept.5,1956

p. 82: Raymond Haas died Nov.7,1978

p. 32: Angela Dawn b.Nov.21,1978 to Alan Dale and Regina Patterson.

p. 90: Charles Patrick Cocker b. Oct.24,1978 to Kelley and Ellen Coker.

p. 15: Malinda Lee Benfer b.Dec.7,1978 to Russell and Carla Benfer.

p.90: Burel Coker m. Jan.6,1979 to Stacy Fadal b.May 14,1958,dau.
    of Dr.Richard George Fadal and Margaret DeBusk.

INDEX

Adams,Elsie 82
        ,Hubert 52
        ,James 52
Adler,Carleen Frances 35,62
        ,Gus Sr. 35
        ,Gus Jr.29
        ,Louise Marie 35
Addicks,Emil 22
        ,Esther 22
        ,Gustav 22
        ,Joel Thomas 22
        ,Nelson 22
        ,Stacy Alan Roehling 22
Akins,Jack Lewis 50
        ,Jane Ann 50
        ,Odus Otto 50
Alaminski,Albert 72
Albrecht,Esther 48
Aldrich,Laura Clara 39
Alsup,Dorothy L. 17
        ,James Arthur 17
        ,James B. 17
        ,James L. 17
        ,Karen Ann 17
Amanson,Lillie Mae 24,42
Andel,Nancy Jane 79
        ,Willie 79
Anderson,Dean Alan 72
            ,Doyle 72
Andrens,Alma 80
Andrus,Alma 82
Anz,Dorothy 15
Arnold,Nanette Susan 55
Atkin,Josephine 86

Bagby.Carolyn Kay 32
        ,Charley 32
        ,Dennis Wayne 32
        ,Floyd C.32
        ,Mary 32
        ,Shirley Sue 32
Bailey,Jackie 47
        ,John 47
        ,Ralph 47
Bain,Dennis Alan 57
        ,R.T. 57
        ,Shari Renee 57

Barber,Alda 74
Barnett,Jan 82
Banik,Albert 19
Barrett,Ernest 38
        ,Geraldine Lora 38
        ,Lora 38
Barton,Karen Rena 16
        ,Raymond Edward 16
        ,William Frank 16
Bass,Brian Howard 52
        ,Patricia Ann 52
        ,Robert Douglas 52
        ,Sam 52
        ,W.A. 52
Bates,Linda 33
Beachamp,Don 49
            ,Donna 49
            ,Judy 49
            ,Michael Jack 49
            ,Tammie 49
            ,Vita 49
Beale,Rena 20
Beaumier,Ada 2
Beavers,Carla Gail 10
Beeman,Thomas Emmett 34
        ,Wanda Mildred 34
Becker,Emma Louise 6
        ,Carla Gail 10
        ,Clara Louise 6
        ,Fritz Herman 75
        ,Traci 75
        ,Wm. 6
        ,Bertha 64
Beerwinkle,Amy 36,80
        ,Baby 81
        ,Brenda Lou 83
        ,Dale 36,81
        ,David 36,80
        ,Donald 36,81
        ,Esther 37,79
        ,Ewaldine 37
        ,Elmer Otto 83
        ,Florine 40
        ,Fred 40
        ,Fritz 40
        ,Henry 78
        ,Henry Sr 36
        ,Henry Jr. 36

,Henry F. 79
,Joyce 40
,Kenneth 36,80
,Kenneth Allen 36,80
,Larry 36,81
,Leona 83
,Linda 36,80
,Lorine Louise 82
,Louise 37
,Lynn Lorine 83
,Marshall 83
,Marvin 37
,Mellissa 82
,Milton August 83
,Minnie 79
,Otto 76,82
,Patricia Louise 83
,Pearl 37,78
,Rachel 36,80
,Ronald Bruce 83
,Ruben 36,80
,Shelli 36,80
,Shirley 40
,Si Donavan 36,80
,Staci 36,80
,Tammy 36,80
,T.G. 81
,Wesley Henry 83
Becker,Clara Louise Bertha 6
,Emma Louise 6
.Fritz Herman 75
,Traci 75
,Wm. 6
Beckman,Kenneth Lee 64
,Wilbert Gus 64
Beimer,Carolyn 40
,George 40
,Leolo H. 40
,Sharon 40
Benkendofer,Rosa 15
Belz,Charles Herman 65
,Franklin D. 65
,Fredrick Wm.Rev.65
,Fritz 65
,John 65
Benfer,Jerry 15
,Malinda Lee 91
Nathan Allen 15

,Russell Allen 15
Benker,Fritz Sr. 72
,Fritz Jr. 72
,La Nelle 72
,Larry 72
,Valgene 72
Bentley,Le Ruth 89
Bergman,Danny 13
,David 13
,James 13
,James Melvin 13
,Marion 13
,Meltion 13
Berry,Catherine 47
Berryman,Arnold 22
,Doris 22
,Joyce Colleen 22
Bethke,Neta 48
Bettis,Eddie 48
Bierschevale,Cathy 91
Billiot,Frank 69
,Katherine 69
,Nathan Christofer 69
Birch,Casey 80
,Christi 80
,Tommie 36,80
Bischoff, Hulda 75
,Ida 81
,William 75
Bishnow,Bernie 32
,Janet Gail 32
,Joyce 32
Bishop,Cinnamon Kay 44
,David 44
Black, Joan 20
,Miriam 64
Yvonne 20
Blankemeier,David 40
Blankenstein,Alma 19
,Elfrieda 19
,Elsie 19
,Gottfried 19
,Mary 19
,Paul 19
,Richard 19
,Ziegfried 19
Blune,Alvina Rev.62
Blum,Nelda 33

Bode,Henry 19
Boedeker,Adolph 22
        ,Anne 22
        ,Theodore 22
Boehringer,Richard Jay 5
        ,Shannon Marie 5
        ,Shawn Marie 5
Bienker,Amanda 53
Bohlen,Harold 68
        ,Harold James 68
        ,Robert Allen 68
        ,Sharon Elaine 68
Bohne,Annie 73
        ,Bertha 73
        ,Caroline 46,61,75
        ,Caroline Lene 72
        ,Christ.W. 71
        ,Emma 71,73
        ,Fritz David 71
        ,Fritz Fr. 71
        ,Fritz III 71
        ,Henry 72
        ,Karl Fredrich Wilhelm 71
        ,Kimberly 71
        ,Marie Jane 71
        ,Minnie 71
        ,Ronda 71
        ,Willie 73
Bohnfalk,Douglas 69
        ,Erwin 69
        ,Gordon Douglas 69
        ,Kathy Fay 69
        ,Larry Wayne 69
        ,Martha 69
Bohot,Annie Mae 73
Borgsted,Hildegarde 73
Bowden,Jimmie Means 66
        ,John 66
        ,Terry Lynn 66
Boyd,Tricia M. 12
Brands,Johanna 16
Bracher,P.O. Pastor 74
Brackett,Eva 24
Brandes,Hazel 54
Brandt,Willimenna Elnora 46
Branning,Caroline 1
Brashear,Betty Jo 32
        ,Lois 32
Brauner,Rosalee 49

Bravenec,Della 79
Brazzil,Lois 40
Breddin,Hattie 22
Breite,Evelyn Joyce 68
Breiten,Alfred 68
        ,Alfred Ray 68
        ,Bret Allen 68
        ,Emma 68
        ,John 68
        ,John Allen 68
        ,John David 68
        ,Sarah Ann 68
        ,Sean Ray 68
        ,Wilma Alene 68
Brinkman,August 16
        ,Esther 17
        ,Helen 17
        ,Lennor 16
        ,Louise 16
        ,Otto 16
Brockermeyer,Albert 41,44
        ,Allen Wayne 44
        ,Anna 42
        ,Blake Weeks 45
        ,Ben 41,44
        ,Ben Abbie 45
        ,Carl 41,44
        ,Daniel Ray Sr. 44
        ,Daniel Ray Jr. 44
        ,Dora Adel 43
        ,Dorthy Louise 43
        ,Evelyn H. Nesbit 42
        ,Floyd Carl 44
        ,Fred 41,45
        ,Fred Henry 44
        ,Gladiola 44
        ,Henry 41,42
        ,James Floyd 42
        ,Janie 44
        ,Kae Louis 41,45
        ,Karen Lynn 44
        ,Lillie 41,44
Brockermeier,Linda Lee 44
        ,Nancy 44
        ,Nola Marie 44
        ,Ora Dell 44
        ,Rosa Lina 44
        ,Rienhard 44
        ,Ruth Marie 44

,William Brent 45
Brockermeyer,R.W. 41
　　　,Robert 41,44
　　　,Rosa 41
　　　,Rienhard 41
　　　,Sharon Sue 44
　　　,Sophie 41,42
　　　,Walter 44
　　　,Wilhelmina Juanita 42
　　　,Willie 41,44
Brown,Charles 31
　　　,Cynthia 31
　　　,Diana 12
　　　,Gail 31
　　　,Horace Douglas 82
　　　,Jimmie C. 12
　　　,Lori Justine 12
　　　,Steve N. 82
　　　,Tricia M. 12
Brownley,Belle 81
Brynie,Henry 7
　　　,Josephine Oswald 7
　　　,Kristye 7
Buddenburg,Lena 57
Burmeister,Annie 65
　　　,Bertha 1
　　　,Herman 1,63,65
　　　,Lillie 1,65
　　　,Martha Lorina 1,65
Burnett,Beverly June 6
　　　,Jim Sidney 7
　　　,Ruthy Faye Mosely 7
Burton,Wilhelmine 64
Busch,Amanda Louise 39
　　　,George Douglas 37
　　　,Grace Brown 39
　　　,Ray E. 39
　　　,Talitha Ann 39
　　　,Von 39
Bush, Nettie Ruth 13
Byrd, Cheryl Annette 31
　　　,Christian Diane 31
　　　,Stanley Glen 31

Camp,Bob 85
　　　,Gene 85
　　　,Geraldine 85

Canuteson,James Allen 7
　　　,Oren 7
Carberry,Ella 50
Carlew,Fabia Oldham 20
Carlson,Janice 55
Carpenter,Evelyn Louise 17
Carrol,Clarence 10
　　　,Lela 10

Castleberry,Willie 90
Castro,Domingo Peralias 89
　　　,Edmond Lee 89
Cecil,Mary Beth 53
　　　,Bill 53
　　　,Tom 53
Chandler,Lloyd 56
　　　,Michael Lloyd 56
　　　,Opal 56
Chaney,Debra Kay 47
　　　,Kenneth 47
　　　,Kimberly Ann 47
　　　,Tina Marie 47
　　　,Vicci Lyn 47
Chapman,Cora Lee 54
Childress,Albert Leroy 24
　　　,Cathy Elaine 24
　　　,Elrosa 24
　　　,Gary Phillip 24
　　　,Tate 24
Choat,Billy Russell 50
　　　,Herman 50
　　　,Margie 50
　　　,Mellissa Michelle 50
Christ,Elizabeth 63
Christiansen,John 85
　　　,Paul 85
Christinson,Christina 19
Clary,Opal Junice 71
Clemmer,Eliza Bell 74
Clevenger,Arthur M. 55
　　　,Lola Irene 55
Chupik,Betty Jean 20
　　　,Bohus J. 20
　　　,Bohus Jr. 20
　　　,Carl Ann 21
　　　,Doreen 20
　　　,Jason 20
　　　,Jimmy 20,21

,John C. 20
,Kevin 20
,Kimberly 20
,Koreen 20
,Mary 20
,Pamela 20
,Robbie 20
,Ronald Black 20
,Ruth Marie 20
,Shawon 20
,Shelia 20
,Stephen 20
,Stephen W. 20
,Troy 20
Cobbs,Ed 49
,Jim 49
,Steve 49
,Thomas 49
,Tonie 49
Coburn,Ewell 32
,Gladys 32
,Justin Wayne 32
Cocek,Anton 25
,Anton John 25
Coker,Bradley Thell 90
,Burl Dean 90
,Charles Patrick 91
,Christopher Kelley 90
,Curtis Charles 90
,Kelly Russell 90
,Kelly Walter 90
Collins,Cordie 85
,Lilie May 15
,Luella 12
Comer,John Edgar 50
,Nancy Jane 50
,Tina Adelene 50
Conrad,Bertha Ottilie 6
Connally,Eva Nell 74
,Lonie Wade 74
Cook,Elmer,Joe 6
,Joe Paul 6
Conner,Charles 21
,William 21
Connors,Ruby 11
Cottle,Glenda 6
,Dudley 6
Cooper,Charles Richard 64
Copeland,Erlene 54

Cornet,Lola 30
Cottle,Dudley 6
Cox,Nellie 29,34
,Richard 34
Crawford,Jack 30
,Marie 30
,Paul 6
Cronkrite,Omega 38
Crow,Gerald Ray 16
,Marilyn Kay 16
Crump,Christina Marie 20
,James Roy 20
,James Roy Jr. 20
,Joni Lynn 20
Cruthers,Douglas 66
Cummins,Billie Marius 42
,James Homer 42
,Kari Marie 42
,Keith 42
,Ruth Marie 42
Curtis,Jay 34
,Juli Ann 34
,Mellissa Michele 34

Dahse,Louise 56
Danford,Edeline 16
Davis,Alene 64
,Laverne 12
Dawson,Bruce Ray 68
,Gary George 68
,George 68
,Linda Lee 42
,Sandra Joyce 68
,Thad Alfred 68
,Vera 68
DeBusk,Margaret 91
DeFrancesco,Edward Anthony 57
,John Edward 57
,Pasquale 57
Dehnel,Florine 33
Deutscher,Deana 44
Dickschat,Alton Carl 73
,Annie 73
,Bertha 73
,Betty Jane 73
,Brian Keith 53
,Carol 73
,Danny 73

,Dorothy Ann 73
,Edwin Christoph 73
,Frank C. 73
,Frank William 73
,Fred 53
,Joyce Lynn 73
,Linda Kay 73
,Mark Wayne 53
,Nina 73
,Otto Fritz 73
,Peggy Elaine 73
,Raymond 73
,Reba 73
,Rodney Allen 53
,Rosa Karoline 73
,William Henry 73
,William C. 73
Dietz,Louise 2
Dippolito,Levia 57
Ditta,Josephine 2
Dittrich,Henry Joseph Sr. 63
,Patricia Elizabeth 63
Dodgen,Bill 30
,Gary Kim 30
,Ginger 30
Doiron,Charles R. 65
Donnheian Ethel 13
Doughty,Katherine 37,79
Douglas,Alice 82
Draehn,Alfred 22
,Alma 22
,Gloria Ann 22
Drennan,Charlotte 20
,Marvin 20
Dubbe,Alive 62
Sugger,LoeNell 30
Duncan,Edwin 74
,Mary Lee 74
,Robert Ewell 74
Dunlap,Deborah Lynn 13
,Raleigh 13
,Ronnie Wayne 13
,Tom 30
Dunn,Bobby Gene 19
,Charles Bradley 19
,Henry Luther 19
,James David 19
,Larry Wayne 19

,Luther 19
,Mattie 19
,Rual 19
Durst,Anida 77
Duval,David Jay 10
,Rebecca Ann 10
,Janie 10

Eakin,Dolores Faye 50
,Thomas Duncan 50
,Thomas Raymond 50
Easterling,Burnice 23
,Carey 23
,Mary 23
Eberle,Glen Doris 24
Eckert,James Ewald 77
,Jary Lyn 77
,Rodney Wheeler 77
,Patricia Elaine 77
Edwards,Cynthia Dee 24
,Lillie 29,30
,Lewis 30
,Warren Milton 24
Elder,Ann 50
Elliott,Margaret Baumann 5
,Mildred Marie 30
,Robert Leonard 30
,William Ray 5
Elmore,Jackie 51
,Robin Lynn 51
,Wm.C. 51
Emshoff,David Alan 64
,Elmo 64
,Otto 64
,Tina Marie 64
Enax,Marvin Charlie 26
,Marvin Jr. 26
,Norma 26
,Norma Jean 26
,Raymond William 26
,William 26
English,Nona Mae 19
Eppers,Francis 45
Ermisch,Pastor 75
Erner,Mabel 26
,Sybel 26
Eskew,Cecil Eugene 30

,Charlotte Nannette 30
Etzel,Louis 74
    ,Richard 74
    ,Ruben 74
Eum,Katherine Rose 5
Evans,Duran 85
    ,Linda Joy 85
Ewing,Mattie A.Jane 79

Fadal,Richard G.Dr.91
    ,Stacy 91
Fair,Amy Nicole 35
    ,David Alan 35
    ,Harold Wayne 35
    ,Joe Charles 35
    ,Lilly 35
    ,Michael Wayne 35
Fahrenkamp,Clara 72
    ,Emma 71
    ,Fritz 72
    ,Ida 72
    ,Linda Kay 72
    ,Minnie 72
    ,Rosa 72
    ,Willie C. 71
Farkle,Carl 19
Federsisch,Carol Elaine 18
    ,Michael Weldon 18
    ,Patricia Diane 18
    ,Teresa Lynne 18
    ,Thomas Marvin 18
Fehler,Alfred 5
    ,Anna Friedricka 4,8
    ,Bertha 4,8
    ,Bobby John 6
    ,Brian 5
    ,Carl William 4,5
    ,Charles Henry 4,6
    ,Charles William Jr. 7
    ,Clara Louise Bertha 6
    ,Corine 5
    ,Daniel 5
    ,David Anthony 7
    ,Deborah Kay 7
    ,Douglas Ray 7
    ,Doyle Charles 7
    ,Edward Dwayne 81

,Evelyn Margaret 7
,Fred Henry 4,7
,Fritz 1,4
,Folterman,Dora 5
,Harole Elmer 7
,Heather Leigh 7
,Hedwig Louise Emilie 4,8
,Henrietta Frieda 4,6
,Henry 81
,Herbert 81
,James Douglas 5
,Janice Colleen 7
,John Charles 7
,Karie Shea 7
,Judy Ruth 7
,Keith 5
,Kimberly Diane 81
,Luther Gustav 5
,Mary Evelyn 5
,Melita Sophia 5
,Michael Paul 6
,Naioma Daune 5
,Otto 5
,Ronald Carl 5
,Shelly Lynn 5
,Steven Harole 7
,Steven Edward 81
,Tonja 5
,Walter 5
,Walter William 6
,William 6
,William Ray Elliot 5
,Willie Mae 7
Fenke,Dora 22
Fenske,Arthur 48
Fergus,Cindy 5
    ,Gary 5
    ,Julie 5
    ,Nolan Dill 5
    ,Perry 5
Ficke,James Alfred 39
    ,Virginia Ruth 39
Finger,Luciene 69
Finklea,Carol 30
    ,Colleen Beth 30
    ,Helen 30
Finley,Chester 64
Finch,Renda Gale 21
    ,Renita K. 12

Finch,Teresa Nell 12
   ,Thomas Howard 12
Finson,Emilie 13
    ,Sam 13
    ,Selma Pauline 13
    ,Teresa Nell 12
    ,Thomas Howard 12
Finstad,Calvin 49
    ,David 49
    ,Richard Allen 49
Fischgrabe,Clara 33
Fisk(Fick),Irene 78
    ,Carl 78
Fleischlauer,Herbert 71
     ,Raymond 71
     ,Willie 71
Fleishour,Dorothy 48
Fletcher,Connie 85
    ,Harry 85
Folterman,Clarence 47
    ,Dora 5
    ,Douglas Keith 47
    ,Henry 5
    ,Jan Renee 47
Fondren,Gladys 83
Forrest,Charles I 50
   ,Sharla Ann 50
Foster,Albert Z. 34
    ,Carolyn 63
    ,Christopher Michael 74
    ,David 34
    ,Gillian Elizabeth 74
    ,Gretal 74
    ,Jack Ray 14
    ,Malaine Ann 14
    ,Marsha Lenell 64
    ,Mary Nell Finley 64
    ,Nathan Gordon 63
    ,Sherry Lynn 14
    ,Thomas Z. 34
    ,Wade 34
Franke,Ervin 53
    ,Friedrich 1
    ,Fudy 33
Franklin,Alma L. 56
Frase,Florence Emma 82
   ,Ray B. 82
Fredrich,Wm.Theodore 82
Freeman,Mary Antonette 5
   .Vonie Shaw 56

Fudge,Juanita 40
Fuelberg,Arthur Carl 64
    ,Bertha 1,64
    ,Betty Lynn 64
    ,Dora 64
    ,Edward 64
    ,Gene Arthur 64
    ,Hilda 63
    ,Kristine Kay 64
    ,Ludwig 63
    ,Mary Dale 64
    ,Oscar 1,63
    ,Oscar Jr. 1,64
    ,Otto 63
    ,Reinhard 64
    ,Robert 64
Fussleman,Ginger 69

Gabrysch,Mary 56
Gastle,Anna Pace 77
Ganado,Milton Bain 57
Garrison,Jamie Estella 62
Garcia,David 81
Geber,Estelle 82
   ,Alice 83
   ,Cora 80
Gebert,Cora 80
    ,Roudolph 80,82,83
Geltmeyer,Fred 25
     ,Ornel Lydia 25
Germany,Merle 80
Gilbert,Shirley Ann 18
Glasco,Maurice 35
   ,Veronica 35
Glaser,Agnes 28,56
    ,Ervin Henry 59
    ,Fritz 56,59
    ,Katie Mae 59
    ,Laura 64
    ,Louise 59
    ,Paul 28,59
    ,Robert Paul 59
    ,Ronald 59
    ,Vernan Paul 59
Glazeman,Bob 48
Glenn,Minnie 30
Goeke,Elsie Tillie 55
Goellerr,William 61

Goessler,Bertha 71
        ,Bertha Minnie 62
        ,Charles Allen 91
        ,Charlie Henry 62
        ,Edna 61,91
        ,Emma 29
        ,Emma Marie 35,62
        ,Fritz 29,35
        ,Fritz Carl 33,61
        ,Gary Lyn 33,62
        ,Hanna 61
        ,Henry 62
        ,Herbert 62
        ,Hilbert Fritz 33,61
        ,Karl Fredrich 33,62
        ,Kevin Lyn 33,62
        ,Lois 72
        ,Mark Anthony 62
        ,Paul Fredrick 62
        ,Ruby Marie 34,62
        ,Werner David 91
        ,William 33,61,71
        ,William A. 61
        ,William Charles 91
Goff,Jessie 34
Graff,Barbara Annette 69
        ,Frances Bernice 68
        ,Fred Louis 69
        ,Joey Stephen 69
        ,Kathy Marie 69
        ,Louis 68
        ,Robert 68
        ,Robert J. 69
        ,Susan 69
        ,Tommie Allan 69
Graham,Curtis 80
        ,Margaret 6
        ,Maxwell 80
        ,Shelia 80
Grant,Esther Corene 63
Gray,Donna 13
        ,Mary Katherine 16
        ,Walter 13
Grebe,Ella 47
Green,Francis Collin 39
        ,Tom 78
Gregory,Alan 20
Griggs,Arvie 19
        ,Betty Lemerle 19
        ,Carl Joe 19

Grimes,Ernest Carl 12
        ,James Edwards 12
        ,Johnny 12
        ,Kirk Vaughn 12
        ,Malcom DeKalb 12
        ,Marla Yvette 12
        ,Norma Rugh 12
Grimland,Oscar Chris 9
Grube,Carl 61,70
        ,Dorothy 69
        ,Elma 68
        ,Frederick 67,68
        ,Fritz 61,85
        ,Herman 61
        ,Hilbert 68
        ,Louis 69
        ,Melanie 68
        ,Minna 61,70
        ,Otto 68
Grossman,Patricia 42
Gunn,Bradley Stuart 10
        ,Steven Maurice 10
        ,Maurice 10

Hackfeld,Erna Augusta 7
        ,John Henry 7
Haarmeyer,Emma 78
        ,Fred 78
        ,Mabel Caroline 64
        ,Nannie 78
        ,Otto 68
Haas,Albert 79
        ,Anton 76,82
        ,Arthur 37,78
        ,Ben 80
        ,Ben Jr. 80
        ,Bradley 79
        ,Chad Michael 80
        ,Donna 52
        ,Edna 40,79
        ,Ervin 78
        ,Esther 36,80
        ,Fritz 36,37,40,76,78
        ,Jacque 80
        ,James Henry 79
        ,James Paul 79
        ,John 78
        ,Kasi Rachelle 79
        ,Kathleen 82

,Kevin 78
,Kevin Eugene 79
,Kimberly Renee 79
,Lorena(Tommie) 80
,Larry 78
,Marjorie Ann 37,79
,Mike 80
,Raymond 82,91
,Robert 8
,Shirley Ann 78
,Stacy Diane 79
,Stanley 37,38
,Steven Mathew 79
,Walter Henry 82
,Wayne 78
,William 37,79
,William E. 37,79
,Wm.Walter 82
Haferkamp,Alberta 48
,Almo 48
,Esther 48
,Helen 48
,Henry 48
,Linda 48
,Mary 48
,Pee Wee 48
,Vernon 48
,Wilma B.(Pudden) 48
Haegelin,Marie Katherine 59
Hafley,Brian 40
,Malinda 40
,Mark 40
,Sherry Renee 44
,Tommy 44
Hahn,August Bernhardt 12
,Carol Lynn 78
,Helen Ann 77
,Helen Martha 12
,Kathy Lee 78
Hailey,Virginia Ann 89
Halcamp,Henrietta 12
Hamilton,Aurthur 8
,Charles Aurthur 8
,Erlene 8
,Kathyleen 8
Handkost,Rev.Theo 90
Harm,Augusta 22
Harms,Augusta 17
,John F. 17
Hansman,Carlyn 38
,Hermina 38
,Wilbert 38

Harper,Jommy 26
,Laverne 26
,Mabel Marie 26
Hartley,Amanda Denise 43
,Crispin Patrice 43
,James Wade 43
,Rondle Lee 43
,Rondle Lee III 43
Hartman,A.C.Jr.55
,Dana Michelle 55
,Melanie Kris 55
,Tina Renee 55
Harvey,Eunice Josephine 83
Hastings,Losma 12
Hall,James T.73
,Patricia 54
Hansen,Harold 70
,Janet 70
,Polly 70
Hasdorff,Charles 56
,Fred 56
Hatter,Lula Jo 83
Hawes,Norma Anne 24
,William Irving 24
Haydon,Dana Louise 32
,Sterling Ruben 32
,Tommie 32
Heckman,Edie Mae 72
Hedt,Emma 25
Heffington,Tennie 74
Heine,Doris 42
,Helena 65
Helms,Bertha C.7
,Emil 6
,John E. 7
,John Emil 6
,Pauline Louise 6
,Regina Ruth 7
Hemphill,Baby 42
,F.C. 42
Henderson,Amy Marie 43
,Richard Lee 43
Hengst,Debra Lynn 44
,Kimberly Kay 44
,Max Kevin 44
,Max Moretz 44
Henry,E.W.Jr.
Henske,Billy Chris 55
,Ervin Charles 55
,Nancy Ruth 55
,Terry Ervin 55
Hering,Nora 74

Hershey,Anne 77
Herzog,August 22
    ,Elsie 22
    ,August 24
    ,Lillie 24
Hess,James R.32
Hessel,Anna 19
    ,Barry Glenn 18
    ,Billy Gene 18
    ,Dorothy Louise 18
    ,F.H.17
    ,Geneva Ann 18
    ,Henrietta 17
    ,Lonnie Harole 18
    ,Mark Alan 18
    ,Minnie 17
    ,Violet Laverne 18
    ,Willie 18
Hesser,Nora Mae 35,62
Hester,Gerldine 66
Hewett,Marlene Kay 5
Hickness,Kenneth 66
Hildebrand,Faye 22
        ,Jean 22,80
        ,John 22
        ,Lorine 22
Hill,Anthony Scott 21
    ,Belvin 21
    ,Charles Albert 21
    ,Kimberly Dawn 21
    ,Tim Rehna 21
Hobbs,Billy Joe 72
    ,Brenda 72
    ,Roddy Joe 72
Hodde,Henriette 26
Hodel,Herman B. 11,84
    ,John 11
Hodges,Mickel Norman 63
        ,Norman 63
Hoefelmeyer,Sophie 22
Hoehn,Dorothy Louise 7
Hoile,Gloria 6
    ,Jackie 6
Hold,August Jr. 55
    ,Janet Elaine 55
    ,Winston Curtis 55
Holiman,Lanetta 37,78
Holle,Adaline 48
    ,Adolph 46,48
    ,Albert 46

,Adolph W.(A.W.) 49
,Annie 47
,Angela Beth 53
,Alvin 49
,Bertha 48
,Berthold(Bernard) 49
,Bennie 47
,Billy 49
,Billie Lee 48
,Bobby Jean 72
,Bobbie Sue 49
,Betty Joyce 49
,Charlene Olga 47
,C.H. 46
,Charles(C.W.) 47
,Charles 46,72
,Charley 46
,Charley H. 72
,Chris 72
,Christel Wynn 53
,Clara 48
,Dan 49
,Darlene Hazel 47
,David Garick 72
,Dennis 72
,Donald 49
,Donald Wayne 53
,Donna 72
,Frances Anderson 72
,Fred 47
,Fred Jr. 47
,Fredrick W. 47
,Frieda 46,48,49
,Friedrick 46
,Fritz 46
,Gayle 49
,Garth 49
,Gill 49
,Gloria 49
,Greg 49
,Emma 46
,Eric 49
,Erwin Henry 48
,Henry 46
,Hedwig(Hattie) 49
,Ima Jean 49
,Joan Kathleen 48
,Julie 48
,Josephine 47
,Kyle Bradley 72

,Lillie 46
,Linda Lou 49
,Louise 46,48
,Malinda 49
,Margaret 48
,Melvin 48
,Melvin Jr. 48
,Minnie 46
,Otto 47
,Ralph Brian 48
,Ralph W. 72
,Ronald 72
,Sam 48
,Sharon Kay 48
,Scott 49
,Sophie 28,46
,Stacy Renee 72
,Thomas N. 72
,Walter 48
,William 28,46,47
,Wm.Jr. 46
,William C. 46,72
,William Geoffrey 72
,Willie 53
Holmes,James 35
Holtkamp,Charlie 33,62
,Henerietta 10
,Lena 33,62
,Lena Mae 33,62
Hood.Alice 49
Houy,August 76,83
,Barbara Jo 77
,Carl Arthur 77
,Carter Wyckoff 77
,Charles Arthur Jr. 77
,Cheryl Ann 77
,Dorothy Louise 77
,Ernest William 77
,Escher C. 77
,Edward Wesley 77
,Henry H. 77
,Rev.Henry 76,77
,John David 77
,Mary Ann 77
,Stephen William 77
,Verdie Helen 77
Hovend,Charlie 14
,Elmo 14
Howell,Billie Francis 31
,Debra Kay 31
,Donna Sue 31

,Lawrence 31
,Lucille 31
,Tammie Elaine 31

Hueske,Albert 47
,Ruth Marie 47
,Annie Mae 47
,Milton 47
,Louise 47
Hultquist,Albert 56
,Lydia Oaks 56
,Raymond 56
Humpries,Hattie 34
Huntsinger,Bryan Chris 39
,Carl Sue 39
,Gene 39
,Henry Narvell 39
,Linda Lou 39
,Randel Cory 39
Hustfield,Len Anthoney 65
,Mary Jo 65
Hutchcraft,Evelyn 16
Hutyra,Doris Louise 16
,Geralding 16
,Jerry 16
,Martha Ann 16
,Vince 16
Hutzler,Marva Louise 70
,Wilford 70

Ingram.Levina 10

Jackley,Lucy 11
Jahnke,Annie 53
,Dorothy Mae 48
,Erwin 48
,Fredrica 29
Jansen,Johanna 17
Januzewski,Ray 52
,Brandy 52
Jahnke,Roudolph 48
Jaster,Betty Lou 62
,Herman 62
Jeffery,Lois Elizabeth 35
,Robert Lee 35
,Terry Joe 35
Jenkins,Bells 16
,Christine Danyal 16
,Clifton Emerson 16

,Clifton Emerson Jr. 16
,Lula 52
,Mildred Ann 17
,Pete 16
Jenson,Olga 46,72
Jeske,Anne Mae 8
,Charlie 8
,Helen 8
,Hildegard Gertrude 8
Jetter,Willie Maude
Johnson,Dolly 13
,Frank 18
,Harold Joseph 13
,Henry 13
,Henry Russell 13
,Jimmy Carroll 10
,Kim Annette 10
,Lonnie 18
,Sherry 40
,Timmy 18
,Preshie Estelle 13
Jolly,Richard 33
Jones,Alton 44
Jordan,Sue Ann Morrison 25
Jorgenson,Andrew 12
,Helma Gladys 12
,Jessie Wayne 12
,Lois N. 12
,Lonnie 12
,Lonnie Wm.Jr. 12
,Lucille 12

Kadubar,Albina Leona 16
Kamman,Artle 50
,Theodore 50
,Artle Irene 50
Karnowski,Albert 81
,Antonia(Toni) 81,76
,Hella 79
,Henry 79
,Louise 81
,Paul 80
Kaska,Anna 16
,Caroline 16
Kasky(Koukosky),Augusta 54
Kaster,Zella 49
Kattner,Glen 40
,Gordon 40
,Herbert 40

,Rickie 40
,Vivian 40
Keadle,Gene 35,62
,Wyle,Eugene Sr. 35,62
Kelm,Albert 10
,Cythia Ann 10
,Daryl Ross 10
,Lori Michelle 10
,Marcus Dwain 10
,Otto 10
,Richard 10
,Rodney 10
,Sharon Kay 12
Kelling,Joylene 33
,Willie 33
,Willie F. 33
,John 48
,Paul 30
Kemper,Sophie 85
Kerr,Sidney 80
,Warren 80
King,Jenny Lynn 52
,Renee Michelle 52
Kirchner,James 42
Kilcrease,Cynthia Gail 9
,Gary Douglas 9
,James Douglas 9
,Randy James 9
Klier,Jessica 78
,Ronald Keith 78
Klingleman,Lucille 40
,Monroe 40
,Trapp, Hilda 40
Klopstad,Caroline 54
Klostermann,Mithilda 9
Kluck,August 89
,Rev.Carl Wesley 89
,Charley Wesley 89
,Elsie 16
,Emile 89
,Emile F.Rev.90
,Gottlib 89
,Gus 89
,Heneritta 90
,Homer Roy Rev. 89
,Kraig Scott 16
,Lois Marie 89
,Lornze 16
,Marrida 89
,Marguerite Marie 89

,Mildred Ann 17
,Otto 16
,Rosalie 90
,Rose Ellen 16
,Ruth Evelyn 89
,Sharon Dianne 89
,Shelly Ann 16
,Wilhelmina A.Christine
  (Minnie) 89
,William 89
,Willie E. 89
,Willie 88,89
,William Emanuel 90
Knapp,Alice Louise 16
Kneschke,Ferdinand 62
        ,Norma Jean 62
Kiniker,Charles Henry 29
Knox,Billie 8
    ,Danny 8
Kochwelp,Ernest 65
        ,Louise 65
Koehler,Irene 85
       ,Paul 85
Koening,Alice 77
Koeppen,Otto 28,58
Koester,Albert 48
       ,Alvin 48
       ,Bernice 48
       ,Bobbie Sue 48
       ,Bruce 48
       ,Connie 48
       ,Caroline 48
       ,Curtis 48
       ,Cynthia 48
       ,Doloras 48
       ,Josephine 48
       ,Kavin 48
       ,Karol 48
       ,Keith 48
       ,Lucille 48
       ,Kenneth Janks 48
       ,Maryline 48
       ,Milton 48
       ,Paul 48
       ,Stanley 48
       ,Wilburn 48
       ,William 48
       ,Dwayne 48
Kokemor,Arthur 49
       ,Edwin 49
       ,Ervin 49

,Hennie 49
,Henrich 49
,Louis 49
,Roy 49
,Selma 49
Kolar,Barbara 21
     ,Betty Louise 21
     ,Emil 21
     ,Louis 21
     ,Marjorie 21
Kolhorst,Christina Lynn 72
        ,T.C. 72
        ,Todd Christopher 72
Koopman,Martha Elisa 12
Korth,Cora Lee 52
     ,David Wayne 52
     ,Edwin 53
     ,Eleanor 53
     ,Fritz 28,52
     ,Fritz W. 52
     ,Gloria Jean 53
     ,Henry 52
     ,Herbert 53
     ,Howard 53
     ,James Allen 52
     ,Joy Ann 53
     ,Keith Allen 53
     ,Kimberly Kay 53
     ,Lillie 52
     ,Linda Ruth 53
     ,Michael 53
     ,Minnie 52
     ,Ruth Lois 52
     ,Walter 52
     ,Walter Jr. 52
Kosel,Ben 65
Kraemer,Rebecca 55
Kramer,Dennis Robert 12
      ,Donna Marie 22
      ,Laura 22
      ,Norbert 22
      ,Robert 79
      ,Roberta 40,79
      ,Stella 40,79
Krause,Velma 53
Krenik,Ella 19
Krueger,Albert 34,61
       ,Clara 61,91
       ,Elsie 72
       ,Ettie 34
       ,Frieda 29,33

,Malinda 53
,Nelda 47,72
Kuehl,Walter 48
    ,Walter Jr. 48
    ,Janice 48
Kuhlmann,Emma Dorothy 37
Kupott,Lillie 71
Kureger,Malinda 53
Krumnow,Lennie 47
Kuretsch,Bernard 57
    ,Louis 57
    ,Marjorie Ann 57
    ,Weldon 57
Kyzar,Dorothy Sanberg 63
    ,Elmo Ben 63
    ,James Ronald 63

LaCater,Lena 48
Lafgern,Beverly Dee 5
Laird,Joe Mack 32
    ,Joe Shack 32
    ,Marion Elizabeth 32
    ,William Wiley 32
Lambert,James Ennis 23
    ,Renee 73
Lampley,James Oscar 44
Lammert,Carolyn Ann 7
    ,Erika Allison 7
    ,Jerry Don 7
    ,Lonnie Louis 7
    ,Wayne Fredrich 7
    ,Wm. 7
Landry,Ian Louis 18
    ,Margo Renee 18
    ,Meridith Leone 18
    ,Michael Ann 18
La Spina,Jack Jr. 69
    ,Jack Sr. 69
    ,Lisa Michelle 69
    ,Louise 69
    ,Mark Scott 69
Lassiter,Arch Frank 9
    ,Earline 9
    ,Emma Mae 9
    ,Daniel Ray 10
    ,Hugh Frank 10
    ,James Michael 10
    ,Rhonda Deleon 10
Lattner,Robert L. 40
Ledbetter,Debra Sue 89
    ,Doloras Ann 89
    ,Lester 89

Lee,Carl 20
    ,Curtis Eugene 7
    ,D. 20
    ,Elizabeth 20
    ,Rhonda D'Ann 7
    ,Taunia Denise 7
    ,Wm. Randel 7
Legan,Ethel Ann Forest 50
Lehman,Annie 49
Lehmann,Christina 19
    ,Clara 18
    ,Ed 19
    ,Mary 19
    ,Paul 19
    ,Pauline 19
    ,Walter 19
Lehrman,Louise 48
    ,Melinda 48
Leinweber,Elizabeth 68
Lemm,Charles 55
    ,Millie Augusta 55
    ,Ronnie Lindsey 55
Lenning,Glendora 86
    ,Irvin 86
    ,Pat 86
Leuschner,Julius 17
    ,Lance Allen 17
    ,Laurie Ann 17
    ,Lucille 16,17
    ,Shirley Ann 16
    ,Stanley J. 16
Lewis,Biron 66
    ,Carl H. 37,79
    ,David Todd 37.79
    ,David Vaughan 79
    ,Larry 66
    ,Melissa 66
    ,Paula Annette 79
Light,Ida Belle 64
Lightfoot,Angela Kae 30
    ,Aubrey Lee 31
    ,David Paul 30
    ,E.L. 31
    ,Gary Lynn 30
    ,Larry Lee 31
    ,Nettie Killion 31
Lindahl,Don S. 44
    ,Jayson Jay 44
    ,Steven Jay 44
Lindsey,John L. 55
    ,Ronnie L. 55
Linnard,E.A. 12
    ,Pethrica 12

Litchy,Alvin John 34
    ,Daniel John 34
    ,Lynn 34
    ,Thomas John 34
    ,Timothy John 34
    ,Tony 34
Locka,Martha 40
    ,Richard Clay 77
    ,Rose Louise 77
Loesberg,Emma 68
    ,John N. 68
Loesch,Anna 1
    ,Annie 61
    ,Bertha 33,61,63
    ,Carol Lois Carlile 66
    ,Charles Hy 66
    ,Charles Hy Jr. 66
    ,Charlie H. 65
    ,Darla 66
    ,Geneva 66
    ,Herman 2,61
    ,John 65
    ,Johnnie Mae 65
    ,Louise Belle 65
    ,Lucille 66
    ,Mary 65
    ,Melvin 65
    ,Roy 65
Lohmeyer,Bertha 72
Lommer,John Ashley 53
London,Albert 81
    ,Leah Anne 81
    ,Clarence 81
    ,Dennis Neal 81
    ,Ernest Ray 81
    ,James Neal 81
    ,Merle 81
Lovell,Ernest 64
    ,Joel Ernest 64
    Lowe,Margaret 77
Luckmeyer,Mary Caroline 46
Lucky,Shirley Marie Tate 79
    ,Melissa Marie 79
    ,Steven Mathew 79
Luech,Henry 49
    ,Henry Jr. 49
    ,Lonnie 49
    ,Rosena 48
Lueckhoff,Rev.Fr. 72
Luedtke,Betty Ann 8
    ,Donna Kay 8

    ,Ernest 8
    ,F.C. 8
Luhn,Florine Elsie 54
    ,Raymond 54
    ,Robert 54
Lumplin,Calvin Sr. 51
    ,Carroll Ray 51
    ,Laura 51
Lundy,Charles 14
    ,Janette 14
    ,Nadene 14
Lynch,Rick 40,79

MacNutt,Mark Benjamen 75
    ,Robert Carl 75
    ,Thomas Lansing 75
    ,Wm. Phillip 75
    ,Wm. Thomas 75
    ,William 75
Madden,Mike 2
    ,Mitzi 2
    ,Vernon 2
Maier,Mina 3
Malik,Eleanora Ann 57
Marks,Hilda 48
Marsh,Cave 86
    ,Dell 86
    ,Ruth 86
Martins,Carl 1
    ,Friedrich 1
Marshall,Allison Kay 8
    ,Joe 8
    ,Joe Crawford 8
    ,Maryanna 8
Marz,Charlyn 5
Matus,Mary 17
    ,Louis 17
    ,Estelle 17
    ,Josephine Ann 35
    ,Joseph Frank 35
Mattlage,Ester 6
Mayfield,Bill 81
    ,Jewel 81
    ,Diane 81
McCall,Faye Lois 85
McCleary,Betty Ann 14
    ,Bobby Ray 13
    ,Ed 13
    ,Pauline 14
    ,Peggy Joyce 14

McClanahan,Billy Lynn 57
        ,Billie Robert 57
        ,Collier Joseph 57
        ,Diana Marie 57
McCutchen,Billy Fred 40
        ,Billy Mac 40
        ,Eric 40
McDonald,Nelda 39
        ,Roger 39
McElwreath,Mary Ann 40,79
McGehee,Barbara 7
McQueen,Kathy 83
McVey,Laverne 81
        ,Margaret 81
        ,Raystelle 81
Meador,Rita 40.79
Meals,Ila Mae 38
        ,Oscar 38
Meekin,Cecil Elliott 34,62
        ,Danny Joe 34,62
        ,Mace H. 34,62
        ,Pearl 34,62
        ,Rufus 34,62
Meckleson,Lula 13
Meier,Carl 54
        ,Dorthea 15
        ,Elsie Alice 54
Meiske,Anna 24
        ,Emma 81
        ,William 23,24
Meisner,Edwena 2
Melton,Bobbie Gail 70
Menglos,Dennis 78
        ,John Andrea 78
        ,Monica Lynn 78
Menke,Alan 33
        ,Annie 33
        ,Bonnie 33
        ,Jesse 33
        ,John H. 33
Mercer,Henry E. 56
        ,Lucy 56
Meyer,Beverly 66
        ,Charlotte Wilhelmine
        D. 3
        ,Darrel 66
        ,Debora 66
        ,Diana 66
        ,Gene 66
        ,Linda 66
        ,Mary 66

Mick,Brian 5
        ,Daniel 5
        ,Keith 5
        ,Sue Ann 5
        ,Tonja 5
Mikolajewski,Ruth
        Catherine 52
        ,Randy Gene 52
        ,John Victor 52
        ,John Victor Jr. 52
Miller,Anne Frances 55
        ,Athol 71
        ,Colin Clyde 71
        ,Cornelia 38
        ,David Glenn 38
        ,Esta 55
        ,Irene 6
        ,Joan 71
        ,Joe 55
        ,L.J. 38
        ,Stephen Lee 71
        ,Tom Lee 6
        ,Willis Burgess 38
Mitschke,Linda 42
Mnar,Marie 25
Moeller,Elva 38
        ,Eva Mae 38
        ,Hermina 36
        ,Grace 38
        ,Keith Edwin 38
        ,Margaret Ann 38
        ,Tonie 36
        ,Virginia Kathryn 38
        ,Wallace 38
        ,W.E. 36
        ,W.H. 38
Mohr,Frieda 53
Mooney,Audry Dale 13
        ,Bill 13
        ,David Neal 13
        ,Duane 13
        ,Hershal Wayne 13
        ,Opal 13
        ,Opal Laura 13
Moore,Adele 64
        ,Ben 30
        ,Buell 64
        ,Carol 64
        ,Dale 64
        ,Joyce 64
        ,Obe Ebeneezer 64

,Patricia 30
,Thelma 33
Morgan,Alonzo 2
Morrison C.E.25
Muegge,Albert 12
,August 10,12
,Bernice 12
,Emma Louise 10
,Judy 12
,Mike 12
,Roy 12
,Sharon 12
,Sophie 40
Muehlbrad,Emil 64
,Lydia Helen 64
Muller,Louise 47
Murphee,Angela 13
,Clinton 13
,Cloves 13
,Fern Rahne 13
,La Renda 13
Murphy,Alicia Catherine 83
,Cynthia Eileen 19
,Daniel Carl 19
,David 83
,John Henry 19
,Kathleen 19
,Marion 83
,Michael Patrick 83
,Mignon Turner 83
,Patricia 19
,Patricia Eileen 19
,Pearl 19
,Sidney 19
Mutscher,Clarence Gustav 42
,Esther Clara 42
,Glenn Allen 42
,Herman 42
,Jeffery Dean 42
,Keith Allen 42
,Marvin Paul 42
,Ralph Dennis 42
,Randy Wayne 42
,Shirley Mae 42
,Travis James 42
Myrick,Deana 83
,Ernest 83
,John Henry 83
,Sandra Jean 83

Naumann,Ed 52
,Ray Allen 52
,J.F. 52
Namken,Donna Gail 55
,Kathy Elaine 55
,Harry G. 55
NcNeis,Nita Jean 83
Neason,Brownie Katherine 61,91
Neiman,Lora 80
,Lorene 36
,John 36,80
Neikamp,David 66
,Edmund B. Jr.66
,James 66
,Sidonia Charisse 66
Nelson,Anthony Joseph 66
,Dolly Russel 51
,Hershel Lee 51
,Joseph 66
,Joseph Jr. 66
,Kimberly Jo 66
,Michael Ray 51
,Preston Lee 51
Neuman,Louis 69
,Lynn Ray 70
,Michael Ray 70
,Sigmund 29
Neuman,Betty Louise 69
,Charles Larry 70
,Charles Larry Jr. 70
,Clarence 69
,Daniel Louis 70
,Dennis James 70
,Fanell Dorothy 69
,Hulda 28,61,62
Neumann,Laura 90
Nichols,Aimee Denise 30
,C.L. 30
,Davis 81
,Esther 76,81
,Jeane 30
,Larry 30
,Larry Michael 30
,Patricia 36
Nidy,Janet 39
Nitsche,Garry 55
Novasas,John 8
,Mary 8
,Roy 8

Odle,Barry Clint 10
       ,Jerry Olin 10
Oldham,Melvin 20
       ,Rena Beale 20
Oliver,Donnie 34
Olson,Jerald Wayne Hemphill 42
Ondrej,Christine 16
       ,Daniel John 16
       ,Elizabeth Anna 16
       ,John 16
       ,John Daniel 16
       ,Mary Barbara 16
Ostinelli,Charles 20
         ,Diana Clare 20
         ,Lucille 20
         ,Mary 20
         ,Michael Lee 20
         ,Paul Edward Jr. 20
Otto,Roy Sidney 33
Owens,Cynthia 20
      ,Earl 20
      ,Joe L. 20
      ,Mildred 20
      ,Sam 20
      ,Samuel Bohus 20

Pankonien,Alice 47
Parker,Audrey James 5
       ,Brendon 5
       ,Emma 5
       ,James Beldon 5
       ,James Daniel 5
       ,Jeremy 5
       ,John Frederick 5
       ,Kimberly 5
       ,Norma Jean 5
       ,Patricia Ann 5
       ,Vernon Beldon 5
       ,Wendy 5
       ,William Vernon 5
Pate,Nathan 40
Patrick,Carol Ann 79
        ,R.H. 79
Patterson,Alan Dale 32
          ,Angela Dawn 91
          ,Ethel 32
          ,Louis 32

Patton,Blake Freeman 56
       ,Bobby Alton 56
       ,Dee 56
       ,Imogene 56
       ,Kimberly April 56
       ,Sharon 56
Paul,Elbert C. 32
     ,Eva 32
     ,Nelda Faye 32
Pearce,Fannie 57
Peeples,Christie 30
        ,Inghey 30
Pelkemeyer,James Allen 73
           ,Jennifer Leigh 73
Perkins,Martha 6
        ,Neil 6
Person,Melanie Dawn 18
       ,Richard Lee 18
       ,Ronald David 18
Pessarra,Billie Kay 65
         ,Jared Dakota 65
         ,Kelley Marie 65
Peterson,Caroline Holle 47,73
         ,Charles Wayne 73
         ,Judy 73
         ,Susan 73
         ,Clarice 13
Pfeffer,Bobby James 22
        ,Elizabeth 17
        ,Ewald Adolf 17
        ,Frank 22
        ,Frank F. 17
        ,Herman 28,58
        ,James Ernest 17
        ,Judy Louise 17
        ,Karl 17
        ,Rolf 58
Pierce,Diana 20
       ,Lorene 12
       ,Roy 20
       ,Wm. 12
Pogue,Audrey 39
      ,Bryan Charles 39
      ,Christian Harold 39
      ,David Allan 39
      ,Harold 39
      ,Wm. A. 39
      ,William Lisle 39

111

Poindexter,Glenn 26
        ,Glenn Dean Jr. 26
        ,Frank Ray 26
        ,Homer Allen 26
        ,Malinda Nell Marlene 26
Pomikal,Melba Joe 54
        ,Melvin 54
        ,Minnie 54
        ,Stacey 54
        ,Wayne Melvin 54
        ,Willie 54
Possey,Randall 15
Poucher,Donald Earl 7
        ,Joe Ann Bell 7
        ,Louise Carol 7
Prause,Harvey 64
        ,Hazel Mewia Beckman 64
Presley,Carolyn Sue 81
        ,R.H. 81
Prator,Pansy Lie 12
Price,Arthur 32
        ,Brent Lee 86
        ,Erna Wehmeyer 87,88
        ,John Lee 86
        ,Lee 86
        ,Lee Roy 86
        ,Richard Mark 86
        ,Roy Lee 86
Prinz,August 7
        ,Marie 7
        ,Sophie 7
Privette,Allen 23
        ,Cathy 23
        ,Frances 22
        ,James 23
        ,Scott 23
        ,William 22
        ,Wm 22
Pruitt,Alvin 9
        ,Elenor Gail 9
Pryor,Ann R. 50
        ,Claude 50
        ,Elizabeth Ann 50
Pulido,Emil Charles 42
        ,Gregory Anthony 42
        ,Lesha Lynette 42
        ,March Charles 42

Quade,Minnie 74
Qualls,Alfred Perry 50
        ,Billy Jo 50
        ,Debra Sue 50
Quebe,Herbert Oliver 54
        ,Malinda 2,3,26
        ,Mina 26
        ,William 3,26
Quicke,Timothy John Edward 16
        ,William John Edward 16

Rahne,Fern 13
Rann,Johann 1
Rathliff,Dehn Marline 14
        ,Henry 14
        ,Lee 13
        ,Linda 13
Rauch,Daniel Edward 16
        ,Michael Edmund 16
        ,Nancy Elsie 64
        ,Patricia Marie 16
        ,Ronald Edmund 16
        ,Victor Max 16
        ,W.Otis 64
Ray,Bruce Wright 24
        ,Carey Lee 52
        ,Christina Ann 52
        ,Corey Allen 52
        ,Heather Anne 24
        ,Howard 52
        ,James A. 24
Reagan,Mona Sue 18
Reese,Robert 8
        ,Stephen Gerald 8
Reeves,Leta Illa 38
Region,John Wayne 89
        ,John Houston 89
        ,Lynelle 89
        ,Michael DeWayne 89
        ,Tammie Sue 89
        ,Tonya Gay 89
Reichle,Clarence 15
        ,Jan 15
        ,John 15
        ,John Carl 15
Reimer,Lisa Dawn 22

Reise,Robert 8
Renfro,Grace Marie 38
     ,Luthern Burleson 37
     , Vaughn 38
Rentz,Florence E. 81
     ,Lucien D. 81
Reue,Emma 4 9
Richmond,Mary Naoma 64
Richter,A.J. 68
     ,Doris 17
     ,Florence 68
     ,Fritz 56
     ,Helmut 17
     ,Kim 69
     ,Kirk 69
     ,Kris 69
     ,Neddie 56
     ,Wilford 68
Rittimann,Nadine Ruth 33
     ,Nelli Nadine Miles 33
Roberson,Marion 81
Robertson,Justian Lee 14
     ,Penny 48
     , Thomas Lee 14
Robins,Carla Sue 15
     ,Charles R. 15
     ,Leo 15,91
     ,Robin Lea 15
     ,Sandra Jean 15
Robinson,Athlene 79
Rodden,H.C. 52
     ,Janet Ann 52
     ,Linda Ruth 52
Rodenbeck,Annie 53
     ,Carolyn 35
     ,Otto 53
Roehling,David Gene 22
     ,Louie 22
Roese,Carol 72
     ,Christine 71
     ,Edith 73
     ,Herbert 72
     ,John Robert 72
     ,Judy 72
     ,Larry Gene 71
     ,Milton 71
     ,Robert 71
     ,Roland 71
     ,Wilbert 71
     ,Willie 72
     ,Wm.71

Roesler,Johanna 71
     ,Rosa 2
Rogers,Bill 8
     ,Gregory Paul 21
     ,James F. 8
     ,Janet May 8
     ,Karl Patton 8
     ,Martha Lynn 8
     ,Ray 21
     ,Raymond 21
Roliard,Stephen Chad 63
Rosentreter,Fred 52
Rogers,Kristy Renee 63
     ,Nancy 72
     ,Toby Eugene 63
Rose,Effigene(Jean) 30
Ross,Mary Jane 25
Roselius,Janice 83
     ,John Dwight 83
     ,Roland 83
Rosenbaum,Fritz 75
Roussear,Ann 74
Routt,Jack 2
     ,Jackson 2
Row,Garlan Craig 15
     ,Melanie Lynn 15
     ,Rebecca Lee 15
     ,Seymore 15
     ,Tara Ann 15
Rowe,Dorothy Lucyle 10
Roy,James 20
Rude,David 6
     ,James Emery 6
     ,Joseph Emery 6
Ruk,Carl(Pastor) 62
Rush,Mildred 56
Russell,Sidney 81

Salazar,Janie Marie 63
Salberg,Deloras Kay 10
     ,Gerald Ray 10
     ,Milton Jr. 9
     ,Randy Keith 10
     ,Robert Carl 10
Saltzman,Keith 49
     ,Randy 49
     ,Russel 49
Sample,Glenda 61,91
Samuel,Oscar(Pastor) 41,76,89
Samuels,Debbie Jo 43

113

Samuelson,Cecil 14
        ,Michael Dwayne 14
        ,Otto 14
        ,Shelia Laverne 14
Sanders,Betty Louise 10
        ,Buster 6
        ,Christopher James 10
        ,David Glen 10
        ,Elsie Anna 6
        ,Henry 10
        ,Janet Diane 10
        ,Johnnie Edward 10
        ,Julie Ann 6
        ,Lisa Dawn 10
        ,Lonnie 6
        ,Lorence 6
        ,Margie Myrtle 6
        ,Nora Bertha 6
        ,Melissa 34,62
        ,Otto 10
        ,Randell Robert 6
        ,Richard Lawrence 6
        ,Robert Fred 6
        ,Ron Warren 6
        ,Stacey 6
        ,Stanley Gene 6
        ,Tracy 6
        ,Virginia Marie 10
        ,William 6
        ,William Wayne 10
Sandhoff,Betty 52
Sandridge,Margie Ruth 89
Schamberg,Lydia 73
Schawe,Dora 68
        ,Johanna 34,61
        ,Selma 67,68
        ,W.F. 68
Schatz,Hattie 22
        ,Louie 22
Schenkel,Christoph 1
Schiller,Sophie 15
Schlechte,Caroline 75
Schlotman,Bill 49
        ,Lidia 49
        ,Lonnie 49
        ,Otto 49
Schmalriede,Eldon 8
        ,Leo 72
        ,Mary Ann 8

Schmedthorst,Bradley Craig 32
        ,Christi Lynn 32
        ,Fritz 32
        ,Westly 32
Schmidt,Amy 37
        ,Andrew Robert 39
        ,Arvell 39
        ,Audrey Leah 39
        ,Bertha 38
        ,Carolyn Sue 39
        ,Catherine Talitha 39
        ,Charles Arthur 39
        ,Charles Robert 39
        ,Charles Robert Jr. 39
        ,Daisy Nell 39
        ,David Ray 39
        ,Debbie Ann 40,79
        ,Donna 40,79
        ,Doyle 40,79
        ,Edward 40
        ,Edwin Jo 40,79
        ,Ella 38
        ,Emanuel 36
        ,Erna 40
        ,Evelyn Fay 37
        ,Freda Mae 36
        ,Gary 39
        ,Gustave 39
        ,Hanna 36,78,79
        ,Harvey 37
        ,Heneritta 79
        ,Henry 39
        ,Homer 37
        ,Julia Mae 40
        ,Lana Sue 39
        ,Lou Ann 39
        ,Louis 28,36,78,79,80
        ,Mark Anthony 40
        ,Michael Allen 40
        ,Nettie 38
        ,Michael Lynn 40,79
        ,Paul 37
        ,Paul August 37
        ,Peter 37
        ,Richard 62
        ,Ruby 36
        ,Scott 40,79
        ,Sharon 40,79
        ,Steven 40,79

,Steven Allen 39
,Susan 40,79
,Trisha Deene 40
,Vernon 39
,Viola 36
,Virginia Ann 39
,Walter 40
,Weldon Floyd 40
,Willie 39
Schmitt,Theresa 55
Schorn,Bertha 36
,Dennis Eugene 36
,Eugene 36
,Theodore 36
Schroder,Arthur H. Sr. 69
,Arthur H. 69
,Bertha Matilda 7
,Bobby Ray 65
,Bryan 69
,Gesena 6
,Karen 69
,Stephen 69
,Thelma 69
Schroeder,Alma 78
,Louise 56
,Michael Glenn 65
,Ronald E. 65
,Wilbert 65
Schuette,Clara 37
,Wm Henry 37
Schulenburg,Louise 76
Schulz,Fritz 1
,Joachim 1
Schulze,Earline 44
,Reinhard 44
,Velma 44
Schumacher,Rosie 15

Schwartz,Bertha 2
,Doris 73
,Ella 44
,Louise 52
Scharz,Pastor James 75
Schuch,Peggy Ann 77
Schwettman,Freida 2
Scott,Mittie 30
Seale,Annie Mae 19
,Bobby Gene Jr. 19
,John R. 19
,Paula 19
Seeton,Michael Dwain 7

Sembritzy,Coreen Colleen 78
,Sherry Ann 78
,Stephen 77
,Steve Lee 78
Semff,Melvin 36
,Richard 36
,Rosa 36
Shabey,Elizabeth 82
Shank,Lisa 13
Shaper,Christopher 71
,Victor 71
Sharp,Mary Jo 32
,Mary Ruth 74
,Sidney Thomas 74
Shelton,Bobby Lynn 16
,Burl 16
,Danny Lynn 16
,Patty Ann 65
Shoemacher,Annie 7
Schmalriede,Eldon 8
,Mary Ann 8
Shitzer,A.H. 46
Shull,Ben 37
,David 37
,Rachel 37
,Sarah 37
,Timothy 37
Sicks,Betty 10
Simank,Charles 65
,Gracie 65
,Sullie 65
Simmons,Daniel 38
,Rebecca 38
Slovacek,Jessie Patrick 77
Smidt,Kay 54
Smith,Allison Jeanne 56
,Bobbie Gene 6
,Charles Cale 47
,Claude 56
,Dale 47
,Elsie 71
,Gene 73
,Kimberly 73
,Kitty Ann 71
,Mary 30
,Nelson Clyde Jr. 71
,Nelson Clyde Sr. 71
,Robin 73
,Wanda Sue 83

Sommer,John 53
    ,John A. 53
    ,Richard Dean 53
Sorenson,Bryan 13
    ,Conrad 13
    ,De Ann 13
    ,Debbie 13
    ,Dennise 13
    ,James Marion 13
    ,Karen 13
    ,Kathy 13
    ,Lane K. 13
    ,Leroy 13
    ,Marion A. 13
    ,Marynell 13
    ,Mina Fay 13
    ,Tad Marion 13
    ,Troy 13
    ,Troy Don 13
Sparks,Emmett Elwood 62
    ,Garland Leneal 62
    ,Jeffery Scott 62
Spies,Tonie 63
Spreen,Heneritta 71
Spross,Lydia 39
Stahl,JoAnn 85
    ,Roy 85
Stallard,Faye 15
Stammeier,Louise 6
Stanford,Chris 35
    ,Christine 35
    ,Fleta 35
Staudt,Cora Dirks 7
    ,Jeanne Marie 7
    ,Ruben 7
Stchanke,Rose 47
Stegmon,Cora 52
    ,Henry 52
Steinke,Meddie 49
Steele,Charles Wesley 64
    ,Edward Elijah 64
    ,Alvena 49
Sternberg,Helen 52
    ,Louis 52
    ,Louise 46
Stevens,Hazel 51
    ,Mary Frances 51
    ,Morris 51
Stewart,Estell 13
Stienke,Donna Kay 7
    ,Henry Alfred 7

Stienman,Lena 85
Stockton,Audrey 11
    ,Audra 11
Stolz,Herbert William Jr. 73
    ,Kelli 73
Stone,Donna Beth 30
Stuth,Ed 6
    ,Edgar Arnold 33
    ,Ella 29,33
    ,Elmer John 33
    ,Jerry Wayne 33
    ,John 29,32,33
    ,John C. 33
    ,Judy Ann 33
    ,Lydia 29
    ,Lydia Charolette 32
    ,Minnie 32
    ,Pamela Dianne 6
    ,Robert Deryle 6
    ,Robert Edwin 6
Sulak,Albert Paul II 16
    ,Audra Elizabeth 16
    ,Darrell Ronald 16
    ,Ronald Charles 16
Sutton,Betty 8
    ,Hylton 8
    ,Richard Hylton 8
Swanner,Eula Mae (Jean) 59
Swann ,Virgie
Swearengen,Ellen Kay 90
Swonke,Thomas 55
Sykora,Georgia 48

Tappe,Dorothy Mae 65
    ,Erich William 65
    ,Henriette 65
    ,Mary 65
    ,Sadie 44
Tate,Cynthia Ann Holmes 35
    ,Katherine 37
    ,Robert Lee 35
    ,Robert Lee II 35
    ,Leroy 37
    ,Shirley Marie 37
Tedform,Brenda 19
    ,Ted 19
Tegeler,Lydia 56
Teichelman,Darlene Dana 55
Tellis,Beatrice Adaline 12
Temple,Glenda Cottle 6

Thim,Adele 23
     ,Anita 22
     ,Annie 22
     ,Arnold 22
     ,Charlotte 23
     ,Dorotha Ann 22
     ,James 23
     ,John 22
     ,John Weldon 22
     ,Raquel Leigh 22
     ,Roudolph 22
     ,Sandy 23
     ,Schelley Jean 22
     ,Stacie 23
     ,Tracie(Theresa) 22
Thomas,Clyde W. 34
     ,David Charles 34
     ,Dora 15
     ,Dorothy 15
     ,James 15
     ,Naome 15
     ,William 15
Thompson,Amy Christine 83
     ,Charles R. Sr. 83
     ,Charles R. Jr. 83
     ,Dorothy 31
     ,Harry 31
     ,Harry Steven 31
     ,Juanita Hunter 75
     ,Kathleen 44
     ,Rebecca Dawn 31
     ,Robyn Elise 83
Threadgill,Randy 40,79
Tidwell,Donna Kay 12
Tondre,Charles 69
     ,Dianne 69
     ,Fred Louis Jr. 69
     ,Robert Charles 69
Tonies,Valeria 39
Townsend,Jawn 89
Trammel,Winnie 8
Traylor,Bernice 80
     ,Shirley 80
Trlica,Lillie Ann 35
Trolinger,Amy Michelle 16
     ,Christopher Michael 16
     ,Frederick Michael 16
     ,Wayne Eugene 16
Tschirhart,Martha 70
Tucker,Helen 57

Ueckue,(Mrs.Karl Pfeffer) 17
Ulrich,Clara Ann 17
Ullrich,Kathryn 63
     ,Jacob Sr. 63
Underwood,Betty 55
Urbankt,Daisy Lydia 39
     ,Willie 39

Vahrenkamp,Annie 71
     ,Elsie 71
     ,Fritz 71
     ,Henriette 24
     ,Minnie 6
     ,William 24
Vana,Agnes Margaret 30
Varner,Shannon Rhea 73
     ,Shelli Kae 73
VonRuff,David 34
     ,Eddie 34
     ,Edwin 34
     ,Kirk 34
     ,Mike 34
     ,Mildred Louiese 34
     ,Walter 29
     ,Walter John 34
Volman,Ollie 54
Vowell,Amy Lou 39
     ,Hester 39

Wacht,Joe 17
     ,Louise 17
     ,Michael 17
Wade,Archie J. 43
     ,Joyce Marie 43
     ,Meysa Diane 43
     ,Patricia Ann 43
     ,Ronnie Fred 43
Wagener,August 23
     ,Fred 23
     ,Ida 23
Wagner,Charles W. 49
Walker,Ralph Lewis 5
     ,Theodore 5
Wallart,Louisa 78
Warner,Raymond Wilson 73
Ward,Rusty 52
     ,Shannon 52
Wallart,Louisa 78

117

Watson,Jim 14
Wavrusa,Bradley 18
       ,Frank 18
       ,Kathryn 18
       ,Stevie 18
Weaver,Dorothy 75
Webel,Fritz 56
      ,Louise Selma 56
Weber,Alma 38,39
      ,Mildred Lucille 33
      ,Will 39
      ,William Henry Jr. 33
Wedeking,Anna Henrietta 18
         ,Ben Henry 19
         ,Ben Josesh 19
         ,Betty Jean 15
         ,Billy Gene 15
         ,Charles 17
         ,Charles Henry 18
         ,Charline 18
         ,Cynthia Eileen 19
         ,Daniel Carl 19
         ,Danny Ray 15
         ,Darren Lane 17
         ,Diana Clare 20
         ,Donald Wayne 17
         ,Elisa Jo 15
         ,Ella(Ellen) 21
         ,Eric 17
         ,Fred Frank 15
         ,Fritz W. 17
         ,Gregory Alan 20
         ,Henry Otto 18,19
         ,Henry Z. 15
         ,Jeanette 15
         ,Jeremy Lane 20
         ,Jo Ann 17
         ,John Henry 19
         ,John Robert 20
         ,John Robert Jr. 20
         ,John T. 15
         ,John Wayne 15
         ,Jon Paul 19
         ,Joyce Marie 15
         ,Karl Edward 19
         ,Kathleen 19
         ,Lynda Clare 20
         ,Malinda Louise 17
         ,Marie 20
         ,Matilda 16

,Michael Lee 20
,Paul Edward 20
,Paul Edward Jr. 20
,Paulita 15
,Reinhart 15
,Reinhart Jr. 15
,Richard Lee 15
,Rosa 15
,Rose Marie 19
,Terry 20
,Timothy Ray Eugene 19
,Wilfred 15
,Willie Fritz 15
,William 15
,Yvonne 18
Wegner,Bonnie Jean 49
      ,Henry C. 49
Wehmeyer,August 85
        ,Bernie 85
        ,Charlie 85
        ,Charlie William 85
        ,Clara 85
        ,Collins Fred 85
        ,Debra Gail 22
        ,Dona Denise 22
        ,Doretta Ann 22
        ,Doris 22
        ,Emma 85
        ,Erna 85
        ,Fred Henry 85
        ,Frederick 85
        ,Fritz 75,85
        ,Gary 85
        ,Helen 85
        ,Henriette 74
        ,Herbert 85
        ,Herman 74
        ,Jim 85
        ,John Fredrick 74
        ,Lillie 85
        ,Louise 74
        ,Martha 85
        ,Marie Henriette 74
        ,Melvin 85
        ,Minna 61,67
        ,Minetta 71
        ,Otto 85
        ,Walter 85
        ,Willie 85
        ,Wilhelmine 75

Weidner,Annie Appel 52
        ,Lillie Belle 52
        ,O.A. 52
Weimers,Allen 69
        ,James 69
Weis,Ann 74
Weiss,Carlos 75
        ,Christopher Charles 74
        ,Charlotte 74
        ,Ed 74
        ,Harold 74
        ,Harold Charles 74
        ,Martha Louis 75
        ,Mary Corol 74
        ,Robin Beth 74
Weithorn,Annie 7
Weiting,Edna 37
Wellmann,Becky Lynn 63
        ,Brian Scott 63
        ,Dorothy 72
        ,H. 1
        ,Herbert 63
        ,Kathy Renee 63
        ,Lena 28,50
        ,Merle Helen 63
        ,Nathan Herbert 63
        ,Pauline 63
        ,Ralph Reinhard 63
        ,Rodney Alan 63
        ,Toby 63
        ,Tommie Lee 63
        ,Vernon Herbert 63
        ,Wayne Allen 63
Welticke,Marie 63
Wendt,Charles 61,91
        ,David 61,91
        ,Sophie 5
        ,Werner 61,91
Wenzel,Augusta 28,54
Werland,Clyde 7
        ,Dora 7
        ,Larry Dale 7
        ,Stephen Harold 7

Werzbach(Urerzbach),Mildred
        ean 68
Whatley,Doris 36
        ,Oniel 36,80
Whehrmann,Wilhelmine 33
Whittemore,Juanita Marie 50
        ,Lillie 50
        ,M.H. 50

Wiatt,Wanda 71
Wese,Pete 15
Wiede,Adolph 6
        ,Alice Fay 6
        ,Christian 1
        ,Ferd. 1
        ,James Ray 6
        ,Johann 1
        ,Linda Mae 6
        ,Walter Henry 6

Wiese,A.F.Carl 3
        ,Agnes 9,43
        ,Agnes Annie 13
        ,Alan Wayne 74
        ,Alice Agnes 81
        ,Alonzo 1,2,65
        ,Amy 82
        ,Annie 3,22
        ,Anna Caroline 75
        ,Annie Louise 25
        ,Arthur Edward
            Fredrick Jr. 55
        ,August 76,61,70
        ,August Jr. 76,81

        ,Barbara Danielle 30
        ,Barbara Lynn 11
        ,Becky June 56
        ,Bernard(Ben)
            Friedrich 75
        ,Bertha 3,4,28
        ,Bertha Henrietta 24
        ,Betty Lynn 33
        ,Bill 74
        ,Billy Gene 35
        ,Billy James 10
        ,Brenda Joyce 30
        ,Brenda Marie 56
        ,Brenda Vivian 24

        ,Candice Lorraine 54
        ,Carl 3,33,76,78
        ,Carl H. 34
        ,Carl Henry John 25
        ,Carl Hermann Wilhelm 60
        ,Carl Friedrich Wilhelm 73,
                74
        ,Carol Anne 30
        ,Caroline 61,82
        ,Carolyn Sue 2
        ,Carolita Denise 51
        ,Chantelle Lee Ann

,Charles 50,83
,Charley 9,12
,Charley William 12
,Charlie 28
,Charlotte Beth 2
,Charlsey Louise 74
,Chris 28
,Christoph 54
,Christoph Heinrich
        Wilhelm 75
,Clara 9
,Clara Mathilda 14
,Craig Alan 35
,Craig Edwards 24
,Darrell Dean 30
,David Lee 12
,Dawn IdaNell 35
,Debora Ervin 50
,Deborah Lynn 32
,Debra Shannon 82
,Della 56
,Donna Elizabeth 35
,Donna Katheleen 30
,Donnie Milton 50
,Doris Irene 50
,Douglas 56
,Eddie Doyle 56
,Edgar(Eddie)Otto 32
,Edward Fredrick(Tex)55
,Edward Joe 35
,Elaine 74
,Eldon Charles 51
,Elizabeth 2
,Elizabeth Louise 76,77
,Elroy 56
,Ella 9
,Ella Annie 12
,Eloise 2
,Emma,9,28,36,37,40,58,
        76,78
,Emma Louise 12
,Emma Matilda 11
,Emma Sophie Wilhelmine 50
,Ernest 76,81
,Ernest Ray 30
,Ernestine Louise 81
,Ernie 9
,Ernie Louise 14
,Esther 75
,Estelle 54

,Etta 33
,Eugene Everett 54
,Eugene Everette Jr. 54
,Ewin Henry 56

,Fern Lorraine 54
,Frances Loraine 50
,Frankie Clarence West 56
,Fred 28,29
,Freddie 74
,Fredrick Sigmund 30
,Friedrich 74
,Fritz 2,28,61,62

,Gary Layne 50
,Gary Price 33
,Gerald 56
,Gertrude 10
,Gilbert 50
,Guy 2

,Harold 56
,Harold Sidney 13
,Harold Joseph 13
,Helen Christine 30
,Henry 1,9
,Henerietta 76,83
,Heneritta Louise(Setta)9,
        25,61,71,89
,Henriette Wilhelmine
        Charlotte 70
,Henriette 75
,Henry 1,9,28,29,33,61,79
,Henry Jr. 56
,Henry Louis 13
,Hermann Carl W. Wilhelm
                24
,Henry Russel 13
,Heinrich Friedrich Carl 74
,Herman Friedrich 1
,Herman Friedrich William
        1,3
,Henry Chris 54
,Henry Fredrick 28,29,61
,Hulda 29,33,35,61

,Ida 76,82
,Irene 81
,Irene Carolyn Louise 81
,Iris Marie 50

,James 2
,James Aubrey 81
,James Howard 11
,Janel 33
,Janice 33
,Jennifer Lynn 32
,Jerry Alexander 54
,Jerry Ray 25
,Jerry Jeffery 12
,Jerry Jeffery Jr. 12
,Jessie Wayne 12
,John 2
,Johann Friedrich 3
,John Henry 54
,John Henry II 34
,Joseph 2
,Joshua Kristof 35
,Joy Nell 30
,Joyce 33
,Julia Errin 35

,Karen Sue 56
,Karla Ann 54
,Kelli Dawn 50
,Kenneth Edward 11
,Kenney Allen 11
,Kim Lisa 51
,Kimberly Susan 55
,Kris Deane 54

,Larry Clevenger 55
,Laura Bell 10
, Leona Amelia 54
,Leroy Henry 54
,Lidia 28,54
,Lillie 29,81
,Lillie Augusta 55
,Lillie Emma 35
,Linda Marie 35,62
,Lisa Marie 32
,Lois 12
,Lonnie 2,9,12
,Lonnie Henry Carl 25
,Lonnie Jr. 2
,Lonnie Wm. Jr. 12
,Lori Beth 50
,Lorina 2,65
,Louise 2,3,15,61,70
,Louise Nell 2,3,15,35
,Luanne 30

,Lucille 12
,Lydia 9,28,29,58,83,84,76
,Lydia Friedricka 33
,Lydia Louise 11

,Malinda 29
,Malinda Emma 34
,Margie Estelle 13
,Marion Thomas 2
,Mark Alan 35
,Mark Dwain 50
,Marie Wilhelmine
        Charlotte 90
,Marie Wilhelmine
        Henriette 60
,Mary Ann 32
,Mary Jiane 25
,Megan Noel 30
,Melinda 28,78,79,80
,Mena 23
,Michael Ray 56
,Mildred 57
,Milton 56
,Minna 74
,Minnie 9,76,82
,Minnie Louise 13
,Nan A. Lois 32
,Nancy 2
,Nancy Claire 34
,Nora 24

,Ora Marie 10
,Oscar Herman 55
,Otto 29
,Otto Charles 32

,Pamela Ann 12
,Pamela Sue 32
,Paula Catherine 35

,Raymond Henry 55
,Rene Charlotte 2
,Regina Martha 55
,Robert 2,29
,Robert Charles 34
,Robert Charles Jr. 34
,Robert Elton 33
,Robert Fritz 34
,Robert Gerald 56

,Robert Joe 30
,Roger Paul 32
,Rose Mary 2
,Roy 2
,Roy Jr. 2
,Roy Fred 30
,Roy Fred Jr. 30
,Roy Frederick 24
,Ruben Will 32
,Ruby 9,13
,Ruth Agnes 55
,Ruth Violet 34

,Sandra Kay 56
,Shirley Jean 35,62
,Shirley Jenise 32
,Sidney Ray 30
,Sophie 5,28,59
,Steven Wade 12
,Suanne 30
,Suzanne 82
,Suzanne Carol 35

,Tammy Lee 11
,Tasha Renea 25
,Terry Wayne 12
,Thelma Louise 13
,Theresa 56
,Thomas 2
,Thomas Edward 75

,Viola L. 57
,Viola Mae 31
,Vivian Louise 30

,Walter 2,29
,Walter Jr. 35,62
,Walter Frederick 24
,Walter Henry 35,50,62
,Wayne Eric 25
,Wilhelmine 74
,Wilhelmine(Minnie)
        24,41,42,85
,Wilhelm Carl 9,12
,William 1,3,10,26,28,29
,William(W.C.) 24
,William H. 58
,William Henry 2
,William Lewis 32
,Willie 2,28
,Zelma 29,34

Wiethorn,Alan Paul 7
        ,Annie 7
        ,Donald Dale 7
        ,Glenn Paul 7
        ,Henry 7
        ,Michael Dwain 7
        ,William Paul 7
Wilkins,Brandon Scott 33
        ,Louie Alexander 33
        ,Rickey Glenn 33
Wilson,Agnes Effie 30
        ,Dennis Clay 32
        ,Dennis Clay Jr. 32
        ,Denise Charolette 32
        ,Jeanette 18
        ,Katherine Louise 30
        ,Lorener 12
        ,Marie(Edna)30
        ,O'Levia Neil 30
        ,Robert Samuel 30
        ,Roger Bernard 30
        ,Roger O'Neal 30
        ,Sarah Jane 50
Willhite,Darrel Layne 17
        ,Donna Marie 17
        ,Gloria Ann 17
        ,Harold 17
        ,Harold Wayne 17
        ,Lester Louis 17
Williams,Carolyn 52
Windt,Ida 52
Winkleman,Hattie 32
Winkler,Bernie 38
        ,Beberly Ann 38
        ,Brian W. 38
        ,Carrie Lynn 38
        ,Chas. A.38
        ,Chris Allen 38
        ,Daphne Lynn 38
        ,Gerald Sidney 38
        ,James Carl 38
        ,James Daniel 38
        ,Joseph J. 78
        ,Katherine 38
        ,Lawrence Edward 38
        ,Mark Milton 38
        ,Milton 38
        ,Otto 38
        ,Rebecca Lynne 38
        ,Timothy Craig

```
          ,Walter F. 78
          ,Weldon Homer 38
Wise,Myrtle Lena 51
Wiseman,Talitha Virginia 39
Witte,Christine 8
Wolf,Marie 89
Wolske,Ben 48
          ,Chris Carl 35
          ,Marisa Jan Glasco 35
Woods,Charlotte Beth 2
Worley,Charles Edward 25
          ,John Phillip 24
          ,Liane Marie 91
          ,Margaret Elaine 24
Wright,Bruce 24
          ,Esther 24
          ,John D. 37
          ,Martha Ann 37
          ,Minnie 37,39
          ,Minnie Sue 8
Wyckoff,Richard 77
Wyle,Ruth 77

Yarbrough,Ellen 2
Yorke,Annie Myrtle 24
Young,Helen 13
          ,Oliver 13
          ,Martha Barbara 25
          ,Norbert W. 25
Yum Wol Mae 56

Zahn,Elisa 15
          ,Henry 15
Zeir,Arnold 69
          ,Patsy 69
Zettner,L. 52
Zdansky,Caroly Joan 57
          ,Julius Joseph 57
```

www.ingramcontent.com/pod-product-compliance
Lightning Source LLC
Chambersburg PA
CBHW081431270326
41932CB00019B/3168